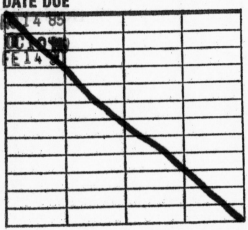
Tm

in

The American Political System in Transition

Harry Lazer

THE CITY COLLEGE
OF THE CITY UNIVERSITY
OF NEW YORK

Thomas Y. Crowell Company

New York / Established 1834

Library of Congress Catalog Card Number: 67-14292

Designed by Laurel Wagner

Manufactured in the United States of America
by Vail-Ballou Press, Inc., ██████████████

To my father and the loving memory of my mother

Preface

The theme of this book is the adjustment of the American political system in the twentieth century to the forces of social and economic change. It is a theme that emerges from a much larger one with which I have been concerned; the adjustment to change of established political systems in general, and those of Great Britain, France, and the United States in particular. I believe that such a focus reveals in a country's political events a coherence and significance that might otherwise elude notice, and that it also encourages especially instructive comparisons between the political institutions and experiences of different countries.

Good reason lay behind the halting of the larger project in order to concentrate solely on the American political system. Living in these years of dramatic change in the area of civil rights and of a potential displacement of political power by legislative reapportionment, an American political scientist can scarcely remain indifferent to the intellectual excitement and challenge of these events. If he considers himself primarily a student of comparative politics, the challenge may be all the greater, because the implications of these years can be seen to transcend the limits of the United States.

This analysis of American political institutions meshes the historical and analytical approaches of presentation because I am concerned with both the significant historical currents that have influenced our politics and the resultant effects upon the operation of its institutions. For this purpose, I have tried to bring together the essence of much of the principal literature in the field. Here, too, I believe a new appreciation is gained—

through the consideration of these studies and their insights within such a synthesis. I have attributed sources wherever possible, but when attributions might have too distractingly interrupted the exposition or too greatly swelled the number of footnotes, the bibliography has proved useful for a fuller listing of sources. It has sometimes been difficult to bring down to earth the source of an idea that is in the air. It should be remembered, however, that this work is intended not for the specialist, but primarily for the college student and for the intelligent layman concerned with public affairs.

Despite all attempts at objectivity, I am nonetheless aware of the effect on the presentation and analysis of my own political values. More than one effort at objectivity has paralleled Samuel Johnson's description of the motivation of his own reporting of parliamentary debates—to see to it "that the Whig dogs never got the better of the argument." The very choice of institutional adjustment as a theme presupposes, of course, an emphasis upon both the value of stable institutions and the primary need for flexibility if they are to be suitable instruments for coping with the real problems of a national society. Thus, the judgments expressed in this work will likely invite denial by those for whom any shift in the character and operation of our political institutions is repugnant, as well as by those who believe the political and social structure so unsound as to require fundamental reconstruction. Nevertheless, whether the reader finds himself in agreement or not, my hope is that he consider the views set forth here not as dogmatic assertions simply to be accepted or rejected, but as interpretations that may serve as springboards for discussion and inquiry.

During the preparation of this work, I have become deeply indebted to friends and colleagues who have encouraged me toward its completion. The list of persons who have been kind enough to read the manuscript, or parts of it, seems almost in inverse proportion to its modest size. I am happy to acknowledge from City College, Allen Ballard, Jr., Arnold Bornfriend, John Davis, Ivo Duchacek, Stanley Feingold, Alan Fiellin, Samuel Hendel, and Sandra Levinson, as well as Morton Cowden of Briarcliff College, Thomas Peardon of Swarthmore College,

Roberto Socas, Jr., of Fordham University, Susan Goldsmith Tolchin of Brooklyn College, and Margaret Cowden, Sybil Langer, Thea Maitinsky, Abby Ziffren, and the late Rosalind Cohen. In addition, comments from Joseph George Chall of City College, Bruce Feld of Columbia University, Irving Fisher of Bowdoin College, and Donald Avery have proven useful. Despite the advice and criticism of the aforementioned, I alone, of course, am responsible for the views expressed in these pages.

In addition, I wish to thank Sylvan Feldstein, Evelyn Fredericson, Adrienne Katz, and Leo Skir for their help in the proofreading of the footnotes. Also, Gerald Barrett, Sarah Hope, Shirley Lerman have done yeoman service in their deciphering of my handwriting as in their admirable typing. I would like also to thank my publishers for their encouragement and understanding, particularly Novello Grano for his guidance, and Julanne Arnold and Herman Makler for their keen editorial insights. I wish to conclude with a word of thanks to my students, whose interest has stimulated me to clarify my concepts of the political process and to whom I have turned, both consciously and unconsciously, to consider and test my views.

H. L.

New York, N.Y.
January, 1967

Contents

I: Stability and Change in American Politics   1

II: The Political System: Establishment and
       Operation   10
Post-Civil War Politics, 12
The New Political System, 14
The Madisonian Philosophy, 21
Progressivism, 26
Wilsonian Liberalism, 29
The Era of the 1920's, 32
The Divided Democrats, 36

III: The Political System: Dissolution and
       Renewal   40
The Depression, the New Deal, and Roosevelt, 40
The Machines, 44
The Negro and the South, 48
The Philosophy of the New Deal, 51
Reaction: Phase One, 54
The Impact of World War II, 62
The Republican Reaction to the New Deal, 63
Reaction: Phase Two, 72
Civil Rights, 76
Kennedy and Urban Change, 81
Reaction: Phase Three, 84

IV: Representation and the Legislature   88
Malapportionment, 94
The House of Representatives, 105
The Senate, 107
Congressional Practice and Power, 112
The Filibuster, 122
The World of the Legislators, 126
"The House without Windows" and Plato's Cave, 131

V: The Countervailing Forces   135
Federalism, 136
Political Parties, 151
The Executive, 161
The Presidency, 163

VI: The Supreme Court and Judicial Review   182
The Court and the Country, 193
Constitutional Adjustment, 195
The Judicial Balance, 198
The State and Free Enterprise, 200
Civil Rights after the Civil War, 206
The Court-packing Controversy, 213
The Implications of the New Court, 217
Civil Rights after the New Deal, 219
The Aftermath of the Brown Decision, 227
Legislative Apportionment, 229
The Conservative Counterattack, 235
The Court Today, 238

VII: The Demands of the Future   240

Bibliography   249

Index   263

Chapter I

Stability and Change in American Politics

This work examines how the American political system has attempted to adjust to a changing society. Such an analysis can be significant not only for its purely historical insights but also for the light it can shed upon the prospects for successful adaptation to future change.

Although the currents of change are charged with vitality, they also carry a potential destructiveness to the political institutions with which they come into contact. There is, thus, an unceasing tension between these institutions and the forces of change. Political institutions, if they are to work effectively, must be made up of regular and stable elements that give an appearance of order and durability. No matter how insistent the pressure for change, a new constitution cannot be written and a new political structure arranged each year. The institutional structure, however, must react in some way to the continuous pressure exerted upon it by the forces of change. "Sheer resistance to change," wrote James Willard Hurst, "by only damming a gathering current, does not conserve, but insures destruction when the dam finally breaks." [1] Our political system, therefore, has faced —and is still facing—a challenge common to all: whether it can successfully meet these changes and adjust to times that are fundamentally different from the particular historical period of its establishment.

Because technological and sociological changes usually occur

[1] James Willard Hurst, *The Growth of American Law: The Law Makers* (Boston: Little, Brown, 1950), p. 359.

[1]

so gradually and imperceptibly, many persons do not realize their full significance. Thus, men often find themselves with an out-moded view of their society—and even their world. Daniel Boorstin wrote: "Old ideas do not suddenly become obsolete; rather they gradually become irrelevant." "And," he added, "in all societies, people are slow to discover the irrelevance of their tra-ditional vocabulary." [2] Just as generals instinctively tend to fight the battles of the past generation rather than those of the present, politicians and political scientists, as well as the general public, show a similar time lag in recognizing and meeting the most pressing political problems of their day.

If we compare the United States of today with the United States at the time of its formation near the end of the eighteenth century, the contrast is a stark one because the changes are as ob-vious as they are significant. We have developed from a small, rural, agricultural society, hugging the Atlantic seaboard, into an industrial, urban one of continental proportions. Despite the many threads to the past, the United States has been transformed into a truly different country.

The nature of this change can best be appreciated if, in addi-tion to comparing the rural America of 1790 with the urban America of 1960, we consider as well the country in the years around 1900 because this period was, in many ways, the turning point when the early culture decisively changed into the modern one, the Great Divide between the two major eras in our history. As we shall see, 1890 opened the decade during which the country's population first realized the potential scope and force of the changes in which it was involved and made the first attempt to adjust the political system accordingly. We shall examine the nature and success of this political system in our next chapter.

The most striking contrast in the 170 years of the country's history is in territory and in population. The thirteen coastal states with an area of 888,811 square miles expanded into a coun-try of 3,615,211 square miles, stretching from the Atlantic to the Pacific, extending even to Alaska and Hawaii. By 1890, the physi-cal dimensions of the modern country were already evident since our westward expansion was virtually closed with the official end-ing of the frontier in the census of that year.

[2] Daniel J. Boorstin, quoted in Hans Kohn, *American Nationalism: An Interpretative Essay* (New York: Collier Books, 1961), p. 211.

Our change in population was even sharper. The 3,929,214 people listed in the census of 1790 grew to 179,323,175 by 1960. The rise in population was particularly apparent in the transition period of the 1890's, as the census showed almost 63,000,000 people in 1890 and about 76,000,000 in 1900. Indeed, from 1870 to 1910, the population, on an average, increased by more than half every two decades.[3]

In 1790 the population was heavily rural, with only 4 per cent of the people living in urban areas of over 2,500 persons; by 1900, the urban proportion of the population had jumped to 40 per cent, and by 1960 it had reached 70 per cent. This process of rapid urbanization was felt with particular force at the end of the century. In 1880, one-fifth of the population lived in cities and towns of 8,000 inhabitants or more; by 1900, this segment had soared to one-third. The rural dwellers could easily realize in these years that their numerical superiority was rapidly dwindling and that the projection of the population trend to the city could only result in an eventual urban majority. This realization colored their political outlook and was a prime force in shaping the politics of the next half century.

The shift to the cities might not have had such an overpowering impact upon American politics if it had not been accompanied by the entrance of over 37,500,000 people into the United States between 1820 and 1930 in one of the largest and most important migrations in the world's history. This wave reached its crest at the end of the nineteenth century and the beginning of the twentieth. More than 14,000,000 immigrants entered between 1860 and 1900, with more than 3,500,000 entering between 1891 and 1900. By 1900, there were over 10,000,000 persons of foreign birth and 26,000,000 first- or second-generation Americans, more

[3] These population figures and those and the immigration figures that follow come from Department of Commerce, U.S. Bureau of the Census, *Statistical Abstract of the United States* in *The U.S. Book of Facts: Statistics and Information for 1966* (New York: Pocket Books, 1965); E. E. Shattschneider, "Urbanization and Reapportionment," from "A Symposium on *Baker v. Carr*," *Yale Law Journal*, LXXII, 1 (November, 1962), 7; Marian D. Irish and James W. Prothro, *The Politics of American Democracy*, 3d ed. (Englewood Cliffs, N.J.: Prentice-Hall, 1965); Harold U. Faulkner, *Politics, Reform and Expansion, 1890–1900* (New York: Harper and Row, 1959); Samuel P. Hays, *The Response to Industrialism, 1885–1914* (Chicago: University of Chicago Press, 1957.)

than one-third of the country's entire population. And most of these aliens had settled in the city.

Not only did immigration increase at the end of the nineteenth century; its character fundamentally changed as well. Although the earlier immigrants had come primarily from the countries of northern and western Europe, the newer wave came mainly from southern and eastern Europe. By 1896, the latter had surpassed the former; by 1900, about seven-tenths of the country's foreign population had migrated from southern and eastern Europe. We should remember that when the country was formed, its white population was in great measure homogeneous in ethnic composition since it consisted almost wholly of natives and immigrants stemming from northern and western Europe, particularly the British Isles. The population that emerged in the twentieth century was fundamentally different since its Anglo-Saxon character had been heavily diluted by a variety of new national elements. Thus, the instinctive concern of the countryside about the rising number of urban inhabitants was aggravated by the alien character of so many of that number.

The huge immigration into the country and the clustering of people in the cities was primarily a response to still another dynamic transformation in our history, the change from an agricultural economy into an industrial one. In 1790, about 90 per cent of the population derived their income from farming; by 1960, fewer than 20 per cent found themselves in this category. As with the size and character of the population, the period when the nation irreversibly changed from a predominantly agricultural economy to a predominantly industrial one was in the decades before and after 1900. "By 1890, for the first time," stated Louis Hacker and Benjamin Kendrick, "the value of the country's manufactured goods was already greater than that of its agricultural products; in another ten years, manufactured products were worth twice as much as those of the farm, the orchard, and the dairy." [4]

These simple statistics show clearly that the United States began as a society whose relatively homogeneous population was settled primarily in farms and small towns and was essentially

[4] Louis M. Hacker and Benjamin B. Kendrick, *The United States since 1865,* 3d ed. (New York: Crofts, 1946), p. 186.

occupied with agriculture; the country is today, on the other hand, a society whose heterogeneous people live mainly in densely populated metropolitan centers and who earn their livelihood within a vast industrial and commercial complex, which is characterized by a highly developed technology. Moreover, the statistics indicate that the turning point from the one society to the other came approximately in the years after 1890. "The 1890's," wrote Harold Faulkner, "separated not only two centuries but two eras in American history. These years saw the gradual disappearance of the old America and the rather less gradual emergence of the new." [5]

There have been critics of modern American life who have bemoaned this historical development. They have maintained that the America of 1900 or 1870 or 1830 was a far simpler and happier place in which to live than our country today and that a thriving, wholesome rural culture was heedlessly sacrificed to the demands of the machine and the city. We will not consider here, however, whether this change has been a beneficial one or whether it has been purchased at too high a price in the basic decencies and comforts of human life. Nor are we concerned with an allied question as to whether this transformation was inevitable or whether it could have been guided in another direction. Such issues of historical development, sociological change, and philosophical values are unquestionably fascinating but largely out of our focus. We rather assume the fact of the mammoth transformation and examine how our political system has adapted itself to it and how well it has performed in meeting the problems of the new American society.

Living in large cities has raised important issues about housing, health, education, crime, transportation, and recreation. The problems, of course, are not new since men have always in recorded history been concerned with the necessities of civilized life. But the concentration of huge masses in metropolitan centers has transformed what was primarily the concern of the private family into a major responsibility of government. Walter Lippmann pointed out this truth when he wrote:

People collected in big cities need more public expenditure than do people who live in the open country. . . . They cannot get along in

[5] Faulkner, *op. cit.*, p. 1.

the cities, as could their grandfathers in the country with private wells, private cesspools, unpaved streets, no police force, a volunteer fire department, private transportation. They must have the facilities and the amenities that are essential once they have moved from the country into the city.[6]

Closely linked to the problems of an urban society are those of an industrialized one. These, too, are basically extensions of perennial problems, particularly the attainment of economic well-being. Our country, throughout its history, has experienced both prosperity and depression. New dimensions have been reached, however, by virtue of the modern economy's span, complexity, interrelatedness, and technological character. As a result, the fundamental relationship between the government and the economy has changed. Admittedly, the government has always been, in some sense, involved in the economy. In the past, nevertheless, we could still maintain our formal adherence to the classical laissez-faire theory that the economy should operate according to the dictates of the free marketplace and should be unchecked by the restrictions of government. Economic freedom unquestionably meant freedom from government.

Our current prevailing theories, derived from modern experience, recognize many more facets to economic freedom. In considering the government as a positive and even beneficial force, they not only explicitly acknowledge its role in the economy, but consider it an indispensable element. By these standards, the government has no more important domestic function than the guarantee of economic stability, the maintenance of a check upon prices and wages, and the support of optimum employment.

In addition to encountering the characteristic problems of a modern industrial urban society, the United States has also been facing the special ones inherited from its past, particularly the integration of persons of diverse backgrounds and traditions into one political culture. The most challenging part of this problem has unquestionably been the incorporation of the Negro population into the mainstream of American political and social life. So

[6] From a 1962 Lippman column reproduced in Clinton Rossiter and James Lare, eds., *The Essential Lippmann: A Political Philosophy for Liberal Democracy* (New York: Random House, 1963), pp. 347–348.

important has this one subject become that the word *integration* in ordinary usage refers primarily to Negro-white relationships rather than the general sociological process. The attempted solution of these problems, as in the cases of urbanization and industrialization, has changed our meaning of individual freedom and has expanded the role of government. In response to overriding necessity, civil rights legislation today, like social legislation of a generation ago, has invaded what was formerly considered the private sphere of human activity.

The irrepressible forces that have expanded the scope of government have, at the same time, upset the previous federal balance between the state and the national government. Thus, our changing society has been reflected not only in our conception of the role of government, but also in our basic attitude to the various governmental levels. In the early years of our country, the average citizen tended to identify himself with the government physically closest to him. He would thus be more suspicious of the state government as the source of a possible encroachment upon his liberties than the local government. Similarly, he would be most suspicious of the national government with its authority encased in distant Washington. Today, however, because of our acceptance of a more positive role for government and our experience of the failure of state and local governments in the Great Depression, we instinctively look to the more powerful, wealthier national government for significant action. Moreover, experience has shown in recent years that when an individual's civil liberties have been invaded, it has usually been by a transgression of a state or local government rather than the national. In the field of civil rights, a similar pattern has been evident. Athough many states have passed antidiscrimination legislation, those citizens who have been most severely denied their rights, particularly in the southern states, have instinctively looked to the national government for aid.

We can, therefore, realize that life in our modern society has caused a transformation of our basic political ideas and values, a change reflecting the transformation of society itself in the last century and a half. In studying our political system, we will see that the key to the way it has adjusted to change lies in the conflict between the forces reflecting a changing society and those committed to the values and interests of the old order and intent upon maintaining intact all its elements.

This book is an attempt to describe not only the operation of our political institutions in a time of flux but also their own role in the dynamics of change itself. There are obvious disadvantages in studying institutions in a transition period, marked by great change, since they seem to lack the stability and regularity that would make them more fitting subjects for scholarly analysis. A description of the politics of the present dynamic period becomes dated almost at the moment of writing; the present trips over the past, and the future becomes the present. In these disconcerting circumstances, one can well understand why some cautious scholars dismiss as "journalism" anything written less than fifty years after the described event.

The unsettled nature of this transition period, however, renders it a particularly felicitous time to study politics. We are close enough to the era of the previous system to be able to understand the motivation of its participants and to appreciate their values. At the same time, the changes we are witnessing allow us a rather clear indication of the future pattern of American politics. Thus, at this bridge between the past and the future, we have a perspective denied before and difficult to achieve later.

Such insights will be difficult to attain decades from now. With the further dilution of laissez-faire and the securing of full civil rights for the Negroes and equality of representation, persons will accept the permanence of a new set of institutions and be at a loss to understand how the previous pattern could have been tolerated. By "understand," we do not mean a primarily intellectual comprehension since this is, after all, readily possible with the reproduction of past arguments. Future generations will lack, however, the ability to feel the compelling force of these views because they did not live at a time when they were generally accepted. Thus, in the fullest sense of the word, they will not be able to understand why people accepted the ebb and flow of the business cycle as a semidivine phenomenon which could not be regulated by the government; they will not be able to understand why the white population tolerated and why Negroes submitted to a degrading double standard at odds with our basic principles of equality and liberty; they will, also, be unable to understand why the urban majority of the population acquiesced to the political domination of the farmers and the residents of the small town. Although the flux of our present politics impedes the task of balanced analysis, it is this very quality that demands our careful attention.

A study of politics in a period of change is particularly valuable because it forces persons to ponder the fundamentals of a system whose institutions and practices they could easily take for granted in more placid times. To acknowledge the necessity for our political institutions to adjust to change is not enough. We must also consider how far this change can go without threatening our basic political traditions. Since we live in an era so different from that when our Constitution was drafted, we must, therefore, ask what is permanent within our political tradition and what is transitory, what is fundamental and what is contingent upon a particular time, economy, culture, or ethnic group, what must be retained at all costs and what can be sloughed off. A delicate sense of discrimination is involved in such a choice since men, carried away by the passions of the moment or lulled by the familiarity of accustomed practice, often confuse the permanent with the temporary. Such an insight can secure the proper synthesis between stability and change within which the American principles of free government can be as meaningful in this period of unprecedented technological and social change as in the century of their birth. We thus begin our study of the adaptability of the American political system when the machine and the city first cast their shadow upon the country and began the challenge to our people to meet the problems of a new world.

Chapter II

The Political System:
Establishment and Operation

Once a country makes the irreversible commitment to industrialization, its paramount problem becomes that of adjusting its political system to reality. In our history, the Civil War was just such a turning point; the impetus for intense industrialization unleashed by military necessity was to continue for decades and to fashion a new America. The main concern of our politics since that time has been the necessity of adjustment to this new social and economic life.

The fundamental character of the United States until the war was clearly rural. To be sure, a rising and spirited industrial and commercial element was dominant in the urban areas of New England and the Middle Atlantic states; its members had been particularly important in drafting the Constitution and in the young government's first years of operation under the Federalist party. The prevailing political tone of the country, however, was set by its agrarian majority. The city may have erected the political apparatus, but the countryside primarily operated it.

The limited political activity of the young country reflected the interests of the small farmers. Although other groups, such as eastern businessmen and western settlers, could perceive definite advantages in a strong government, the farmers generally felt it would little benefit them, and they were content to be left alone. It is no accident that the most energetic activity of the national government at this time was the acquisition of territory, the only policy obviously advantageous to the land-hungry farmers, and one of the major causes of our two wars in these years. In both its inactivity and its dynamism, the national government clearly expressed the interest of the most important socioeconomic group of the period.

Socioeconomic groups, however, do not have their interests reflected automatically in the political arena. It required the political genius of Thomas Jefferson to organize the Republican party (whose name was changed in the Jacksonian period to the Democratic party) as an effective instrument of agrarian interests. He achieved this by hammering out an alliance of the various groups opposed generally to the power of the mercantilist Northeast, and particularly to Alexander Hamilton's financial policies. Although the alliance combined a number of diverse elements, its backbone was a rural one with the western farmer, particularly the small farmer, in partnership with his southern counterpart. Thus reflecting the needs of the country's majority, the Republicans were able to secure a position of virtual political domination that endured for more than half a century.

The Jeffersonian Republicans, therefore, became the prototype of the successful American political party which, by bringing together different geographical, economic, and social groups, could secure a long-standing majority. Although these various elements might be conscious of their differences, they would usually recognize, especially under stress, the common element holding them together.

The dynamic growth of slavery after the 1830's jarred this agrarian coalition. First, it caused the slave-owning element in the party's southern wing to secure a dominant position. Secondly, the slavery system's prodigal use of land generated an appetite for more territory. This pressure eventually brought southern slave-owners into conflict with western farmers, who, struggling with them for control of the same acres, became increasingly conscious of their erstwhile party allies as hostile southerners rather than as fellow farmers. The opposition of these farmers to the advancement of slavery proved to be the chief factor in upsetting the old coalition. When they sensed that slavery was a direct threat to their way of life, they turned to the eastern financial and industrial interests, and discovered new areas of common concern with their former foes. A new alliance began to emerge from the broken pieces of the old.

The Republican party, formed in 1854, took advantage of the farmer's hostility to slavery and his alienation from his Democratic moorings. Abraham Lincoln, in particular, aided this process by depicting the advance of slavery as an attack against the way of life of free men. Such a phraseology, as Richard Hofstadter has pointed out, masterfully brought into the same camp those opposed to slavery on moral grounds as well as economic.[1] Furthermore, the Republicans reinforced their appeal to the West by the passage of the Homestead Act, which generously gave each settler 160 acres of free land. The party was thus in an excellent position to dominate national politics after the war.

Post-Civil War Politics

One of the main results of the Civil War was, of course, the freeing of the southern Negro from slavery, which brought with it the problem of fitting him into the fabric of established American life. At the same time, the war stimulated the dynamic growth of northern industrial capitalism. Indeed, so remarkable was industry's progress as compared with its former modest rate of advance that it could be considered as much a newly freed force on the American scene as the southern Negro. Moreover, the voracious demand of this growing industrial giant for manpower encouraged the great migration from Europe. Thus in the period following the war, the country was faced with the problems of accommodating into the American scene the freed Negroes, the power of big business, and, somewhat later, the mass of newly arrived immigrants.

The first three decades after the Civil War were primarily devoted to groping for a solution to the problem of the Negroes and the large capitalists. The Supreme Court, through a gradual step-by-step process of interpreting the Fourteenth Amendment's "equal protection of the laws" clause, practically eliminated its ostensible purpose, the guarantee of the southern Negroes' rights. By a similarly hesitant unfolding of judicial interpretation, it gave the amendment a new constitutional and economic significance

[1] Richard Hofstadter, *The American Political Tradition and the Men Who Made It* (New York: Vintage Books, 1956), pp. 110–117.

by establishing it as a protection of business from state regulation.

The uncertainty of the Court's position was a true reflection of the times, mirroring a similar ambiguity in both South and North. There was to be no strict rigid pattern of restricting the Negro's social and political rights until a national political system would be firmly established with the triumph of southern white supremacy as one of its major bases.[2]

From 1872 to 1896, there was not, as there had been previously, one single party in dominant control with a solid majority coalition behind it. The closest approach to such power was found in the continuation of the Civil War's Republican alliance between the eastern industrial and financial interests and the western farmers. By this arrangement, basically conservative forces, closely identified with ascendant industrialism, dominated the country's politics. The only conceivable cloud for the conservatives could come from another Jeffersonian agrarian alliance between the South and the West against the East.

Such an alliance seemed an unlikely possibility. The experience of the Civil War was still too near to allow the western farmers to reenter a Democratic party so closely associated with the South. Whenever the war's fiery memories showed any signs of dying down in the popular mind, the Republican leadership had few moral qualms about rousing them once more by "waving the bloody shirt." Even when the farmer was most disillusioned by the big business coloration of the Republicans, he could hardly find the Democrats, often controlled by the same eastern interests, an inviting alternative. In addition, a notable part of the Democratic party's northern electoral strength came from the unsavory machines of the cities. Such things made the image of the Democratic party a repellent one to the mass of western farmers, and discouraged its possible emergence as a vehicle of agrarian protest against the rising power of industry and finance. If there was to be another Jeffersonian agrarian alliance, it could not likely occur within Jefferson's own party.

[2] C. Vann Woodward, *The Strange Career of Jim Crow* (New York: Oxford University Press, 1955), ch. 1. See also Guy B. Johnson, "Freedom, Equality, and Segregation," *The Review of Politics*, XX, 2 (April, 1958), 149–152.

A fundamental change seemed likely to come in the wake of a bitter depression that hit both the western and the southern farmers in the 1880's and 1890's. They instinctively looked to the moneyed strongholds of the East as the source of their economic troubles. If the tide of swelling industrial power could have been checked, this would have been the favorable moment. The western farmers, now suspicious of Republicans as well as Democrats, organized a series of third parties to voice their demands. The most powerful of these agrarian parties was the Populists, whose strong appeal enabled them to transcend their regional limits and to continue their success in the South. The country, therefore, was on the verge of a fundamental political realignment as a new major party, with its small-farmer base in the West and South, appeared ready to take the Jeffersonian torch from the Democrats. The apparent climax of this movement came in 1896 when the Populists supported the presidential candidate chosen by a radically dominated Democratic convention, William Jennings Bryan. There could be no misjudging the depth of the farmers' protest, nor misinterpreting Bryan's attack upon "the cross of gold." With the country sharply divided, our future politics seemed destined to be a clash—and probably a crude, bitter one—between a radical agrarian party and a conservative industrialist one.

The New Political System

The likely result of such a battle is open to conjecture. A lasting victory for the farmers at this time had probably little chance of success in the face of their inability to achieve a partnership with the labor movement and the vigorous strength of their opponents, who possessed unquestioned control of the Northeast, great power in much of the Midwest, and even significant support in the Populist strongholds in the South and the plains states. The conflict, however, did not take place. The country's future political pattern was not to be fashioned upon the seemingly strong and clear division of 1896 because this proved too simple for the complex American society of the early twentieth century. Social and cultural pressures of massive force diffused and divided this battle array with the result that the northern industrial interests were not only saved from the threat of a determined agrarian alliance, but also became the keystone of a new conservative political system.[3]

In the South, the Negro question was the basic social issue which deflected the economic division and shattered the Populist movement. C. Vann Woodward has convincingly shown that southern conservatives, fearful of the threat to their property and privileges, raised the race issue to break the ranks of the party.[4] Appealing to long-standing prejudice, they warned of a potentially drastic increase of Negro political power, particularly in a party with a rural, lower-class base. With the success of these tactics, the South, generally under conservative leadership, became a one-party area in order to guarantee white supremacy. The southern Negro, as a result, became the forgotten man of American politics, a cipher in all power calculations. The political monopoly of the Democratic party in the South, intensely preoccupied with the particular character of its society, facilitated the Republican party's ascendancy in the rest of the country. Under the control of its eastern financial interests, it generally maintained political power until the period of the Great Depression and the New Deal, when the established political pattern began to dissolve.

In the Midwest (the former West), however, the rapid decline of Populism cannot be attributed to one primary cause. Rather, the Populist emphasis upon economics was outflanked by divergent social issues, such as prohibition, anti-Catholicism, and woman suffrage, which prevented the maintenance of a true radical coalition. Moreover, economic discontent was sharply dissipated by increasing prosperity, as well as by the nationalism engendered by the Spanish-American War.[5] With the weakening of their party, the ranks of the midwestern Populists divided, with some joining the Democrats and others becoming potential re-

[3] For an examination of the concept of the displacement of political conflict, see E. E. Schattschneider, *The Semisovereign People: A Realist's View of Democracy in America* (New York: Holt, Rinehart and Winston, 1960), ch. IV.

[4] See his *Origins of the New South, 1877–1913* (Baton Rouge: Louisiana State University Press, 1951).

[5] Walter T. K. Nugent, *The Tolerant Populists: Kansas Populism and Nativism* (Chicago: University of Chicago Press, 1963), pp. 153–209.

cruits to later third parties, while still others returned to the Republican fold and thus buttressed its national political domination.

At first glance, it would seem paradoxical that any of these farmers could have forgotten the bitter memories of but a short time earlier and could ally themselves with their former economic foes. But the bitterness of the farmers in the previous decades had been much more than a reaction to economic hardship. They had, also, been watching with increasing suspicion the rise of the large cities and, in particular, those on the Atlantic Coast swelling with southern and eastern European immigrants. The aggressiveness and selfishness of the eastern financiers were seen as part of a broader and more inclusive threat, that of the growth and impending power of a new urban way of life based upon a combination of large impersonalized speculative finance and a cheap labor supply of masses of alien, unassimilated persons.[6] An industrial economy and an urban culture, it was felt, could destroy the simple, upright society of rural, small-town America, by the sheer force of its technology and the insidiousness of its immorality. Before the Civil War, farmers had viewed slavery as a fundamental threat to their free way of life; now, many believed that the city and the machine were closing in on the countryside and the free individual.

Within this setting, former Populists who returned to the "Grand Old Party" could feel they were justified in their action. By alliance at the state level with the more prosperous farmers and other conservative elements in the rural areas and small towns, they were fitting into the new pattern of American politics and were thus in a position to defend themselves from the effects of feared changes. Although the resultant political control of the

[6] The degree of nativism in the Populist movement and the larger question as to whether it was primarily a progressive or reactionary force in American history is debatable. The most influential historian who has highlighted their regressive qualities has been Richard Hofstadter, *The Age of Reform from Bryan to F.D.R.* (New York: Knopf, 1956), pp. 60–93. For rebuttals to this critical re-interpretation, see C. Vann Woodward, *The Burden of Southern History* (Baton Rouge: Louisiana State University Press, 1960); "The Populist Heritage and the Intellectual," Nugent, *op. cit.;* and Norman Pollack, *The Populist Response to Industrial America: Midwestern Political Thought* (Cambridge: Harvard University Press, 1962).

states was reflected in some degree in Congress, it was mainly important in its own right because rural values could be most effectively defended at the state and local levels. Those in power, therefore, resolutely intended to retain their majorities in the state legislatures in the future as well.

If the cities could not be checked in the steady advance of their population, at least this increase could be nullified politically in the apportionment of representation. In the crucial transition period from 1890 to 1910, this rural domination was, for all practical purposes, written into a number of state constitutions, whether in the drafting of new ones or in the revising of the old. When this permanence of rural domination was not specifically enacted, it was achieved by indirection and neglect. Thus, many state legislatures retained their rural majority by refusing reapportionment to meet shifting demographic currents. In 1950 and 1960 we, therefore, would find legislatures that did not represent their contemporary urbanized population, but rather the rural one of 1900.

Malapportionment was by no means restricted solely to the Midwest. It proved extremely popular in the Northeast, where rural suspicion of the cities may even have been greater because of the heavier concentration of persons of southern and eastern European background. Since the population of the rural areas, with the exception of the Pennsylvania Dutch, was predominantly Anglo-Saxon in ancestry, the contrast between city and country was sharp. The distinction was often seen in rural eyes as the basis of a contest between the Puritan virtue of the farms and the alien immorality of the cities with their malodorous political machines. Malapportionment was also usually encouraged by the dominant financial and industrial northern interests, even though they were nominally located in the cities. Their leaders shared with the state's rural population not only a common ethnic origin, but a general conservatism and a prejudice against the city population as well.

The political system developed at the beginning of the century thus deserved the description of "conservative" because at every level of its operation it was concerned with the maintenance of the status quo. It was definitely keyed to the interests of big business because northern industry was in the dominant national political position. By taking advantage of deep-seated social feelings in the rural areas and in the South, they had not only frustrated the formation of a hostile political coalition, but had also secured allies, the farmers and the southern whites, as insistent as they upon maintaining authority within their own bailiwicks. Within this conservative pattern of politics, with power distributed on a fragmented local basis, even the machines of the large cities found their niche. As the southern whites and midwestern farmers acquiesced to national control by northeastern finance and industry, so did the machines, at their level, accept the rural domination of their states in order to guarantee control of their own territory.

The political system seemed fundamentally stable and durable because of the balance secured by this distribution of power. The balance, in truth, was never a perfect one and there would often be minor displacements. Conservative reformers would at times oust city machines; liberal urban forces would win state capitols; and the Republican party would even lose the presidency in the Wilsonian period. These changes, however, were basically short-lived and were usually regarded as exceptional events. There were also points of friction and differences of view among the conservative forces. Nevertheless, consciously or half-consciously, all were usually aware of their stake in the prevailing system and avoided any steps that might upset it.

One can easily understand why the system appeared a strong, even an infallible, one. Its chief losers, the Negroes in the South, were impotent since they were deprived of the vote and relegated to a lower caste status. Negroes who moved North were insignificant politically because the Republican party had to do very little to retain their traditional support. Living in harsh economic circumstances in the large cities, moreover, they were easily manipulated by the political machines.

The immigrants, also, were politically weak, primarily because they had to devote the greater part of their energies to securing a living and adjusting to what must have appeared to them a bewildering society. Because of their unfamiliarity with the English language and the American political process, they, too, furnished ready fodder for the political machines, whose leaders had no real desire to upset the prevailing political equilibrium.

Even had there been marked and widespread dissatisfaction with the existing system, there was hardly any method for translating it into politically effective action. Third parties, which might have channeled protest, were discouraged by law as well as by the institutional structure. The method of apportionment guaranteed that the voice of urban discontent would be a muffled one at best. At times, it seemed that only action by the courts could slash through the political maze—but they were as much a part of the existing system as the legislatures themselves.

Despite the impressive strength and elegant composition of the political structure, it had the compelling fault that its two main purposes were opposed to American ideals. First, it established a clear-cut hierarchical division of political power by discriminating between groups of citizens. Second, it attempted to set up a wall against the forces of social and economic change.

Equality has been inbred in the American character and is considered, along with liberty, the foundation of our concept of democracy. In other countries, these values had to be achieved slowly or won violently in the face of powerful conservative institutions and traditions. Here, we were already committed to them; indeed, they had been one of the main purposes of our founding "a new nation, conceived in liberty and dedicated to the proposition that all men are created equal." This original dedication was constantly renewed by the public school, the pulpit, and the press, but also each time an immigrant disembarked—and more likely, even before he boarded ship.

In no act was the citizen practicing the ideals of liberty and equality more consciously than in his voting, the most basic function of democracy. By the use of malapportionment, the devisers of the new political system flouted the principle of the equal vote to insure the maintenance of political control in rural, Anglo-Saxon hands. The unfamiliar pattern of a permanent majority and a permanent minority was imposed upon the traditional equality of our politics. The country could not openly acknowledge its action because that would have been a declaration against its own ideals. Due homage was paid to democratic virtue by granting the new urban dwellers the vote—but it was not fairly counted.

The authors of the new political system felt justified in their

disregard of our egalitarian beliefs because of their great fear of the new century's pressures for change. This fear of change and the resultant desire to secure an unnatural stability were a desertion of our basic tradition, since the chief identifying characteristic of our whole previous historical experience had been a willingness to face uncertainty and change. In moving to a "New World," the first settlers on the continent literally accepted the challenge of new conditions. With the official ending of the frontier in 1890, after almost 300 years of conquering and settling a vast territorial expanse, came a desire to refrain from new challenges, particularly those of a completely new dimension. If we criticize this desire to avoid the difficult and new, such criticism must be marked with a sympathetic understanding, because the problems confronting the American people were by objective standards of immense proportions. But in the refusal to acknowledge these problems, to recognize their magnitude, and to attempt to solve them, they established a static and rigid political system that virtually ignored the country's fundamental social and economic changes.

Such a conservative system assumed that the politically handicapped groups, especially the Negroes and the urban ethnic minorities, would remain content in their subordinate position. Little thought was given to the possibility that change in their social and economic status might increase their political expectations. The dominant powers thus believed that the dynamics of politics could be ignored.

When we discuss legislative representation in Chapter Five, we shall note that our eventual break with the practice of malapportionment and the conservative political system which it supported parallels rather strikingly the British experience with the Great Reform Bill of 1832. Thus, Trevelyan's description of the Tories' hostile reaction to reform fits the similarly limited vision of American conservatives at the turn of the century—and even later:

> The opponents of the Bill . . . in their honest attachment to the country's noble past and not ignoble present, refused to consider the possibilities of the future and to take counsel how the best of the past could be preserved for service in a new age. Their mistake did not consist in preferring rural to city life, or aristocracy to bourgeoisie—

matters of taste wherein many will agree with them to-day and most of the Whig leaders agreed with them then. Nor did their mistake lie in their prophecy that larger changes would follow in the wake of the Reform Bill if once it were passed. The Tory mistake consisted in thinking that no change would follow if it were thrown out.[7]

The Madisonian Philosophy

Given the motivation of the new political system, we can understand the emphasis in the twentieth century upon the anti-majoritarian theories of James Madison and John C. Calhoun, particularly the assumption that theirs was *the* American political theory. This school of political thought visualized American society as composed of groups or localities of varying sizes, and considered the main aim of the political process was to achieve a consensus among them rather than to reflect the will of an abstract majority of single individuals. By this apparently practical approach, no one group, or "faction" in Madison's phraseology, could dominate the government and exert its will over the others.[8]

Although it is possible to attack the logic of Madison's philosophy,[9] his defenders maintain, nevertheless, that such an analysis is irrelevant because he was not writing a political theory per se. Rather than being a closet philosopher, he was deeply involved in the politics of his day, and his primary concern was to secure a stable, effective government. His ideas, therefore, are not to be measured by the logician's standard but rather in terms of their political sagacity and practicality.

[7] George M. Trevelyan, "The Great Days of Reform," in *The Times* (London, June 7, 1932), reproduced in Robert Livingstone Schuyler and Herman Ausubel, *The Making of English History* (New York: Dryden Press, 1952), p. 494.

[8] For a presentation of the Madisonian philosophy, see his writings in *The Federalist*, particularly numbers 10, 37, 47, and 51. For the allied theories of John Adams and John C. Calhoun, see George A. Peek, Jr., ed., *The Political Writing of John Adams: Representative Selections* (New York: Liberal Arts Press, 1954) and C. Gordon Post, ed., *A Disquisition on Government and Selections from the Discourse* (New York: Liberal Art Press, 1953).

[9] Robert Dahl, *A Preface to Democratic Theory* (Chicago: University of Chicago Press, 1956), ch. I.

If we judge Madison's works by these latter criteria, our verdict is a mixed one. We can realize that within the limits and experience of his own time, he justifiably rated the intellectual respect of his contemporaries. We cannot infer from this, however, that Madison's prescriptions are necessarily pertinent today. His fear of strong political power brought him—as it did Calhoun—perilously close to the point of demanding unanimity of all groups and localities before any government action could be undertaken. This prescription, with its emphasis upon individual freedom, was uncomfortably similar to the maladroit *liberum veto* of medieval Poland, whereby one noble could check a plan desired by all of his fellows. Thus, the Madisonian philosophy, because of its concern for individual liberty, definitely hobbled the possibility of positive governmental action. Such a limited role for government, however, did not conflict with the needs and character of late eighteenth-century America. There was little, by our standards, that even an energetic government could accomplish in domestic affairs. As James M. Burns, in *The Deadlock of Democracy,* has pointed out, since modern problems and needs have caused us to turn increasingly toward government, the Madisonian political stalemate became accordingly less tolerable.

Some of Madison's assumptions, moreover, are as dated as his prescriptions. With most of his colleagues at the Philadelphia Convention, he was absorbed with the menacing potential of majority rule. The fear of the Founding Fathers of an unpropertied majority intent upon plundering an industrious minority had been distilled by them from the history of earlier civilizations and from contemporary events in Europe. Although this was at odds with immediate experience, they nevertheless believed that our country could not be uniquely immune from this persistent historical pattern.

Their concern about the evil instincts of an unpropertied majority has been proven needless by our experience. Only a tortured reading of American history could discern a continued attack of the majority upon the wealth of the minority. There have, it is true, been clashes between economic classes. What the poorer elements of society have usually desired, however, was not to topple the minority from its perch on the economic ladder, but rather to have free access to its rungs. Louis Hartz has ably shown, in his *The Liberal Tradition in America,* that despite the exaggerated language of this struggle in various periods of our history, it was, nevertheless, of a fundamentally different and milder character than the economic strife the Founding Fathers feared. Not only had they misjudged the nature of American society, but the Constitution they had drafted has been applied successfully only because of this error.

Similarly, from our modern perspective, we can see the naïveté of Madison's belief that concentrated political power was absolutely dangerous to freedom and that it must be diffused by a constitutional frame of separation. To be sure, in this century of the totalitarian state, we can well appreciate his suspicion of political power and his prime valuation of freedom. The rise of the dictators, however, has contained more than one moral. It has shown that constitutional devices, by themselves, are extremely weak protections against grasping political power. We have seen too many paper constitutions burnt by deep emotions or ripped by hard-faced iron men. The true defense of a free people derives less from their formal governmental structure than from their history, their traditions, and their temperament, from what Montesquieu termed "the spirit of the laws."

Furthermore, the success of political institutions, even more than their failure, has called into question the Madisonian distrust of power. Parliamentary systems, where powers are fused rather than separated, tend to allow their majorities full political control, but not necessarily at the cost of significant minority rights. The British political structure is an excellent example because its majority party, through its control of the ministerial apparatus and its disciplined ranks in the House of Commons, has virtually unchecked constitutional power. Despite this lack of an institutional brake, British governing majorities have not committed any of the extreme actions predicted under the pessimistic Madisonian view. The minority has not been trampled upon, and civil liberties are as safe as in our own country—the British would claim, even safer. Thus, we have further indication that history and tradition are more significant in politics than constitutional structure. A constitution is not a generator of a people's political genius as much as its product.

Although Madison's assumptions have not been borne out by

political experiences either here or abroad, his philosophy retains nevertheless, a particular prominence in the twentieth century. Furthermore, one might assume that John Calhoun's companion theory of the concurrent majority, developed in the early nineteenth century, was discredited by the Civil War, which apparently had definitively decided whether one section of the country had a veto over all the others. Calhoun's reputation, however, has enjoyed a revival in recent years and the phrase "the concurrent majority" has been increasingly used to describe the operation of American politics.[10] Clearly this antimajoritarian tradition, despite its glaring weaknesses, must have had certain compelling points of strength.

The authority of Madison, Calhoun, and John Adams, the greatest political philosophers the country has produced, was used to rationalize practices that would otherwise be difficult to justify. Were the weighting of the vote and the denial of political equality alien or subversive to our basic ideals? The defenders of the system could convincingly deny this and, rather, claim that, in supporting the rights of the minority, they were protecting the individual liberties which were the cornerstone of our political beliefs. Was this static system an impractical retreat before the leading social and economic forces of the time? No, according to the theory, it was a realistically structured politics, keyed to actual economic interests and geographic areas, rather than one based upon an abstract world of perfectly equal individuals. The men in power could thus proclaim that they were in the very mainstream of the American political tradition.

In performing this rationalizing function, the theory helped to blur the nature of political tension in the first half of the twentieth century between the dynamic forces of change and the conservative elements determined to maintain the status quo. Instead of a clear-cut line of battle, there was a confusingly complex series of crosscurrents which deflected and confounded the essential conflict. These crosscurrents—economic, social, and cultural —reflected the complexity and diversity of the country. An attempt at a purely economic interpretation of American history,

[10] See John Fischer, "Unwritten Rules of American Politics," *Harper's Magazine,* CXCVII (November, 1948), 27–37. See also Herbert Agar, *The Price of Union* (Boston: Houghton Mifflin, 1950), pp. 267–269, 333–334.

for example, would dilute its richness and distort its significance. The relationship between social, racial, ethnic, and religious groups has often been as significant as that between economic classes. Although much of a man's life is by sheer necessity concentrated upon the size of his loaf of bread, we shall see that at many times he is even more concerned about whom he can break his bread with and what he is able to drink with it. Even though national political campaigns have seldom openly revolved about such questions, they are often brooding beneath the surface.

Because of these crosscurrents, it was not surprising in this period that an individual or group, liberal on one or two points, could at the same time be rigidly conservative on others. Contemporary and later observers, as well as the chief political actors themselves, were often confused by the speckled nature of political groupings and they failed to realize that the controversial issues of the times were really manifestations of the basic conflict between stability and change, between the desire to maintain the existing political system and the pressure to undo it. Thus, many erstwhile liberals possessed only a limited liberalism because they were, in essence, committed to the preservation of the system.

Similar crosscurrents appeared earlier in the Populist movement, in which radical economic protest was streaked with intolerant provincialism and crude nativism. These characteristics meshed into a fundamental reaction against an impending tide which, the Populists felt, threatened their whole way of life. Their targets, therefore, ran the gamut of the modern world. Thus, the Bryan who was the liberal hero against the forces of privilege in 1896 was the same Bryan, fighting what he considered another battle in the same war, who would in the 1920's refuse to support a public criticism of the Ku Klux Klan and would defend fundamentalist religion against the teaching of Darwinian science in the public schools.

When writers in the 1940's and the 1950's threw a sharp spotlight upon these illiberal facets and muted the harsh reality of the farmers' economic plight, Populism easily invited condescension. Its followers, however, were by no means the last group whose liberalism could be questioned by its opposition to the pressure of change.

Progressivism

The century's first reform wave, the Progressive movement, illustrated this ambiguity, this meshing of contradictory interests.[11] The interests of its adherents, mainly of the urban middle classes, were broader and more diverse than those of the Populists, and their program seemed to reflect a more sophisticated knowledge of modern American society and a surer grasp of what could be achieved through politics. Within a few years, their success was remarkable and they generated from their midwestern base a strong democratic tide throughout the country. Successful campaigns were launched for trustbusting, municipal reform, the primary, the direct election of senators, woman suffrage, and the limitation upon the autocratic power of the Speaker of the House of Representatives, and their cumulative effect raised hopes for the transformation of the political and social system. Yet no such transformation did take place—and, moreover, could not in light of the movement's nature.

The Progressives could not transcend the limitation of their conservative conceptions. Like the Populists, their middle-class members were concerned with the threatening implications of a modern industrial and urban civilization. Their defense also assumed the character of a crusade, appropriate to the primarily Puritan heritage of its clientele. "We are at Armageddon," exclaimed Theodore Roosevelt at the start of his Bull Moose campaign, "and we battle for the Lord."

Organized vice was an obvious target for a reform movement strongly grounded in religious morality. The local attacks upon the gambling hall, the brothel, and the saloon were transferred to the national scene with the passage of laws prohibiting the interstate transportation of lottery tickets and women for immoral purposes. The high point for the penchant of legislating morality came with the passage of the prohibition amendment, achieved through the successful combination of the urban reformers' anti-

[11] The analysis of Progressivism in this section leans heavily upon Richard Hofstadter's interpretation in *The Age of Reform from Bryan to F.D.R.*, pp. 131–269.

saloon feeling and the rural fundamentalists' antiliquor sentiment. The reformers were particularly concerned with the neighborhood saloon because they considered it the focus of the city's political as well as moral corruption. It was often the center of the machine's precinct activities, and the saloon-keeper played a prominent role in local politics. In New York City, it was alleged that nothing could dissolve a meeting of Tammany district leaders more quickly than the cry, "Your saloon is on fire."

Although these campaigns against the machines and vice unquestionably possessed a purifying, wholesome character, they contained, at the same time, a dark side which severely cramped the Progressive movement and limited the effectiveness of its reforms. This moralistic preoccupation betrayed a general ethnic and class bias which upset any possibility of forming an alliance that could transform the system. The base of the machine was in the city's slums, with their masses of newly naturalized immigrants, and later of Negroes from the South. In addition, the "respectable" urban elements suspected that the patronage of other forms of immorality came largely from the same sources. The Progressives were thus not able to secure a true and lasting rapport with the bulk of the cities' population, without whose support full reform in the twentieth century was an impossibility. Richard Hofstadter has written: "The insulation of the Progressive from the support of the most exploited sector of the population was one of the factors, that for all his humanitarianism, courage, and vision, reduced the social range and the radical drive of his program and kept him genteel, proper, and safe." [12]

Almost no facet of Progressive reform was free of this crippling prejudice. Many of their proposals, such as woman suffrage and literacy qualifications for naturalization and for voting, revealed some balance between a liberal humanitarianism and a restrictive class and ethnic bias. Even in their most humane and sympathetic endeavors, like the establishment of slum settlement houses, a trace of condescension could still be detected. At their most intolerant, there could be little doubt about the bent of Progressive emotions. Their advocacy of immigration restriction measures clearly showed their hostile reaction to the new groups

[12] *Ibid.*, p. 184.

which seemed to upset the previous balance of the population and which threatened to change the very character and face of the city.

The Progressive record, however, should not be underestimated since its political reforms, on balance, advanced democracy and blew a clear fresh blast of air through all levels of the governmental apparatus. Despite their zeal for innovation, the Progressives were basically conservative in wanting to maintain the existing political system as a dam against the forces of change.

The ambiguous position of the Progressives and the dual nature of their reforms is best illustrated by their attack upon the political machine. Although the machine was an engine of evil to the city's middle-class Anglo-Saxon minority, it had a fundamentally different appearance to its immigrant population. The latter generally found the American political system a cold and bewildering one. The machine, in giving them refuge and guidance, quickly initiated them into the political process and often gave them their first sense of identification with American life. This was not an achievement to be measured lightly, and the new citizens gratefully paid with their votes. Any doubts or suspicions about the machine which they might have entertained were usually dispelled when they realized the bias of its opponents. Thus, when the reformers pressed a campaign against the selfishness, corruption, and sordidness of the machine, they usually failed to secure a solid mass electoral base upon which to remain in power.

The lack of stable success was only one aspect of the futility of the antimachine campaign. What the Progressives failed to realize was that the machine had its particular niche in the existing political balance of power. Thus, the reformers and the machine politicians were both conservative since they were fundamentally interested in maintaining the status quo. In the short run, consequently, the immigrant groups were being manipulated by the machine to preserve a power system that was not to their advantage. In the long run, however, the role of the bosses was an ironic one because they were introducing into politics a potentially dynamic force that would eventually be instrumental in upsetting the system, and with it, the machines as well. The irony to the reformers was even sharper because the demise of the machine, their long-sought, elusive goal, would only take place—and really could only take place—through the cooperation of those they disdained, and only as part of a fundamental change in a system they wanted to preserve.

Wilsonian Liberalism

A new opportunity for liberalism occurred when the Democratic party returned to national power in 1912 after the Republicans had temporarily split. This loss of political control by the large northern industrial interests carried with it the exciting potentiality of a realignment of the American political scene and the formation of a permanent progressive alliance. The resurgent Democratic party, with its main core of strength in the South but with solid support in the West, seemed to be a modern version of the old Jeffersonian rural alliance against the industrial East, the coalition which Bryan had failed to reconstruct.

Despite its Jeffersonian roots, such an agrarian alliance, as the Populist example showed, might not prove liberal in an age of increasing industrialization and urbanization. A rural attempt to check industrial power in the hope of reversing the clock and reviving the Jeffersonian and Jacksonian ideal of an agricultural, small-business society would be an inadequate and inappropriate response to modern needs. In relation to the realities of the period, the Republicans, despite their links with the vested interests, might readily have qualified as the more liberal party because of their acceptance of the industrial age. It was no accident that the Progressive movement was primarily a Republican effort or that the party received at this time considerable support from labor, urban ethnic groups, and intellectuals. In contrast, the Democrats, with their strong southern and western rural coloration, appeared an outmoded party.

Wilson's first legislative efforts fitted this party character despite the fact that they were well received by liberals because they favored the small businessmen against the large, and the poorer states against the wealthier. In essence, however, the reduction of the tariff, the establishment of the Federal Trade Commission and the Federal Reserve System, and the passage of the Clayton Antitrust Act generally reflected the desire of the more backward elements of society to secure a freer and looser economic system, similar to the free competition the country supposedly enjoyed before its commerce was dominated by the industrial giants. Indeed, historians critical of Wilson believe that, despite his intellectual power and moral breadth, he may never have graduated from the nineteenth-century, small-town, laissez-faire training of his youth, and consequently did not feel a true rapport with the city and modern technology. Moreover, his insight into the operation of a complex society was probably not aided by a moralistic Calvinism in which, as with Populism and Progressivism, the forces of righteousness were ready to do battle with the army of evil.

The attitude toward Negroes of an administration in which many southerners were serving under a southern-born president was another barrier to fundamental political change. In the Wilsonian era, the Negroes' status in the country was lowered, and both Washington and the federal government were more segregated after his period in office than before. This was a dubious legacy for a liberal presidency because white supremacy was maintained in the South under the auspices of the conservative political system.

In the face of these negative attributes and handicaps to a true liberalism, what is remarkable about the Wilson administration was the degree of its success, the breadth of its appeal, and, especially, its inspiration for the future. A part of the answer lay in Wilson's character. From the first, by his vigorous leadership, scholarly intellect, and moral stature, he made a very strong impact upon groups not normally attracted to the traditional Democratic rural alliance of the South and the West. In addition, the urban votes he may have forfeited by his hostility to Democratic machines were more than balanced by the support of their opponents.

The content of his politics, moreover, did not seem to contradict its style. Despite the fact that his initial legislative program could be considered somewhat anachronistic in the light of modern industrial life, it struck, as noted before, a responsive liberal chord in the country. Upon this foundation, Wilson later carried through reforms supported by labor groups and Progressives. Thus, at the midpoint of his presidency, the broadest and strongest possible liberal coalition seemed to be forming, composed of the old Populist forces of the South and West, the trade unions and minority groups in the cities, and a number of the Progressive middle-class reformers.[13]

This potential liberal grouping, however, never completely materialized. Its attempt to gloss over the fundamental clash between stability and change could not survive the pressures of our involvement in World War I. As the war progressed, the small town and the countryside reasserted their dominance over the city, and liberal disillusionment with Wilson increased. Sentiment against entrance in the war was strong in the Midwest, the center of Progressivism, and there was also marked pacifistic feeling in the large cities, especially among radical and some ethnic minority groups. The small-town ethos of the administration which had earlier manifested itself in its economic program showed another face in a harsh antipacifistic, antiradical campaign.

The dimming of the aura of liberalism in the last phase of Wilson's administration fitted the pattern of early twentieth-century reform movements: they showed great promise, made their mark in history, and yet failed to change the character of American society. Their failure stemmed directly from their limited conception of the basic conflict, to which all others were secondary, the battle between stability and change. A fundamental change in the system could occur only with a concerted attack along the whole line of battle by all groups opposed to the status quo. The reform movements, whether Populism, Progressivism, or Wilsonian liberalism, however, had neither the will nor the imagination to form and lead such an alliance. Furthermore, limited as each of these movements was in both purpose and support, it was nevertheless broader than its predecessors; this trend indicated that eventually a successful reform coalition could be established.

The immediate aftermath of the Wilson administration was a negative one. A direct clash between city and country had been impending from the very inception of a political system designed to check the city. This battle, deflected by the crosscurrents of

[13] Arthur S. Link, *Woodrow Wilson and the Progressive Era, 1910–1917* (New York: Harper and Row, 1954), pp. 224–227, 239–240, 249–251.

politics, particularly in the rise and fall of liberal movements, came out in the open as the rural areas took the offensive.

The Era of the 1920's

The years from the end of World War I to the New Deal seem to be relegated in the American mind to the position of an unimportant interregnum between the two great Wilson and Roosevelt administrations, both characterized by significant reform and involvement in a world war. Contrary to surface comparisons, however, the 1920's were some of the most significant years in our history.

The war and its aftermath had brought to the surface most of the fears which had been generated in the small towns and rural areas by the thrust of modern life. Realizing that the face of the country was changing, rural white Protestant America was determined to use its strong position in the established political system, not in a passive defense, but rather in a deliberate counterattack. As Daniel Bell wrote:

These skirmishes of the 1920's were the first defensive attacks of the nativist and the old middle-class elements. They arose in reaction to the entry *into* society of formerly disfranchised elements, particularly the children of immigrants and members of minority ethnic groups—an entry made through the urban political machines, the only major route open to them. In short, it was a reaction to the rise of a mass society.[14]

The most important example of this rural counterattack was prohibition. One of the main reasons we tend to dismiss the 1920's as frivolous is because they were so preoccupied with a subject apparently much less significant than economic policy, civil rights, or foreign policy. Within the context of the nation's social divisions, however, prohibition was of major importance. Although supported by some elements in the cities, basically it pitted the rural American culture directly against the urban. The consumption of alcohol was considered sinful by the fundamentalist Protestant denominations which were strong in the country-

[14] Daniel Bell, "The Dispossessed—1962," in Daniel Bell, ed., *The Radical Right* (Garden City, N.Y: Doubleday, 1963), pp. 19–20.

side, especially in the appropriately named Bible Belt. Their population was thus imbued with a moral zeal against this evil so indelibly linked with the mores of the cities' inhabitants. The small town and the country, realizing that they could not halt the swelling tide of the population of the cities, attempted rather to transform their way of life. Denis Brogan, in his *Politics in America*, ably placed prohibition in the defensive rural cast of mind:

Prohibition, looked at historically, was a rearguard action, fought by the elements in American life that urbanization, the motor car, the decline in the "old-time religion," were steadily weakening and would have weakened, nearly as fast, if prohibition had remained a rural fad. It was said that the South, in 1861, went to war against the Census of 1860 that showed the immense economic superiority of the North. The Drys, in a sense, went to political war against the Census of 1910 which revealed, for the first time, that the American farmer was now a member of a declining minority group. Almost everything economically, socially, philosophically, was against him. Radio, the movies, the cheap magazines, the comparative ease of travel were undermining his traditions and his way of life. He was a man with a grievance, and prohibition was, among other things, an expression of that grievance. It was also, and here it deserves more sympathy, an expression of a real and genuine alarm that the new urban world would eat away the habits and beliefs on which rural America had prospered. The fear was well-founded, the remedy was imbecile.[15]

One of the main reasons for the harshness of Brogan's verdict of "imbecile" upon prohibition was that its effect was quite the reverse of what had been expected by its advocates. The desired change in urban morality did not occur. On the contrary, the exigencies of evading the strictures of prohibition resulted in a much laxer morality throughout the country. In addition, powerful criminal elements, through their services as bootleggers, secured positions of influence in the country's political and commercial structure which they probably still retain to this day. The effort to transform morals by law failed and its failure weakened popular respect for law and order. With cruel irony, the America shaped by prohibition began to approach the worst of the pro-

[15] Denis W. Brogan, *Politics in America* (Garden City, N.Y.: Anchor Books, 1960), p. 160.

hibitionists' former fears. Even in terms of short-run political advantage, the "noble experiment" failed its backers. Many city dwellers, who had possessed only a casual interest in the ordinary fare of politics, were angered by this presumptuous interference with their private lives.

Prohibition was by no means the only example of the rural attempt to reverse the tide of history or of the ironic results of failure. The prevailing sentiment in the small town held that the city was alien territory because its heavy number of immigrants, particularly from southern and eastern Europe, threatened the traditional American way of life. As a result a streak of nativism, which had cropped up to the surface previously in our history, assumed nationwide proportions. In addition, influential anthropological theories buttressed these sentiments by emphasizing the innate cultural differences between biologically separated races.[16]

A ground swell, therefore, developed for checking the flow of these aliens. In this endeavor, the predominantly rural forces gained valuable and influential allies within the cities themselves by securing the support of the middle-class Progressives and the trade unions, each with its own particular bias against the immigrants. Thus, a quota system was introduced, whereby out of a limited total of yearly immigrants, each country would be allotted a quota in direct proportion to the number of persons in the United States in a particular year who could trace their descent from it. The restrictive nature of the immigration laws was evident in the fact that earlier censuses were usually used as a base for calculation: the 1910 census for the 1921 act, the 1890 (!) census for the 1924 act, and the 1920 census for subsequent ones until recently. Restrictive immigration, which remained on our statute books for more than forty years, not only limited immigration in general, but cut down drastically the number of immigrants from southern and eastern Europe.

As with the case of prohibition, however, the ultimate effects of this restriction were contrary to the expectations of its advocates. They overlooked that newly arrived immigrants had performed a necessary service in a dynamic economy, that of a labor force doing the hardest, dirtiest, and least remunerative work.

[16] The most popular presentation of these theories is in Madison Grant, *The Passing of the Great Race* (New York: Scribner's, 1921).

With the normal source of supply limited, industry had to tap other outlets. Alan Grimes has noted that, as a result, a major inner migration took place in our country from the South to the North. Although many poor whites followed this path, it was primarily the Negroes who left the South. Thus, the percentage of American Negroes living in the South dropped from 90 per cent at the beginning of the century to less than 50 per cent today. Since they were drawn to the large cities in their move to the North, the urban slums remained and still contain an "alien" population; all that has changed is the nature of their alienation.[17] Nathan Glazer and Daniel Patrick Moynihan, in their study of minority groups in New York City, have written:

> The Negro population is still in large part new to the city. In 1960 half of the entire nonwhite population of the city above the age of 20 had come from the South. These Americans of two centuries are as much immigrant as any European immigrant group, for the shift from the South to New York is as radical a change for the Negro as that faced by earlier immigrants.[18]

This influx into the northern cities exerted a significant impact upon the established political system, under which the southern Negroes were the most handicapped group in the country, deprived of political influence and the basic civil rights. Those who did move to the North, although hardly achieving full equality, did secure the vote. This proved to be not only the means to improve their own position, but also the potential political leverage to aid the members of their race they had left behind. Thus, the addition of the Negroes to the other ethnic minorities in the city aggravated the tension between it and the countryside and hastened the downfall of the existing political system.

The underlying clash between the rural and urban cultures on the question of change can be discerned on a whole gamut of issues in the 1920's. If one incident symbolized this division, it was the Scopes case in 1925, Tennessee's famous "monkey trial," which concerned the violation of the state law prohibiting the

[17] Alan P. Grimes, *Equality in America: Religion, Race, and the Urban Majority* (New York: Oxford University Press, 1964), pp. 64–68.

[18] Nathan Glazer and Daniel Patrick Moynihan, *Beyond the Melting Pot: The Negroes, Puerto Ricans, Jews, Italians, and Irish of New York City* (Cambridge: M.I.T. Press and Harvard University Press, 1963), p. 26.

teaching of the Darwinian theory of evolution in the public schools. Here was another effort to protect part of the country's religious foundation, in this case the fundamentalist interpretation of the Bible, from the apparently corrosive influences of the university and the scientific laboratory. The backwoods rural forces, in their effort to prevent change, struck at the advancement of knowledge itself. As Plato pointed out in theory and as modern totalitarians have shown in practice, there must be a rigid check on books and ideas if a static system is to be maintained, because these could easily become precipitants of change.

The trial's character as a rural-urban debate on freedom of knowledge was set off in sharp focus by its *dramatis personae*. The chief spokesman for Tennessee was William Jennings Bryan, the hero of rural protest in 1896 and the Democratic presidential candidate in two subsequent elections as well. His opponent was the liberal and iconoclastic Clarence Darrow, a man as contemptuous of the traditional pieties as Bryan was their earnest advocate. The biting questioning by Darrow of Bryan's religious beliefs typified to the faithful followers of the "Great Commoner" the cynical urban undermining of moral values. To the rest of the country—and to much of the world—the narrowness and ignorance of Bryan's answers were disillusioning. Those urban forces which had formerly supported him flinched as they realized the limits of Populist liberalism. The climax of the trial did not come with its perfunctory verdict, but with the death of Bryan immediately afterwards, which seemed to symbolize the end of an older pattern of American life.

The Divided Democrats

This struggle between basic social forces that dominated the 1920's was not reflected politically in the contest between the parties, but rather in the tensions within the Democratic party. The Democrats achieved this distinction mainly as a result of their own weakness. The effects of the World War and the spread of isolationism in the Midwest slashed the party's strength and stripped from its ranks most of the new recruits it had secured in the Wilsonian period. Virtually its only sources of support were the two traditional ones, the machines of the large cities and the solid South with its rural western allies. At a time, therefore, when American politics was primarily based upon a city-rural battle coinciding with an immigrant-nativist clash, the Democratic party contained as its two chief elements the most rural sections of the country with the heaviest concentration of native-born Americans along with the most urban and the most immigrant-conscious parts. Although the Democrats had never been strangers to intraparty strife—and could seldom fight the erstwhile foe with the same enthusiasm as they could each other—the stark confrontation of these two forces presented a struggle of burning intensity and fateful consequences.

The party's most dramatic conflict occurred in its 1924 convention when the delegates battled through 103 ballots before nominating a presidential candidate. Since human physical resources are finite, men usually would not ballot 103 times unless something of great significance was at stake. The two chief contenders for the party's nomination typified its warring wings. William Gibbs McAdoo of California, a former Georgian and a former member of the cabinet of Woodrow Wilson, his father-in-law, was the representative of the rural sections of the party and was supported by William Jennings Bryan, the party's leading spokesman for the Populist tradition. His opponent was Governor Al Smith of New York, a fitting representative of urban interests and political machines because he came from our largest city and was a product of the country's most famous—or infamous—machine, Tammany Hall. His symbolical character was further enhanced by his Irish descent and Catholic religion, as well as by his strong opposition to prohibition. In addition, those sympathetic to a political system attuned to the true character of the country recognized that he was one of the best examples of the efficient administrators who were trying to adjust the political mechanism to modern social and economic conditions.

Even before the marathon balloting, which ended in the dark-horse compromise candidacy of John Davis, a New Yorker with West Virginian roots, the split in the party had already broken out in a debate on whether the platform should explicitly condemn the Ku Klux Klan. The Klan, which had played a major role in securing southern white supremacy over Negroes in the last stages of the Reconstruction period, had been revived during the World War with a broadened scope and base of operations. No longer limited solely to being an anti-Negro force in southern territory, its anti-Catholic, anti-Semitic, and anti-immigrant influence was felt throughout much of the country. Thus, the Klan, by its direct attack against the groups in American society most closely identified with the large cities, became the vanguard of the rural, small-town assault upon them. This role became evident when the Democratic convention, by a very narrow margin, refused, despite the Klan's emphasis upon distrust and hate, to accept a proposed platform clause against it.

The position of forces in the Democratic party as reflected in the stalemate of its 1924 convention shifted in the succeeding years. By 1928, its urban wing was in the ascendancy. Smith, aided by the rising population tide in the cities as well as by his increased personal prestige gained from a longer term in office, defeated the southern and small-town forces on the first ballot. This signal victory transferred the conflict between city and country to a larger theater, the national election campaign between Smith and the Republican candidate, Herbert Hoover. Hoover won a resounding victory with the overt benefit of being a Republican candidate in a period of Republican prosperity and with the surreptitious aid of nativistic, anti-Catholic, and anti-urban feeling. Buoyed by this wave, the Hoover forces even managed to crack the solid South.

Beneath the surface of overwhelming defeat, the Democratic party and the urban forces could have detected optimistic signs for the future. The electoral statistics revealed that a majority of the voters in the country's largest cities were in the Democratic column. Although this majority was a small one, it indicated a shift from the party's previous minority urban status.[19] This Democratic majority was impressive not only because the number of persons living in the city was increasing, but also, as Samuel Lubell has pointed out, because it reflected the heightened political consciousness of the second generation of its immigrant groups.[20]

[19] Samuel J. Eldersveld, "The Influence of Metropolitan Party Pluralities in Presidential Elections since 1920," *American Political Science Review,* XLIII, 6, (December, 1949), 1194; V. O. Key, Jr., *Politics, Parties, and Pressure Groups,* 5th ed. (New York: Crowell, 1964), pp. 530–531.

[20] Samuel Lubell, *The Future of American Politics, 2d ed.* (Garden City, N.Y.: Anchor Books, 1956), pp. 29–43.

The continuation of both of these urban trends at an accelerated pace in the 1930's had important consequences upon the fortunes of the Democratic party and the balance of its internal forces. The identification of an increasing urban majority with the Democratic party had its most visible impact in laying the foundation for its national supremacy by insuring a victorious or near-victorious margin in the large populous states which had a heavy weight in the presidential Electoral College. Within the Democratic party, the rising influence of the cities would correspondingly weaken its southern element. Although the city machines were the immediate gainers from this urban vote windfall, they, too, would in the long run suffer from its consequences.

The changing character of the Democratic party would have a profound effect upon the political system since the groups most handicapped under it, the ethnic minorities in the cities and the Negroes in the South, were now able to exert political influence. The system itself, therefore, would dissolve in the succeeding decades and its various elements would regroup in a new political pattern.

Chapter III

The Political System: Dissolution and Renewal

The Depression, the New Deal, and Roosevelt

In the 1930's, the direct confrontation between city and country did not take place because it was deflected by the Great Depression and the New Deal, which ripped apart the cohesiveness that had kept the conservative forces of the old de facto coalition together. A new political realignment took place with Franklin D. Roosevelt masterfully establishing a broad, dominant coalition which, at first, largely isolated the large businessmen, the chief beneficiaries under the old system. The new coalition was united upon a wide-sweeping energetic governmental program designed to check the effects of economic dislocation. The ultimate impact of these policies would change the function and significance of the government.

The political engine for the vast change was Roosevelt's Democratic party. Because of its disunity and its conservative characteristics, it was an unlikely candidate for such a decisive role. Its colorful history gave small hope that the party could long keep together in one coalition not only its own warring elements, but also those Republicans who had switched sides under the pressure of the depression. E. E. Schattschneider did not exaggerate when he wrote:

The Democratic party in the 1930s became the reluctant instrument of a revolution it did not plan and did not produce. It is hard to imagine a party less prepared for its new responsibilities than the Democratic party was at the time of Franklin Roosevelt's first inaugural.[1]

The very choice of Roosevelt as presidential nominee was hardly a portent of great change since it could be considered a victory for the rural and small-town elements of the party. Although the governor of New York, his strength at the Chicago convention came mainly from the southern and western delegates rather than those from the cities, most of whose machines were still faithful to Al Smith.[2] The agrarian brand on the party stood out even more clearly when the vice-presidential nomination was given to John Nance Garner, whose delegates from California and his home state of Texas had thrown their support to Roosevelt on the final victorious ballot. The embittered city spokesmen, some of whom refused to join in a final unanimous vote for Roosevelt, viewed his emergence primarily as a piece of good fortune thrown at the feet of the most regressive forces in the party, who had been searching since 1928 for a suitable figure to defeat Smith.[3]

It is thus easily understandable why many first considered that the New Deal was in a direct line of descent from the traditional heroes of the Democratic party, Jefferson, Jackson, Bryan, and Wilson. Just as Wilson had developed the formula of adding a measure of social workers and labor leaders to tincture Bryan's agrarian compound, so Roosevelt seemed to improve on this precedent by allowing the cities and labor an even greater—although still secondary—role in his administration. A good part of the early New Deal program with its interest in agriculture, its lowering of the tariff, its support of silver, its stimulation of small business, its encouragement of other centers of financial power

[1] E.E. Schattschneider, *The Semisovereign People: A Realist's View of Democracy in America* (New York: Holt, Rinehart and Winston, 1960), p. 86.

[2] Edward J. Flynn, *You're the Boss: The Practice of American Politics* (New York: Viking, 1947), p. 95. Flynn, the Democratic leader of the Bronx and one of the few machine men supporting Roosevelt, also noted that "most of the agricultural states supported Roosevelt, while practically all the industrial states were opposed to him" (p. 92).

[3] Oscar Handlin, *Al Smith and His America* (Boston: Atlantic–Little, Brown, 1958), pp. 142, 152–153, 159–166.

besides Wall Street, and its initial genuine desire to operate in partnership with business seemed a broader and more ambitious extension of Wilson's program. Even Roosevelt's enhancement of the presidency was in the Wilsonian tradition. Conservatives could, therefore, believe that American politics would follow traditional grooves and that fundamental change had been averted.

These judgments grossly underestimated Roosevelt himself. Today it is difficult for us to realize that his contemporaries in 1932 did not fully perceive his warm humanity, daring imagination, and brilliant political skill, and that some considered him a potentially weak president. Walter Lippmann was not alone in his view when he dismissed him as "a pleasant man who, without any important qualifications for the office, would very much like to be President." [4]

These contemporaries also failed to appreciate his sensitivity to the realities of all levels and facets of American life and his recognition of their changes. His background, wealth, education, and previous experience aided his acute observation. Unencumbered by the agrarianism of Bryan or the nineteenth-century outlook of Wilson, the Harvard-educated New Yorker recognized the importance of cities and the permanence of large industry in modern America. Unlike the self-made men whom the Republicans usually presented for the presidency, Roosevelt held no particular reverence for the barons of finance and the captains of industry, and looked at their pretensions and power with a skeptical eye.

Roosevelt's understanding of contemporary American politics complemented his sense of social and economic reality. His programs were skillfully attuned to the dynamic changes in the character of the electorate. The generating political force at this time was in the vote of the large cities. We noted that in the presidential election of 1928, the majority of their voters had gone over to the Democratic party. In 1932, this urban wave increased, and by 1936, it became a flood tide. These large cities proved to be the cornerstone of the new dominant Democratic alliance, because in this period they usually carried with them the large

[4] Walter Lippmann, *Interpretations, 1931–1932*, ed. Allan Nevins (New York: Macmillan, 1932), p. 262.

electoral states in which they were located.[5] Consequently, much of the New Deal program in relief, public works, labor relations, and social security was designed to benefit an urban clientele.

Urban political sentiments, however, can be seriously misunderstood if too strong an emphasis is placed upon the economic benefits of the New Deal to the cities. Although the ethnic minority groups unquestionably responded favorably to the economic benefits, they were even more deeply moved by his humanity and liberalism. Their enthusiasm was primarily fired by their realization that the New Deal was undermining the hierarchical values which suffused the political system. They recognized that when Roosevelt indicated to an unenthusiastic audience of the Daughters of the American Revolution that nearly all Americans were descended from immigrants, he was really speaking to them. Thus, they no longer considered themselves as hyphenated second-class citizens, alien elements in the body politic, but rather as significant members of a broad coalition in the very bloodstream of American politics.

This rapport between the ethnic minorities and the New Deal explains in large measure why it played a role in American political history fundamentally different from that of Progressivism and Wilsonian liberalism. Despite the probable descent of many of its programs from the former movements, the measures of the New Deal reflected a freedom from the prejudices which had cramped its predecessors.[6]

Similarly, this aspect of the New Deal provoked a sharp hostility among its enemies, who railed against "that man in the White House." [7] The irrationality and the bitter depths of this response could not be attributed solely—and possibly not even primarily—to economics. Eric Goldman quoted an incisive observer about this aspect of the feeling against Roosevelt:

[5] Samuel J. Eldersveld, "The Influence of Metropolitan Party Pluralities in Presidential Elections since 1920," *American Political Science Review*, XLIII, 6 (December, 1949), 1195–1206.

[6] Samuel Lubell emphasizes this aspect of the New Deal in *The Future of American Politics*, 2d ed. (Garden City, N.Y.: Anchor Books, 1956), pp. 44–85.

[7] Arthur M. Schlesinger, Jr., *The Coming of the New Deal* (Boston: Houghton Mifflin, 1959), pp. 567–569.

For quite a while I have lived in a commuter community that is rabidly anti-Roosevelt and I am convinced that the heart of this hatred is not economic. The real source of the venom is that Rooseveltism challenged their feeling that they were superior people, occupying by right a privileged position in the world. I am convinced that a lot of them would even have backed many of his economic measures if they had been permitted to believe the laws represented the fulfillment of their responsibility as "superior people." They were not permitted that belief. Instead, as the New Deal went on, it chipped away more and more at their sense of superiority. By the second term, it was pressing hard on a vital spot and the conservatives were screaming.[8]

The Machines

Although the importance of the rising urban vote was well recognized at this time, there was considerable doubt as to its significance. The main reason for this ambiguity was the position of the Democratic city machines since there was a natural tendency to credit them with delivering the vote. The machines were more than willing to take the credit—and with it, their share of federal patronage. Their leaders overcame their original coolness to Roosevelt not only by their pragmatic appreciation of his campaigning prowess and his electoral success, but also by their realization of the unprecedented patronage opportunities for a political party, which had been out of office for twelve years and which was about to embark upon an ambitious program requiring a vast bureaucracy. Roosevelt, on his part, was respectful of the machine leaders and considerate of their interests, even though they generally felt that the New Dealers were insensitive to their broad patronage demands. To contemporary observers, the president and the machines were inextricably linked together in mutual support. Neither the observers, the machines, nor even Roosevelt himself realized that if one could kill with kindness, he was committing this act against the machines.

The imposing urban majorities at the elections were not being delivered primarily through the efforts of the machines, but rather through the magic of Roosevelt's name and the appeal of

[8] Eric F. Goldman, *Rendezvous with Destiny: A History of Modern American Reform*, rev. and abr. ed. (New York: Vintage Books, 1956), p. 289.

his program. Indeed, the machines were dependent upon Roosevelt's appeal to carry them, as illustrated by the story about the 1932 election of a candidate for a local judgeship in Boss John McCooey's Brooklyn Democratic organization. The candidate had become concerned because:

he hadn't seen his name mentioned in the papers and he was sure he was going to be licked. He stood in McCooey's receiving line one Monday morning, intending to unburden himself on the county boss. But his local district leader saw him first, knew what was on his mind, and yanked him by the ear over to a corner.

The leader said: "Look. You've seen a ferryboat pull into a slip. When it pulls in, it pulls a lot of garbage in with it. Stop worrying. Roosevelt is a ferryboat." [9]

Since these organizations did not have to exert themselves unduly to win apparent successes, they grew weak and flabby. With their customary efficiency enervated and their customary corruption intact, they became model foils for tough, lean Republican state organizations which in the later 1930's would begin a vigorous counterattack under able, moderate leadership.

Even the substance of the New Deal, which gave such rich electoral dividends to the machines, proved to be another factor in their undoing. Their traditional largesse—the picnics in the summer, the food baskets at Christmas, and the ubiquitous dollar bills at election day—paled before the material gains of a sophisticated social welfare program. Only with the more recent immigrants could the machines picture themselves as the necessary transmission belt for these new benefits. To most of the machines' former clientele, their social service function was taken over by an impersonalized Washington bureaucracy and performed more rationally and honestly. The welfare state robbed these local organizations of their raison d'être and hastened "the last hurrah" of the old-time political leaders.

Moreover, the bosses' enthusiasm for the New Deal was slackening at the very time it was increasing among their apparent followers. The broad liberalism of the New Deal, which generated such a warm response among the minority ethnic groups, aroused their misgivings. This division between the

[9] Warren Moscow, *Politics in the Empire State* (New York: Knopf, 1948), p. 131.

operators of the machine and the urban population should not have been surprising since it was latent even before the beginning of the century. The machines, as noted earlier, were basically conservative because of their place within the political power system; the minority ethnic groups, on the other hand, with their subordinate status, were a potentially disruptive force. A break between them, although paradoxical on the surface, was almost destined to occur once strong pressure was applied against the system.

This division might possibly not have been so deep and the machines might have adjusted more readily if there had been no ethnic and religious complications.[10] The machine leadership had traditionally been a Gaelic preserve with the Irish leading the other ethnic minorities in the large cities by virtue of their seniority, their numbers, their knowledge of the English language, and their ready political talents. With the increasing tide of immigration, however, the percentage of Irish dropped. The second generation of the newer immigrants grew restive under their seemingly permanent monopoly of local political power. The Irish leaders attempted to check the spread of this rebellious sentiment by granting some bits of patronage and office to other ethnic groups when the political pie was being cut. Such tokens were usually inadequate and the leaders found themselves battling for sheer survival in their positions of power.

Usually the Italians were the largest nationality group next to the Irish, and in many instances outnumbered them. In New England, New York, and New Jersey, they, therefore, took the lead in wresting control from the Irish. When other ethnic groups, particularly the Jews, entered the fray, it became even more complex. At this stage, moreover, the conflict at times transcended the question of machine control into one of machine

[10] This section on the ethnic clash in urban American politics has been strongly influenced by the sensitive delineation of the conflict in Nathan Glazer and Daniel Patrick Moynihan, *Beyond the Melting Pot: The Negroes, Puerto Ricans, Jews, Italians, and Irish of New York City* (Cambridge: M.I.T. Press and Harvard University Press, 1963), particularly in the excellent chapters "The Irish" and "The Jews." James Q. Wilson in his study of Democratic reform groups points out their particular ethnic character, *The Amateur Democrat* (Chicago: University of Chicago Press, 1962), esp. pp. 13–16, 28, 79, 303–304.

survival. These newer elements would not only challenge the leadership for domination of the organizations but would also set up counter-organizations and, in New York, even minor counter-parties.

To complicate the struggle still further, the New Deal had attracted to its banner in the cities many liberals, who were Anglo-Saxon in ancestry and Protestant in religion. Although they were dissatisfied with the conservatism of the Republican party, their temptation to rebel had often been counterbalanced earlier by the traditional sleazy image of the Democratic city machine. This significant body of recruits thus was joining the party at the very time its old leadership was being threatened by new forces. Simultaneously, the second and third generations of the newer immigrant groups, with many members in the middle and professional classes, found increasingly more in common with their liberal Protestant counterparts and less with the Irish Catholic machine leaders.

The popularity of the New Deal, combined with the charismatic nature of Roosevelt's leadership, served to keep the warring elements in the party together. In the years after Roosevelt's death, however, the surface of party unity in the cities was broken. The issue of anti-Communism in the McCarthy period intensified the intraparty antagonism by reinforcing the conservatism of one faction and the liberalism of the other. The presidential candidacy of Adlai Stevenson in 1952 and 1956 deepened the fissure. The machines, despite their support for his nomination in 1952, developed reservations early in the campaign about his popular appeal and his decisiveness. The intellectualism, wit, and eloquence which convinced them that Stevenson was an irresolute, academic "cold fish" were precisely the qualities which appealed to the urban Protestant and Jewish voters and gave him an almost heroic status among them. Their anger at the token support they charged he received from the machines added another element of bitterness and misunderstanding in the conflict between them.[11]

The machines in the post-New Deal period, therefore, faced the most powerful and sustained attack leveled against them. This assault overcame the failings of the previous Progressive

[11] Wilson, op. cit., pp. 47, 52–55, 74, and 113.

[47]

antimachine campaigns, which, as we have seen, proved fruitless because of the mutual lack of understanding between the old stock reformers and the immigrant population of the cities. The machine bosses, who had never appreciated the irony of being conservative leaders of a potentially liberal population, often proved unable to cope with the shifting social character and heightened political consciousness of their erstwhile clientele.

The Negro and the South

Urban politics became still more complex with the addition of another unsettling factor encouraged by the New Deal, the demand of the Negroes (and in New York City, the Puerto Ricans as well) for their due recognition. Some of the new Jewish and Italian leaders and legislators found themselves in the same predicament as their Irish predecessors, with a following and a constituency fundamentally different from that which had brought them into power. Although the political demands of the Negroes followed the pattern of previous minority groups as they rose up the social and economic ladder, their unique characteristics of color, geography, and history raised particular problems and gave them a special role in American political life.

Although the northern Negroes were in a comparatively better position than those in the South, their status was, nevertheless, a low one, even before its worsening by the depression. Consequently, they felt, even more than other minority groups, the tonic effect of the New Deal, and their response was accordingly enthusiastic. The shift of their vote to the Democratic party, which could hardly be detected in 1932, assumed landslide proportions in 1936. This changeover was no passing phenomenon since the Negroes would remain the most faithful of all the groups within the New Deal coalition.

This electoral transformation was an unusual one, since the previous record of the Democratic party hardly justified the American Negro's looking to it for succor. The Negro was first attracted to the Democrats in reacting against a Republican party which had long taken his vote for granted. This insensitivity increased after the 1928 presidential election when Hoover carried part of the formerly Democratic solid South. The tantalizing vision of a permanent stronghold in the South encouraged the formation of "lily-white" Republican state organizations.[12]

The New Deal's economic program capitalized upon this initial jarring of the Negro's traditional adherence to the Republican party. Since the urban Negro, "the last hired, the first fired," was the heaviest target of depression unemployment, the New Deal's relief program had its greatest impact upon the Negro community. At the very time, therefore, when the Negroes' intangible benefits from the Republican party were dissolving under the pressures of political expediency, their tangible gains from the Democrats became the most important part of their existence. Moreover, as with other minorities, the confidence of the Negroes in Roosevelt transcended the economic and "stemmed from the conviction that he was trying to facilitate their long hard struggle to attain full citizenship." [13] Little wonder that in 1936, J. E. Spingarn, president of the National Association for the Advancement of Colored People, could declare that Roosevelt had "done more for the Negro than any Republican President since Lincoln." [14] By that time, the mass of Negro voters were ready to take the advice originally proferred by the Negro publisher Robert Vann in 1932: "My friends, go home and turn Lincoln's picture to the wall. That debt has been paid in full." [15]

The fusion of present economic help and future social equality was symbolized in the Negro mind by the first family itself. Franklin Roosevelt personified the politically practical priority of meeting immediate pressing economic needs. His wife, Eleanor Roosevelt, by her words and actions, represented the idealistic goal of future social equality, thereby provoking both a devotion and an antagonism unlike that accorded any other first lady.

Although Roosevelt never released his full power in a legislative struggle over civil rights,[16] and although future

[12] Henry Lee Moon, *Balance of Power: The Negro Vote* (Garden City, N.Y.: Doubleday, 1948), pp. 108–113.

[13] *Ibid.*, p. 27.

[14] Louis W. Koenig, *The Chief Executive* (New York: Harcourt, Brace and World, 1964), p. 113.

[15] Arthur M. Schlesinger, Jr., *The Politics of Upheaval* (Boston: Houghton Mifflin, 1960), p. 430.

[16] Richard P. Longaker, *The Presidency and Individual Liberties* (Ithaca, N.Y.: Cornell University Press, 1961), p. 11.

administrations were actually to accomplish more, as the New Deal developed, the eventual achievement of civil rights for the Negro became less utopian. The pressure of the large cities upon the political system would inevitably work to the advantage of the southern Negro, whose subordinate position was one of its integral parts—as well as one of the chief reasons for its establishment.

At first glance, such a development appeared unlikely since the South seemed to be the most favored region of the country at this time. Roosevelt believed that the revitalization of its economy deserved a high priority and he termed the South "the nation's no. 1 economic problem." Thus, the South, with its neighboring areas of the border states and the Southwest, gained heavily from federal funds. It was appropriate that one of our greatest experiments in governmental operation, the Tennessee Valley Authority, was conducted in this territory.

In addition, many southern Democrats had strongly favored Roosevelt's nomination in 1932 and played a prominent role in his administration. This was especially the case in Congress where southerners were among his chief spokesmen, and where their combination of seniority and political acumen seemed to guarantee them a permanent preeminence. Many an old Wilsonian in Washington felt justified in his view that the South in half a generation had come back once more to dominate the political scene.

Despite its traditional overlay, Roosevelt's administration was to have a different impact upon the South from Wilson's since it would eventually curtail southern political influence, and the pressures released by the New Deal would work toward the elimination of racial segregation. This lessening of political influence was least evident in Congress, which the South dominated. Yet, in the post-New Deal period, this domination would be of lessening value because the position of Congress itself was falling. On the other hand, while southern influence upon the presidency was declining, the power of the office was increasing. The chief influence upon the presidency had become the large cities, whose ever-increasing population felt justified in using their electoral power as leverage for achieving a broader-based political equality and ending a political system under which southern whites had maintained segregation. The white South had much opportunity in the years after the New Deal to appreciate the gulf between the era of Woodrow Wilson and that of Franklin Roosevelt, and to reflect upon whether it had shortsightedly forfeited its political and social heritage in order to attain a degree of economic protection and security.

These later-shifting tides of political power hit the white South with particular ferocity in its own stronghold, the Democratic party. It lost its party domination because the urban population was growing as the city vote was swinging heavily to the Democrats. The electoral returns, reflecting the stark population figures, revealed that the balance of power in the party had shifted and that the South was no longer the foundation of Democratic victory. Roosevelt's elections had shown that if the large cities were strongly Democratic, the South's electoral votes were not essential to success.[17] Even the elections of Truman and Kennedy, close as they were, were secured despite the cracking of the solidly Democratic South.

The southern influence in the presidential sphere was also diminished by the elimination in 1936 of the two-thirds rule at Democratic conventions. Since candidates were henceforward to be chosen by a simple majority vote, this change deprived the South, in effect, of its virtual veto in the convention's choice of candidates. The changes begun under the New Deal, therefore, would result in succeeding years in presidential candidates and platforms committing the party to a progressively greater fulfillment of a program of civil rights. The South, thus, found itself demoted within its "own party" to a secondary position in the determination of policy and the choice of presidential candidates.

The Philosophy of the New Deal

In the light of the New Deal's conflicting characteristics and implications, many of its contemporaries found difficulty in labeling it and were confused about its underlying philosophy. Some could even discern the distinct outlines of neo-Fascism or

[17] Alexander Heard, A Two-Party South? (Chapel Hill: University of North Carolina Press, 1952), p. 17.

Communism. Observers were also divided as to whether the New Deal was primarily a progressive or a conservative force.

A part of the theoretical ambiguity surrounding the New Deal is primarily semantic. Even our brief references to its dynamic and unsettling qualities are enough in themselves to justify it as a progressive movement, indeed radical enough to dissolve the existing political system and to lay the basis for another. At the same time, nevertheless, a strong case can be made for the conservatism of the New Deal if two of the meanings of the word are recognized. In this work, we have usually used the word in reference to a particular political system established in the 1890's with its special economic and social characteristics. Conservatism, however, can possess a much broader frame of reference, and we can, thus, describe the New Deal as "conservative," not of a special age or system, but rather of the country's basic traditions and political structure.

This clarification of conservatism is significant in the division between what is fundamental in our heritage and what is secondary or peripheral. In a time of crisis, the drawing of this line is particularly challenging because too intransigent a defense of the temporary may endanger and subvert the permanent. Roosevelt was conscious of this basic responsibility in these troubled years as he attempted to adjust the institutional structure to the degree necessary for survival in the modern world. Arthur Schlesinger, Jr., has shed light on his theoretical motivation by a revealing quotation from his 1932 campaign:

Say that civilization is a tree which, as it grows, continually produces rot and dead wood. The radical says: "Cut it down." The conservative says: "Don't touch it." The liberal compromises: "Let's prune, so that we lose neither the old trunk nor the new branches." This campaign is waged to teach the country to march upon its appointed course, the way of change, in an orderly march, avoiding alike the revolution of radicalism and the revolution of conservatism.[18]

Roosevelt's conception of his role and the importance of his mission were recognized by the British economist John Maynard Keynes, who wrote Roosevelt at the end of 1933:

[18] Schlesinger, op. cit., pp. 648–649.

You have made yourself the trustee for those in every country who seek to mend the evils of our condition by reasoned experiment within the framework of the existing social system.

If you fail, rational choice will be gravely prejudiced throughout the world, leaving orthodoxy and revolution to fight it out.

But, if you succeed, new and bolder methods will be tried everywhere, and we may date the first chapter of a new economic era from your accession to office.[19]

Keynes was an appropriate figure to have stated the importance of Roosevelt's mission because his theories, which would dominate the economic thinking of the democratic world, furnished a philosophical basis for many of Roosevelt's policies.[20] His application of Keynesian thought showed his careful differentiation between laissez-faire economics and the essentials of the American political tradition, and his willingness, in the face of pressing economic needs, to limit the former in order to protect the latter.

Roosevelt, however, could not be considered a consistent follower of Keynesian economics. Indeed, he could not be considered a consistent follower of any one particular social or economic theory. His eclectic and skeptical approach to ideas caused much of the theoretical confusion about the New Deal because those who analyzed it in terms of theoretical categories missed the dominant spirit of Roosevelt's own pragmatic outlook. Although familiar with the realm of ideas, he lived in a world of facts. To quote Arthur Schlesinger, Jr., again: "He respected clear ideas, accepted them, employed them, but was never really at ease with them and always ultimately skeptical about their relationship to reality." [21]

Thus Roosevelt was little troubled by outward consistency and coherence of policy but was vitally concerned with its tangible results, particularly in its effect upon the well-being of the population. His standard of priorities is best illustrated by a conversation he had with Senator George Norris shortly before the bill establishing the Tennessee Valley Authority was sent to Congress:

"What are you going to say when they ask you the political philosophy behind TVA?" Norris laughed.

[19] *Ibid.*, p. 656.   [20] *Ibid.*, pp. 649–654.   [21] *Ibid.*, p. 649.

"I'll tell them it's neither fish nor fowl," Roosevelt laughed back, "but, whatever it is, it will taste awfully good to the people of the Tennessee Valley." [22]

Reaction: Phase One

This analysis of the New Deal's philosophy—or lack of it— shows that it could be considered as exemplifying American political conservatism in its broadest interpretation. On the other hand, its effects were unquestionably harmful upon conservatism in the narrower sense, that is, upon conservatism that was a defense of the current political, economic, and social status quo. These conservative forces were alarmed at the strength of the new dominant majority, within whose broad consensus were found many who had previously supported the older system: the white southerners, the farmers, and a sizable segment of the business community.

The Democratic vote at this time was singularly impressive. The presidential election of 1932, which showed one of the great shifts of party voting in our history, was the beginning of a trend which would give the Democrats national political control for a generation. In 1934, the tide increased, as they gained seats in the midterm congressional elections, an almost unprecedented feat for a party which had won the previous presidential election. The crest of the wave came with Roosevelt's great victory in 1936 when he carried every state except Maine and Vermont. In that unhappy year for the Republicans, their seats in the House of Representatives were reduced to 89, and in the Senate, to a mere 17.[23] More than one premature obituary was written for the Republican party at this time, as well as for the conservatism it represented.

The forces of conservatism, however, had not been decisively defeated, but had only been driven back to their strongholds where they were preparing a counterattack which would partially check the advance of the New Deal. The conservatives had loyal followers, financial resources, and strategic positions of advantage

[22] Goldman, *op. cit.*, p. 263.
[23] *Politics in America: 1945–1964* (Washington, D.C.: Congressional Quarterly Service, 1965), p. 91.

which should not have been underestimated even at the lowest point in their fortunes. By 1935, with a discernible change in the temper of the country, some of the New Deal's marginal supporters joined forces with its hard-core opposition. This change was caused by a number of events: the criticism engendered by the substance and application of New Deal policies, some relief to the harshness of depression conditions, and, most importantly, the fact that a serious crisis had passed. Because of the timely aid of governmental intervention, many businessmen and farmers recovered their faith in the principles of rugged individualism and felt free to rejoin the Republican party. Even though Alf Landon suffered a humiliating electoral defeat in 1936, he did receive 16,679,583 popular votes to Roosevelt's 27,751,597.[24]

Furthermore, all the opposition to the New Deal was by no means reserved to the Republican party. Roosevelt became increasingly aware of the deep conservative elements within Democratic ranks, especially in the South, and recognized the potential threat of a congressional coalition of conservative Democrats with the members of a revived Republican party. In his first term, however, Roosevelt generally secured exceptional cooperation from Congress for his energetic policy in a prolonged "honeymoon period." At the time, the enemy of the New Deal and the recognized fortress of conservatism was not an apparently pliable Congress; rather, it was a stubborn Supreme Court.

THE SUPREME COURT BATTLE

Since the Supreme Court of the early New Deal was markedly conservative, it was at odds with the new political temper of the country. Moreover, operating contrary to the traditional cautiousness of the judiciary, it declared an unprecedented number of major administration measures unconstitutional. It was thus unhesitatingly moving into a direct clash with a president and a Congress that represented a heavy majority of the people. Roosevelt accordingly responded by proposing in 1937 to change the character of the Court's membership through a plan of appointing a new member for every judge over seventy who did not retire.

[24] Ibid., p. 92.

Although Roosevelt's "Court-packing" bill was defeated, he achieved his ultimate objective, since the Court did shift its position on the constitutionality of major New Deal legislation. Although this change was recognized as important at the time, the dimensions of the Court's adjustment could be realized only in succeeding decades. Its later decisions on race and apportionment would reveal that its commitment to change was not limited to the economic sphere but would eventually encompass all aspects of the old political system. With the future pattern of American politics consisting largely of a liberal president facing a conservative Congress, Roosevelt achieved a major victory by determining the character of the Court. In the perspective of the fundamental tension between stability and change, it weighted the balance on the side of our adjustment to reality.

In winning this war, however, Roosevelt did lose the battle, indeed the first stage of a campaign which, for all practical purposes, checked the New Deal. His attack upon the Supreme Court brought a sharp reaction far beyond the ranks of his opponents. It antagonized many of his nominal Congressional supporters who usually suppressed their misgivings about him and the direction of his program. Even some of his most wholehearted followers felt that here Roosevelt had gone too far.

In noting the sharpness and, at times, the virulence of this opposition, we should remember that in this period, one democratic system after another had either reverted to authoritarianism or succumbed to the newer lures of totalitarianism, and many of the remaining democracies looked none too sturdy or attractive. In such a dynamic and threatening atmosphere, the image of a powerful executive attempting to dominate an independent judiciary, after having already cowed the legislature, seemed to many a menacing rejection of the traditional bases of our liberty, the principle of the separation of powers and the system of checks and balances. Moreover, with constitutional structures crumbling under the exigencies of depression or extreme nationalism, any attack upon a body whose very existence was bound up in the defense and interpretation of the Constitution could easily be considered an attack upon the Constitution itself.

THE CHECKING OF THE NEW DEAL

The next year, Roosevelt's bill for reorganization of the executive branch was defeated in the same atmosphere, because the predictable congressional suspicion of an even stronger presidency was reinforced by an instinctive coupling in the popular mind of executive efficiency with totalitarian dictatorship. This setback was a remarkable one because, unlike the still controversial subject of the power of the Supreme Court, the rationalization of the executive office has, at present, secured the approval of conservatives as well as liberals. Probably the most impressive breakthrough in the field of executive reorganization has been made as a result of the reports of the Commission on Organization of the Executive Branch of the Government, the Hoover Commission, chaired by Herbert Hoover.

These defeats revitalized the flagging conservative opposition to the New Deal in both Congress and the country, and put a virtual halt upon the economic advances of the New Deal. The financial climate, with the recession of 1937 and 1938, also added to the disillusionment with spirited reform. From that time forward, no further major piece of domestic legislation was secured, except for the Wages and Hours Act of 1938—and that only after a long struggle and many enervating concessions. The conservative characteristics of Congress, which had been submerged by a strong executive at the height of his popularity, now came to the fore. These conservative features—malapportionment, localism, and seniority—were mirrored as well in practically every state by the unrepresentativeness of its legislature. Thus, the country's conservative forces, although not able to throw back the New Deal, took advantage of their positions of strength to check its thrust. A continuing stalemate between Congress and the presidency developed and became the regular pattern of our national politics.

THE PURGE

The brooding Roosevelt was concerned not only about his immediate frustrating position, but also about the future prospects of American liberalism. How could he, or future presidents, outflank conservative chairmen, mainly from the South, with their many years of seniority and sources of power? He did not move directly against the political structure itself, but rather attacked those who held power within it. In 1938, he thus entered the home states of these conservative magnificoes and attempted to purge them by campaigning in the Democratic primaries for their liberal opponents.

Although this step showed a sense of vision for the future, it was a political blunder for the immediate present. In the first place, the foray probably cost Roosevelt some public support because it tended to reinforce the image of an overambitious leader who, in this instance, was trying to stamp out the vitality of local and state political life. Still more significant, Roosevelt had begun a process of changing the character of the Democratic party, but he had seriously overestimated what he could quickly achieve against the grain of the American party system.

By entering the state primaries, he had seemingly overlooked the obvious fact that our parties are to a great degree not national parties at all, but rather shadowy and unsubstantial organizations, temporarily collecting the truly powerful state and local parties together to conduct a presidential election. Since Roosevelt became involved in these primaries as the head of a weak national organization warring with the leaders of strong state ones, his defeat along practically all the line of battle was not surprising. In only one instance was an incumbent legislator who had been under Rooseveltian fire rejected by the Democratic voters. This exception, however—Congressman John O'Connor of New York, the chairman of the powerful House Rules Committee—served only to prove the rule of localistic supremacy in party affairs since New York was Roosevelt's home state.

The president was correct in realizing that the power of the state parties, with their great local interests and their entrenched bases of strength in the congressional structure, could only be met effectively in the long run by strong, disciplined national parties, keyed to the country's majority. The modification, however, of a party system so deeply embedded in the structure and tradition of American politics could not be changed in the space of a few months.

In seeking to establish a strong national party, Roosevelt's primary desire was to fashion a guaranteed political instrument to carry out a liberal program. This could not normally be attained with a party in which conservatives and liberals could placidly live together under the same roof. He felt that progress could be achieved only by a committed party and not one which was inhibited by one-half its own forces—and often the more powerful half. Roosevelt's faith was not in the Democratic party per se, but in a liberal Democratic party.

He was again correct in foreseeing that the ideological question could not be evaded permanently and that the blurred political lines would eventually be sharpened. Nevertheless, the clear division of parties upon principles was contrary to the spirit of our political history. An ideological test for party qualification, however reasonable and logical in theory, had "un-American" overtones. Furthermore, many Democrats had misgivings about a Democratic president's opposing faithful party members upon a criterion as ephemeral as policy support. Many intraparty convention battles would have to be fought over credentials and loyalty oaths, and many persons would have to bolt the party a number of times before Democratic leaders would recognize the significance of policy in the modern political scene.

Under these circumstances, one can easily understand why in 1944 Roosevelt, a Democrat throughout his life, would even consider scrapping the existing party system, with its encrusted values and associations, and joining with Wendell Willkie, his Republican rival in 1940, in establishing a new party to bring together the liberal elements of the Democrats and the Republicans.[25]

THE CONGRESSIONAL ELECTIONS OF 1938

Roosevelt's second term, won by the historic victory of 1936, proved to be a period of frustration for him as the conservative reaction halted his reform movement. The first two years of this

[25] Samuel I. Rosenman, *Working with Roosevelt* (London: Rupert Hart-Davis, 1952), pp. 423–424; Donald Johnson, *The Republican Party and Wendell Willkie* (Urbana: University of Illinois Press, 1960), pp. 300–303; James MacGregor Burns, *The Deadlock of Democracy: Four–Party Politics in America* (Englewood Cliffs, N.J.: Prentice-Hall, 1963), pp. 173–176.

term witnessed one defeat after another: the Supreme Court bill, the reorganization bill, and the Democratic primary "purge." In 1938, he suffered still another loss, whose impact shifted the nature of political conflict in succeeding years. In the midterm Congressional elections, conservatism made an impressive gain as the Republican party recovered from its previous weakened position. By securing 169 seats in the House of Representatives and 23 in the Senate, it could function as an effective formal opposition.[26]

The gain to conservatism cannot be measured solely by the added Republican legislators since their increase in number was primarily significant because it virtually insured a working conservative majority whenever the conservative Democrats joined forces with the resurgent Republicans. Thus, a de facto political coalition was formed which, transcending party lines, sharpened the ideological division between conservatism and liberalism. The basic fact of political life in the next quarter century would be the domination of Congress by this coalition. Although this majority was not infallibly cohesive, its success in checking the president, especially in domestic affairs, was the most striking characteristic of Congress' entire record in this period. Even when the conservative coalition would actually lose its numerical majority, it was still usually able to control the legislative situation because of its power positions, particularly the committee chairmanships guaranteed by the seniority system.

The rural areas and the small towns, therefore, which had been thrown off balance by the dynamic upheaval of the New Deal and the vigorous presidency of Roosevelt, now regained their footing and were able to stop the advances of the urban population. The more prosperous farmers, the businessmen, the white southerners, the so-called "wasps" (white, Anglo-Saxon Protestants), all of the dominant groups in the old system now regained control of Congress. As a result, Congress was intimately linked with the older rural way of life, just as Roosevelt's identification with the modern urban culture would be transferred to his successors in the executive office.

The conservatives gave little thought to the possibility that a Congress with such a regressive nature might drop in popular

[26] *Politics in America: 1945–1964,* p. 91.

prestige and influence, and might invite serious attack upon its unrepresentative character and the antiquated mode of its operation. These long-range effects were hardly imagined in the exultation over their ability to halt what they considered an executive juggernaut. Indeed, thoughts of the future more likely consisted of heady dreams of winning the presidency, the very citadel of the opposition. In the late 1930's, many conservatives assumed that a conservative president, preferably but not necessarily a Republican, in partnership with a conservative Congress, could bring back the old system with its comforting features of privilege and stability. They did not realize that they were living through an era of fundamental change, rather than a disconcerting interregnum in the established pattern of national life.

One reason for their misjudgment of this period lay in the prevalent identification of its events with Roosevelt's personality and character. The strong emotions he provoked, ranging from venemous hatred to adoring acclamation, seemed to justify the contemporary view that he was primarily responsible for what was occurring. Conservatives could, thus, reasonably hold that the New Deal would not survive Roosevelt's presidency, especially if the executive office were once more returned to "safe hands." The termination of his presidential tenure in 1940 seemed within the range of possibility. Even if the anti-third-term tradition would not inhibit the iconoclastic Roosevelt, it might allow a more conservative Democrat to win the nomination, or a Republican, the election.

The 1938 election fired Republican optimism by uncovering a number of attractive political personalities, men whose appeal might even possibly rival that of Roosevelt. One such figure was Thomas Dewey of New York, whose dynamism in office established the crusading district attorney as a modern American folk hero. Dewey was a leading contender for the 1940 nomination, even though he had been defeated for governor in 1938—but only narrowly, and by the esteemed Herbert Lehman.

The most significant Republican thrown up by the victory of 1938 was the new senator from Ohio, the brilliant and intractable Robert Taft, the man who, until his death in 1953, would so well represent the conservative reaction to the New Deal that he would be considered its very embodiment in Congress, particularly in the Senate. Despite his practically unchallenged recognition as the veritable "Mr. Republican," the chief spokesman of conservatism, Taft was never given the presidential nomination of his party. Although this denial was considered by his supporters as an ungenerous act of political opportunism, it was nevertheless appropriate that the man who represented conservatism and the Republican party should be identified with Congress rather than the presidency, because the legislature, not the presidency, was the conservatives' true stronghold.

The Impact of World War II

The onset of World War II halted the revival of the conservatives and punctured their chances of defeating Roosevelt. The president who had guided the country in a period of dire domestic emergency was now its leader in time of international stress and, eventually, war itself. Despite the immediate check upon conservative electoral hopes, the international situation paradoxically seemed to make definite the demise of the New Deal. Roosevelt apparently recognized this fact officially when he mentioned in a press conference that "old Dr. New Deal" had been replaced by "Dr. Win-the-War." This interpretation, however, is only partially true. Although admittedly, no new installments of progressive legislation were presented during the war, the reforms and the spirit of the New Deal proved to have a durability quite unprecedented in American history. This liberal spirit was partially supported by our conscious desire not to experience a reactionary relapse similar to that caused by World War I. With a more sophisticated concept of wartime patriotism, we realized that a war need not necessarily stifle liberalism even though it might tend to restrict some freedoms. With the exception of the Japanese on the West Coast—a tragic exception of great proportions—there was comparatively little of the petty persecution of individuals and the unnecessary restrictions on liberties which had occurred in World War I. On the contrary, liberalism itself became a means of waging an ideological war. Although "Dr. New Deal" had been officially retired, he was often a silent consultant.[27]

[27] Longaker. *op. cit.*, p. 28.

Because of their depressed status, the Negroes singularly benefited from this wartime liberalism. Although the dissolution of the old political system gave implicit promise that discrimination against them would eventually be eliminated, the stimulus of war undoubtedly hastened its fulfillment. To Alan P. Grimes, the governmental acts in favor of the Negro seemed less concerned with the substance of civil rights than with the winning of the war. The nature of these gains, however, clearly indicated that they were not terminal but installments toward a full payment.[28]

The Republican Reaction to the New Deal

In the field of party politics, our involvement in international affairs had its greatest impact as a divisive force within the Republican party, sharpening a cleavage which had existed almost from its formation between an industrial eastern wing and a rural midwestern one. Although living under one party roof, the two factions were often at odds with each other. The eastern seaboard was the heart of Republican conservatism, while the Midwest was heavily in favor of progressive measures. The midwestern Republicans understandably resisted eastern dictation of party policy, and their rebellious senators were pungently described by a New England colleague as "the sons of the wild jackass." After World War I, there was increasing friction between the two wings of the party on the subject of farm legislation, with the progressives in Congress allying themselves with the Democrats in an effective agricultural bloc. Their persistent efforts for commodity price supports were dashed by the veto of Republican presidents, who reflected the eastern position. The party split was aggravated by a difference of outlook on foreign policy, with the Midwest being the center of American isolationism and the East Coast much more sympathetic to our involvement in world affairs.

In the first half of the Roosevelt era, the two wings of the party had presented an apparently united front against the New Deal. The hopes of effective party unity, however, faded as international relations entered the center of public discussion in the 1930's. The debate between interventionism and isolationism

[28] Alan P. Grimes, *Equality in America: Religion, Race, and the Urban Majority* (New York: Oxford University Press, 1964), pp. 68–69.

renewed mutual suspicions and led to party division based on foreign policy. Thus, it was foreign, rather than domestic, policy which induced the eastern wing at the 1940 Republican convention to secure the nomination of the most interventionist candidate, Wendell Willkie. The midwesterners, in turn, were disillusioned with the eastern coloration of the party organization, particularly when the choice of Willkie was made only a few days after Roosevelt had named the former Republican Secretary of State and the former Republican vice-presidential candidate to be his secretaries of the Army and the Navy. Even in later periods, this division was paramount. It was fear of Taft's foreign policy which impelled the eastern wing to have Eisenhower successfully challenge him for the nomination in 1952. It was a similar fear which explains much of the reason for its distraught attitude in 1964 with Goldwater's successful bid for the nomination.

In the domestic sphere, the division among Republicans was less perceptible and developed more slowly than in the international. Although there was no complete unanimity of Republican disapproval when the main parts of New Deal legislation were being considered in Congress, it was after these programs had been passed and had become integral parts of the nation's social and economic machinery that a definite fissure emerged in Republican ranks on domestic policy. With the exception of a segment of former midwestern Progressives who had become committed to the New Deal, Republicans in the rural areas and in the small and medium-sized towns retained their suspicion of its program, while those in the cities, particularly in the Northeast, accepted it.

Because of their differing response to liberal social legislation, the eastern wing was labeled the liberal, and the midwestern, the conservative. At first glance, this terminology is perplexing because, as we have noted, earlier in the century the liberal and the conservative wings were in the opposite geographical locations. The earlier distinction between liberalism and conservatism, however, was not a comprehensive one because the midwestern farmers, in their hostility to urbanism and in their suspicion of industrialism, could justifiably be considered more conservative than the eastern Republicans who had to establish a working relationship with these rising forces. Similarly, the split between the two wings on foreign policy can be seen as, in essence, another facet of the fundamental division between the escape from reality and the adjustment to it.

The Republican domestic division in the latter New Deal period, therefore, should not have been surprising. To the midwesterners, the major social reforms were the inevitable fulfillment of their fathers' warnings that urban industrial life would stifle the free individualism of a rural society. The Republicans in the northeast, however, responded differently to these programs. They followed the lead of the major business and financial interests who accepted them as necessary, if not particularly palatable, facts of life because they were faced with the practical problems of financing and conducting large-scale enterprises within the modern industrial milieu. "'Those who rule' are in the mainstream of American political and economic life," John H. Fenton has written. "Consequently they do not struggle against the main current." [29]

This tolerant attitude was not reflected in all layers of the business community. The small manufacturer, who was much more influential in the midwestern party organizations than in the eastern, tended to continue his original opposition to the New Deal measures. The necessity of dealing with trade unions and of contributing to social security seemed both an economic threat and a violation of his fundamental political views. The large industrialist had a different perspective since he could handle these matters in an impersonal, regularized manner. Indeed, some believed that these devices actually facilitated the rational operation of industry by eliminating some of the former frictions and uncertainties.[30]

This position of the large American industrialists in the reformed economic system did not qualify them as liberals, New Dealers, or as "traitors to their class." On the contrary, they realized that business could effectively influence governmental decisions without any radical dismantling of the system that had been established under liberal auspices. Thus, although accepting

[29] John H. Fenton, "Liberal-Conservative Divisions by Sections of the United States," *Annals of the American Academy of Political and Social Science*, 344 (November, 1962), 124.

[30] *Ibid.*, p. 125.

the federal regulatory agencies as permanent fixtures in the economy, they nevertheless believed that agency members should have a benevolent attitude toward business in general and a sympathetic understanding of the regulated industry. In effect, they were accepting Roosevelt's basic conception that institutions could be preserved only by necessary reform. As conservatives, however, they laid great stress upon Falkland's advice: "When it is not necessary to change, it is necessary not to change." [31]

In analyzing the division between the Republican liberals and conservatives, therefore, we should realize that the "liberals" felt themselves to be the true "conservatives." They dismissed their opponents as reactionaries, whose insistence upon outmoded dogmas would lead to disaster for the party and bitter divisiveness for the country. To the party's erstwhile "conservatives," however, their liberal brethren were, at best, flaccid "me-tooers," carried along with the contemporary progressive tide, or, at worst, traitors to the basic concepts of democracy and free enterprise, which were usually linked as one entity.

On the record, the liberals appeared to have defeated their conservative opponents in a remarkable run of successes and to have had their view prevail as Republican policy. At all presidential nominating conventions in the 1940's and the 1950's, the liberal forces named the party candidate. From 1944 through 1952, these Republican battles were primarily encounters between the two leading party personalities of the period, Governor Dewey and Senator Taft, each symbolizing one wing of the party—even though in only one of these years, 1948, did Dewey and Taft personally oppose each other for the nomination.

Thomas Dewey was a felicitous choice as the representitive of the eastern liberals. In his administration as governor of New York and in his program for the presidency, he exemplified their acceptance of the modified welfare state and their goal of brisk efficiency in its operation. With his proven electoral success in the most populous state of the Union, which contained its largest, most diversified city, he had proven that the eastern liberals' concept of conservatism could detach a sizable part of the New Deal alliance.

[31] R. J. White, ed., *The Conservative Tradition* (New York: New York University Press, 1957), p. 127.

Senator Taft, on his part, was identified with the party's conservative wing. Although personally he was more progressive than the general run of conservatives, he, nevertheless, represented rural America's distrust of the liberal urban political trend, its suspicion of a large national government, its desire for a greater role for the states, and its hope for a return to a simpler world.

In each of the conventions in these years, Dewey's forces defeated Taft's. Dewey won the nomination from John Bricker, Taft's fellow senator from Ohio, in 1944, and from Taft himself in 1948. In 1952, Taft ran once more, but Dewey that year supported General Eisenhower, whose success gave still another victory to the eastern wing of the party. The 1952 battle was a particularly dramatic conflict between the two forces because the heart of the majority of the delegates was clearly with Taft. There was, however, no break in the pattern of convention decision-making because when the votes were counted, the liberals were once more in control.

This behavior pattern was so consistent that many persons were convinced that the nature of the American political process necessitated the liberal victory. One was tempted to dismiss Republican conventions in this period as somewhat akin to primitive ritualistic contests, which, despite their color and drama, had a foregone conclusion of which all participants were aware.

We can, thus, understand why neutral observers, as well as liberal Republicans, were caught off their guard by the victory in the 1964 convention of Senator Barry Goldwater, who represented the conservative faction. This defeat of the party's liberals, although far from being predetermined, was yet not a chance or an accidental event, but one derived from the Republican response to the New Deal. Its predicament was not a specifically American phenomenon since practically every conservative party in the Western world is faced with the problem of adjusting to major social reforms. How well it does adjust is not only of crucial importance to the survival of the party, but also to the social peace and stability of the country.

The most successful example of such adaptability is found in the history of the British Conservative party whose adaptability has enabled it to survive as probably the oldest continuous political party in the world. In the second half of the nineteenth century, for example, when the party appeared in danger of being eventually crushed between the forces of large-scale industrialism and rising political democracy, its leader, Benjamin Disraeli, accepted the challenge by educating his party to its new responsibilities and carrying through a program of social reform. One of the most recent major examples of the Conservative party's flexibility occurred after World War II when it easily accepted the Attlee Labour Government's program of nationalization and free national health service. When returned to power, it gave no consideration to dismantling—with the exception of the special case of steel nationalization—the basic structure and character of the welfare state. In colonial policy as well, the Conservatives, the traditional party of British imperialism, overcame their initial hostility to Labour's "liquidation" of the British Empire and continued the process on their own. There were at times, it is true, some rumbles of discontent from a few reactionary gentlemen at what they called unprincipled political opportunism, but they were clearly recognized as eccentric and of little political importance.

Because of our long acquaintanceship with the British system of government and the similarity of our two political traditions, it was natural to draw a parallel between the British Conservatives and the American Republicans. Did not the Republicans accept the gains of the New Deal in the same vein of pragmatic conservatism as their British counterparts accepted the welfare state? Had not the Republican liberals been consistently successful against the party's right wing? Were not all doubts about the nature of modern Republicanism removed when the Eisenhower administration retained the basic liberal structure inherited from the Democrats?

One sharp difference between the Republicans and the Conservatives, however, stood out: unlike the Conservatives, the mass of dedicated Republican party members had never been won over to the acceptance of the modern state. The success of the Republican party's liberals at presidential conventions was not due to the persuasiveness of their philosophy, but to their practical power in securing money and votes. The argument that prevailed in successive conventions until 1964 was not that the conservative philosophy was wrong or out of tune with the modern world, but rather that it could not win a national election. The liberals insisted that a conservative candidate running on a conservative platform would inevitably face defeat because he would win only the votes of that minority of the electorate committed to the Republican party. The successful liberal Republican governors—such as Dewey and Nelson Rockefeller of New York and Earl Warren of California—loomed large at convention proceedings because they had already exhibited proof of their ability to produce votes in the post-New Deal atmosphere.

At the same time, the majority of the delegates still remained committed to their basic small-town, rural outlook and never hid their distaste for the necessity of compromising their faith for tactical reasons. They applauded heartily when the conservatives declaimed their fundamentalist political and economic views; they listened uncomfortably when warned that the party was selling its soul for short-term electoral benefits as it tried to echo the liberalism of the Democrats.

The nature of this tension between the two wings of the Republican party showed little similarity with any modern experiences of the British Conservatives. It did reveal, however, a rather remarkable parallel with the Labour party. Labour, in a somberly introspective mood induced by an unusually prolonged period out of power, was grappling in the 1950's and early 1960's with a comparable intraparty split between theory and practicality. Labour's commitment to socialism, particularly the nationalization of industry, is considered dogmatic by the standards of the pragmatic, untheoretical politics of Great Britain and the United States. The party's right wing maintained that the nationalization program was an albatross around Labour's neck, frightening away the middle-class vote which was needed for victory. These rightists pointed out that since the doctrine of nationalization had been the product of the class conflicts of a previous era, Labour's unyielding adherence to it presented the image of an old-fashioned party unable to adjust to the modern age of technology. The party's left wing declared, however, that the theory was essential since it was Labour's chief distinction from the Conservative party and, indeed, its very reason for existence. The left wing felt that the party should stand committed to its principles regardless of the tides of public opinion because only in that way could it preserve its self-respect and be ready for the call when the people decided that they wanted a true leftist government. To trim principles to the wind, the left maintained, would be both immoral and impractical.

At this point a contrast can be made between the Republican and the Labour parties, a contrast which underlies the essential weakness of the liberal Republican position. The right wing of the Labour party not only argued that nationalization was a political liability, but also insisted that the theory should be re-examined and scrapped if it stood in the way of a clear apprehension of the problems of the modern technological age. By raising this issue, the rightists admittedly intensified party conflict, but they also cleared the air. The party members were, thus, forced to think through their basic political and economic views and not glide over their differences. The party leader, Hugh Gaitskell, pressed the issue even though it resulted in harsh criticism and an open rebellion against his leadership.

The liberal Republicans, on the other hand, went only as far as pointing out the political disadvantages of a conservative philosophy, but stopped short of explaining to the party that their theory was no longer applicable to modern conditions. It is true that when in power at the state level, and to a great extent under the presidency of Eisenhower as well, the liberal Republicans reflected their awareness of governmental responsibility for social services, and their administrations were largely similar to those of their Democratic predecessors. Although the actions of the liberal Republicans were in conformity with modern needs, their words were not. Their speeches, particularly before the party faithful, stressed free enterprise, states' rights, and limited governmental expenditures to achieve the hallowed goal of a balanced budget. A liberal thread, admittedly, was woven into the texture of these speeches, but it was so smoothly blended within the general conservative tone that it appeared more like a shading or reservation rather than the content of a different set of principles. It became the practice of observers, scholars, and reporters in analyzing such speeches or programs to cut through the conservative ritualistic ideological verbiage to its substantive liberal essence. This apparently sophisticated mode of analysis probably distorted the significance of what was taking place. The recognition accorded the conservative ideology in speeches was truly important because it revealed that the liberals were not willing to face the consequences of openly challenging it.

The liberal leaders, therefore, made no real effort to educate their party in the responsibilities of political power in the twentieth century. There was no Disraeli or Gaitskell among them. They were rather men who felt that the degree of their political success was justifiable reason for not dividing the party in bitter ideological strife.

Only one figure on the liberal Republican side, Wendell Willkie, can be considered an exception to this rule, since he did try to modernize the party. Willkie, however, was an atypical figure in American politics with a limited impact upon his party. He had had absolutely no political or governmental experience before his nomination in 1940 and had no solid organizational party base. In addition, he had an extraordinarily short political career since he died in 1944.[32]

The Republicans gave their titular leadership to the liberal wing not out of respect for its philosophy but out of admiration for its political skill and recognition of its financial strength. The liberals had not reformed the party or captured its heart. Thus, the recognition accorded the liberals and their high level of visibility in the public eye gave a misleading impression as to what was happening in the party as a whole.

Far closer to the actual sentiment within the party was the conservative contingent of congressional Republicans, whose legislative position was quite at odds with the liberalism of the party's presidential candidates. This was even true of the legislators from the small towns and rural areas of the East, where the state parties were under the nominal control of the liberals. The Democratic presidential nominees, therefore, made their most telling thrusts against the Republican record in Congress rather than against the positions taken by their opponents. Roosevelt initiated this tactic with his concentration in the 1940 campaign upon the conservative congressional trio of "Martin, Barton, and Fish" rather than Willkie. In 1944, he largely ignored Thomas Dewey and saved his memorable attack, possibly the most

[32] Johnson, *op. cit.*, p. 318.

humorous in our political history, for the hapless Republican congressman who injudiciously suggested that federal funds were being needlessly wasted to transport Roosevelt's dog, Fala. Mr. Truman carried on this tradition with his campaign in 1948 against the Republican 80th Congress, which he termed the worst in American history (later promoted to the second-worst out of deference to the claim of the radical Republican Congress that enacted the Reconstruction program).

When observers in the postwar years spoke of the modernization of the Republican party and its acceptance of the modified welfare state, they highly exaggerated the degree of its conversion. Mr. Dewey, the symbol of the Republican adjustment to modern economic and social needs, may have received the party's nomination two times, but he was never "Mr. Republican." That honor was accorded Mr. Taft, the hero of the mass of the party, the acknowledged spokesman of the small-town and rural areas. These conservative elements suffered disillusionment in the postwar era—even when Republicans captured the White House—because the period was in great degree shaped by the New Deal and was a fulfillment of its basic trends.

Reaction: Phase Two

It might appear difficult, initially, to credit the view that the years after Roosevelt's death were a true continuation of the progressive trend begun by the New Deal. On the contrary, there seemed to be much evidence to indicate that the New Deal was an exceptional, but transitory, break in our history that had been caused by the fortuitous combination of a world depression and a powerful personality. With the elimination of the harsh economic circumstances and with the death of the charismatic figure of Roosevelt, it might have been assumed that a conservative tide would recur and that the old political system would return.

The circumstances for a conservative revival seemed far more favorable than the initial abortive attempt in 1938. At that time, the forward advance of the New Deal had been checked; in the 1940's and the 1950's, this limitation appeared as the dominant political motif of a conservative age. Congress exemplified this conservative spirit because its Republican–southern Democratic

conservative majority was larger than before, particularly when the Republicans secured majorities in 1946 and 1952. Although Roosevelt's successor, Harry Truman, presented an ambitious extension of his policies called the Fair Deal, most of its provisions failed to pass their legislative hurdles. Congress, however, was not content with merely halting the progressive tide, but sought to reverse it as well. Over Truman's veto, it enacted the Taft-Hartley Act, which restricted the activities of labor unions and clipped some of the gains made by labor under the New Deal. In similar fashion, it passed the McCarran-Walter Act, which retained the quota system of immigration selection.

In the face of this vigorous congressional conservatism, there seemed to be little hope of a significant liberal response. The institution of the presidency was apparently ineffective in this period of Congress' supremacy. Truman lacked the dynamic appeal of Roosevelt and was constantly frustrated by Congress in the domestic field. Moreover, in the Truman years, the spirit of the executive office had changed in accordance with the prevailing ethos of Washington. The ubiquitous flock of idealistic reformers of the New Deal period had dispersed; in their place returned the courthouse politician and the machine hack, who carried with them the smell of petty corruption.

In 1952, the presidency itself fell into Republican hands with the election of General Dwight Eisenhower. He was a fitting choice for the conservatives because his limited conception of the office's potentiality was in accord with their own suspicion of it. Under Eisenhower, the tone of the executive office, which had begun to change under Truman, was transformed still more. The reformers and the intellectuals were shunted even further to the side as businessmen predominated in the executive departments and in the regulatory commissions. The presence of these men reassured the conservatives that the Eisenhower administration would undo the "sins" of the New Deal and free the country from the regulation of a government that had allegedly usurped the liberties of individuals and the powers of the states. One can see why liberals, who had felt frustrated under Truman, were appalled by Eisenhower. More than one person believed that the era of Harding and Coolidge was being repeated.

The conservatives in Congress, however, were not satisfied by these comforting appearances. They had been so thoroughly shaken by their experience with Roosevelt that they had resolved soon after his death not to risk another strong, liberal president. They pushed through the draft of the Twenty-second Amendment, limiting the presidential tenure to two terms, and easily secured its approval from the conservative state legislatures. In the same vein, they seriously considered the proposed Bricker amendment which, as we shall see in our later discussion of the presidency, was a drastic restriction of the president's power to conduct foreign affairs.

With an apparently weak presidency facing a strong conservative Congress, could the liberal forces expect any support from the Supreme Court, which had shown such strong evidence of committing itself to change? The Court seemed a shaky haven for liberalism at this time. The Roosevelt Court quickly lost its homogeneity as it divided up into liberal and conservative wings on issues of civil liberties, with the conservatives usually having a safe majority in this period.

Despite these signs of a conservative revival which loomed so prominently in the Truman and Eisenhower years, what stands out in retrospect is how much of the structure established by the New Deal was retained. Even more remarkably, the spirit of innovation and the pursuit of a more rational politics, which were so obviously checked at some points, were, nevertheless, dominant in other areas. On balance, the period was not a return to the times of Harding and Coolidge. It was rather an era whose very conservative features proved that the revolutionary tide could not be checked, but rather could be carried even further through the auspices of conservative, moderate men.

In the field of foreign policy, involvement of the United States in world affairs after World War II would remain unchanged. Our own strength, combined with the results of the war, the expansion of the Soviet Union's sphere of influence, the power vacuum in Europe, the nuclear armament race, and the emergence of new nations in Asia and Africa, pushed us into a position of decisive influence which could not be relinquished without global consequences. Despite Truman's difficulties with Congress in domestic affairs, he worked his will in the realm of foreign policy. The Truman Doctrine, the Marshall Plan, the North

Atlantic Treaty, the Point Four Aid Program, and the Korean action—all testified to his firm control. In reacting to the spread of Communism, he pursued a strong policy of resistance, tempered by a desire to avoid a nuclear world war.

Although the Eisenhower administration came into office with a commitment to continue our alliances and to maintain our involvement in world affairs, there was ground for belief from the Republican campaign that in other respects a fundamental change in foreign policy would occur. The promises of stemming the tide of world Communism and of "unleashing" Chiang Kai-shek gave hope of a more spirited offensive in Europe and Asia in contrast to the cautious and defensive approach of the Democrats. In office, however, the belligerency of Republican propaganda was muffled by the awesome potentiality of nuclear warfare. Consequently, Republican actions, particularly in relation to Hungary and the islands of Quemoy and Matsu, were essentially a continuation of previous Democratic policy.

On the domestic scene, the chief characteristic of the period was the maintenance of the New Deal's conception of the role of government in modern society. Although this role was not expanded by legislation during Truman's administration—with the important exception of the Employment Act of 1946—he did guard against its contraction. With Eisenhower, on the other hand, the conservatives had real expectations, as in the field of foreign affairs, that he would institute a fundamental change, a sharp turn to the right from the paternalism of the New Deal. This hope was nourished by his words after his election as well as before. In office, however, possibly the only serious attempt at reversal occurred during the Dixon-Yates controversy when the administration unsuccessfully tried to limit the TVA. On the whole, the existing reformed apparatus, carried over from the New Deal, was retained. The Alsop brothers succinctly caught the irony of the Eisenhower administration's position when they stated that it "merely accepted (and denounced) the basic postulates of the New Deal." [33]

These conservatives were keenly disappointed when they realized that the administration, far from dismantling a social

[33] Joseph and Stewart Alsop, *The Reporter's Trade* (New York: Reynal, 1958), p. 27.

security program that had become an integral part of American life, was actually liberalizing its coverage. Their faith was strained even further on the subject of federal-state relations. We will note later, in discussing the Manion-Kestnbaum report controversy, their unfulfilled expectations of a shift of national functions and responsibilities back to the states. Here, too, the practical necessity of governmental responsibility forced the retention of the New Deal structure because it had been fashioned as the pragmatic machinery for meeting the problems of the modern world. This was the lesson the Republican liberals learned in office, despite the preconceptions of the conservatives and even of Eisenhower himself. This was the lesson, however, that they did not impart to their fellow members.

Civil Rights

Since the death of Roosevelt in 1945, the demands of the dynamic society have been exerting pressures for a degree of governmental action inconceivable in the days of the New Deal. This has been especially the case in the field of civil rights, where the direction of history has carried presidents of both parties further than anyone would have guessed. The subjects of civil rights and legislative representation show how shortsighted was the view that the post-New Deal period was one of a conservative reaction when, in fact, the governmental machinery was adjusting to even deeper changes than in the days of Roosevelt.

These changes were not chance events, but rather were essential parts of the main theme of our history in this century: the formation, the maintenance, and the dissolution of a conservative political system. In its limited duration of approximately a generation, this system protected the big businessmen, the southern whites, and the farmers in their privileged positions by binding tightly, with powerful political and constitutional ropes, the demands of the rest of the country's population—the poor, the Negroes, and the urban ethnic minorities. Facing the mutually reinforcing bonds of Republican hegemony, white supremacy, and legislative malapportionment, the handicapped groups were at a severe disadvantage in the political arena. By virtue, however, of their expanding numbers and the dynamism of the economy, their power increased in the first decades of the twentieth century and pressed strongly against their bonds. We have already noted from some incidents in the twenties how intense this pressure was and how searing the resultant friction. With the depression and the New Deal, the breaking of the bonds began.

The first rope to crack was that of Republican hegemony and with it the companion strands of business protection and dedication to the philosophy of laissez-faire. Thus, during the New Deal period, primary attention was fastened upon these remarkable changes in the role of government in the economic field. The latter half of Roosevelt's tenure and the succeeding years were easily considered as merely maintenance of the status quo since hardly any new changes were occurring in this field.

What was being overlooked, however, was that during this apparently placid time, the second bond of the previous system was being broken, that which held down the Negro, especially in the South. When this social revolution came to the surface in the late 1950's and early 1960's, few could still maintain the thesis that the times were essentially conservative, a relaxing pause from the hectic pace of the New Deal. Furthermore, while the color revolution was taking place, one of the most fundamental transfers of political power in our history became possible with the cracking of the third bond of the old system, legislative malapportionment.

One reason for not recognizing that the bonds of white supremacy and legislative malapportionment were breaking was that this process was taking place primarily through judicial channels, rather than through the expected avenues of political change, the executive and the legislative branches of government. We should remember that the courts made a fundamental adjustment to change in the New Deal period. When the Supreme Court, after much controversy, relinquished its role as the main governmental support of business, it followed through the implications of this change by no longer upholding the other entrenched conservative groups in American society. Thus, at a time when the executive was usually on the defensive and the legislative branch conservative, the Court carried out its commitment to change, particularly with the seminal decisions of *Brown* v. *Board of Education* in civil rights and *Baker* v. *Carr* in legislative apportionment.

The Court's decisions on civil rights were not the only reflection of the demands for racial change. After years of neglected recognition, these pressures eventually made an impressive breach through the defenses of Congress with the passage of the first civil rights legislation since Reconstruction, the Civil Rights Acts of 1957, 1960, and 1964, and the Voting Rights Act of 1965. Thus Congress, especially with the last two measures, made a guarantee of Negro rights, whose broad scope was considered beyond the range of federal statute before the Brown decision.

The actions of our chief executives from Truman through Johnson were still another indication of how inexorable was the force of historic change in this field. At the time of their accession to office, none of these presidents appeared likely to achieve distinction in the field of civil rights. Harry Truman, a man with strong anti-Union roots, from the border state of Missouri, was chosen vice-presidential candidate in 1944 by the city machines and the southerners to defeat the incumbent Henry Wallace, the hero of the liberals and a strong advocate of civil rights. Dwight Eisenhower, the man who broke the solid South for the Republican party, was cautiously skeptical about the efficacy of civil rights legislation and was neutral throughout his presidency toward the Supreme Court's Brown decision. John F. Kennedy was supported by the southerners for the Democratic vice-presidential nomination in 1956 and, at the 1960 convention, "was the *least* popular among Negroes of all Democratic candidates." [34] He had only a moderately liberal senatorial record on civil rights and during most of his presidency tried to avoid a direct clash with the South on this issue. Of all the members of this brace of presidents, the one least likely to make his mark in this field was Lyndon Johnson, who in his early congressional career had been a southern opponent of civil rights legislation. His later role, when Senate Majority Leader, as the purported honest broker in the passage of the Civil Rights Acts of 1957 and 1960, gained him little support in the North and did not affect his status as the South's favorite son in 1960.

[34] Theodore H. White, *The Making of the President, 1960* (New York: Atheneum, 1962), p. 354, White's italics.

Yet despite their backgrounds, their previous records, and even their own predilections, these four men will be primarily remembered in our domestic history because they brought to fruition the Negro revolution. Truman committed the nation to the goal of eventual equality by setting up the President's Committee on Civil Rights and by desegregating the armed services. The committee's report, *To Secure These Rights,* spurred the passage of federal civil rights legislation, and military desegregation, completed under Eisenhower, has been described as "probably the one most influential single step toward the increasing recognition of the Negro citizen's right to full status as a human being." [35]

Under the administration of Eisenhower, the civil rights bills of 1957 and 1960 were enacted. He also sent federal troops into Little Rock, Arkansas, to enforce a court order for desegregation, thereby setting a precedent for executive support of the judiciary in this field. The action at Little Rock affected the balance of forces in the federal system because it proved that in an eventual confrontation between the national government and the state on the question of civil rights, the state must comply. Eisenhower's reluctance to move, even to the point of stating earlier that such an action was inconceivable, underlined the near inevitability of a trend that carried with it a man of marked political restraint.[36]

With the presidency of John F. Kennedy, the United States government committed itself to the full integration of the Negro into American political life, and appropriately his administration proposed the most comprehensive civil rights law of modern times. Here, too, however, the insistent pressure of history could be felt because civil rights had not originally been highest in his scale of priorities, and he leaned strongly toward their fulfillment indirectly and on the oblique through increased Negro registration in the South and through vigorous enforcement of existing executive legal powers. The impassioned flow of events upset this rational calculation of political and social forces. The obdurate stand of the governors of the deep South, the outbreak of violence, and, finally, murder changed the atmosphere and forced

[35] Walter Millis, as quoted in Longaker, *op. cit.,* p. 114.

[36] Emmet John Hughes, *Ordeal of Power: A Political Memoir of the Eisenhower Years* (New York: Atheneum, 1963), pp. 241–245.

the president's hand to decisive, direct action. At the time of his assassination, he was a symbol of the cause of civil rights.

In the wake of the assassination, many parallels were drawn with the similar death of Lincoln almost a century earlier. No parallel, however, is more striking than the image of two moderate, cautious, realistic men, the object of criticism by zealous advocates of Negro rights, who finally, under the pressure of events, took the step that would insure their place in history. The fact that Kennedy and the other recent presidents did not hew with a single-minded purpose to the primary goal of human equality throughout their political careers is no more valid a criticism of them than it was of the Great Emancipator. The period was in the grip of memorable change and these men, in their own way, were its instruments in their recognition of it. Senator Everett Dirksen, a most reluctant crusader for liberal causes, epitomized this sense of history when, in the debate on the 1964 Civil Rights Act, he quoted to his southern colleagues the words of Victor Hugo: "Stronger than all the armies is an idea whose time has come." "The time has come," he declared, "for equality of opportunity in sharing in government, in education, and in employment. It will not be stayed or denied. It is here." [37]

The development of Lyndon Johnson's public position on civil rights legislation was in microcosm the path of feeling that the American people as a whole had followed and of the process that the southerners are still experiencing. His first actions in Congress were in opposition to such measures; later, as Senate Majority Leader, he secured moderate compromises between North and South on such legislation by smoothing its rough edges and drawing some of its teeth; as vice-president, he made his commitment to civil rights legislation but was still reluctant to override established parliamentary procedure; as president, however, he strained for this objective even to the historic point of supporting the smashing of a senatorial filibuster. He also showed vigor in 1965 in pressing for the voting rights bill, which directly attacked the subterfuges used by the southern states to prevent Negroes from voting. Johnson's southern background and his previ-

[37] Speech delivered by Senator Dirksen, June 10, 1964, *Congressional Record,* Vol. 110, pt. 10 (Washington, D.C.: U.S. Government Printing Office, 1964), p. 13319.

ous opposition to civil rights legislation made his case before his fellow southerners in Congress the more convincing and allowed him to achieve a success that probably no northerner could have secured. Since 1954, southerners, especially those in Congress, had undoubtedly seen the writing on the wall. Possibly they were only waiting to have it read to them in the soft accents of the South.

Johnson's espousal of civil rights aimed deeper than any of his predecessors because he committed the resources and power of the national government to eliminate not only the surface manifestations of racial prejudice but also its primary social and economic causes. At the time, therefore, when the Negro was at last within range of securing the goals of civil and political equality, Johnson committed the nation to transcend these former objectives and move to the full integration of the Negro into American society. Again, it was appropriate that a southerner voice these sentiments because white southerners had long suspected that the call for civil rights from the North was hypocritical to a great degree, with racial prejudice as strong above as below the Mason-Dixon Line. Thus, as the South was beginning its granting of civil rights, it could legitimately ask the whole nation to pay in full and with interest the moral debt of equality, a debt, as C. Vann Woodward has shown in *The Burden of Southern History*,[38] incurred during the Civil War period when we lacked the moral resources for repayment.

Kennedy and Urban Change

Drastic as were the consequences of the Negro revolution, it was not the sole manifestation of major change in the post-New Deal period. Indeed, even before the effects of breaking the white supremacy bond could be fully realized, the third and last bond was being ripped, that of rural domination of the legislatures, the last stronghold of the old conservatism. This last bond was, in many ways, the most significant because the deepest characteristic of the old political system was its rural, small-town brand with its domination by the old-stock Americans over the

[38] C. Vann Woodward, *The Burden of Southern History* (Baton Rouge: Louisiana State University Press, 1960), pp. 74–85.

masses of the city with their varied backgrounds. When the consequences of this change would be felt, in conjunction with the others, a different political system would be in operation, one in conformity with the real diversity of the new America.

We shall describe this transformation of power in our chapter on the judiciary because, even more than in the case of civil rights, the prime instruments of change were the courts, especially the Supreme Court. We shall also attempt to analyze the Court's motivation in initiating such a controversial undertaking.

The election of John F. Kennedy as president in 1960 may have indirectly reinforced the Court's attitude that the old bias against the cities and their population of minority ethnic groups could no longer be sustained and constitutionally justified in the urban atmosphere of the latter half of the twentieth century. The country, which a generation before had allowed its rural prejudices to aid in the defeat of Al Smith, elected a man "whose great-grandfather was an impoverished refugee of the Irish potato famine, his grandfather, a saloon keeper and a classical old-time urban political leader." [39] Kennedy's symbolism, however, transcended the particularity of his Irish ancestry and Catholic religion since some other ethnic minority groups probably voted more heavily for him than did the Irish Catholics.[40] The electoral map showed that, with the exception of part of the traditionally Democratic South, the Republicans captured the rural states and the West, the strongholds of the farms and the small towns. On the other hand, with hardly any exceptions beyond Richard Nixon's home state of California, the states with the large cities voted for the Democratic party. "The [electoral] majority which put John F. Kennedy in the White House," wrote one scholar, "was formed by the addition of minorities." [41]

If, however, his election was important in indicating the loss of the country's heavily Anglo-Saxon character, it may have proven even more significant in showing the recognition of this

[39] Fred I. Greenstein, "The Changing Pattern of Urban Party Politics," *Annals of the American Academy of Political and Social Science*, 353 (May 1964), p. 7.

[40] White, *op. cit.*, pp. 354–355; Glazer and Moynihan, *op. cit.*, p. 272.

[41] Leslie Lipson, "The Character of American Politics Today," *Political Quarterly*, XXXIII (April–June, 1962), 157.

change by the white Protestants themselves. Since more than half of Kennedy's votes came from Protestants, a sizable portion of this former dominant group must have made the fateful choice and overcome, according to Theodore White, their "hidden and unspoken reluctance . . . to abandon their past—and not only the past of religion, but the pride of the Anglo-American peoples who had fought the Civil War, who had built America's industry, who had cleared its plains, who found themselves still unable to recognize in the third or fourth generation of the immigrant hordes those leadership qualities that run in the tradition of Lincoln, Roosevelt, Adams, Hay, Wilson, Roosevelt, Stimson." [42]

Even more than being a symbol of the country's social and religious diversity, Kennedy was the representative of its modern urban character, and his election was the repudiation of the absolute identification of American democracy with the small town. As John P. Roche has written:

> Kennedy was our first "modern" President, the first to emerge from the political vortex of urban America, the first to represent the urbane sophistication of the North-east. That he was of Irish ancestry and a Catholic was incidental; what was significant was that he read The New Yorker.[43]

The population of the city had come into its own.

Kennedy's main impact upon our politics extended beyond the symbolism of his election to his making explicit the change that had occurred in a generation, the transformation of government from a somewhat anachronistic device for maintaining the values of an outmoded society to an instrument for rational adjustment to the realities of the modern world. In this respect, he had been immeasurably aided by the example set in the presidential campaigns of Adlai Stevenson, who had prided himself on "talking sense to the American people." Such an attitude was different from that of the liberal Republicans, who could not openly acknowledge their principles of government and their recognition of a changed society. At the same time, Kennedy's style in office, the understatement, the controlled force, the mastery of detail,

[42] White, *op. cit.*, pp. 357–358.
[43] John P. Roche, "How a President Should Use the Intellectuals," *The New York Times Magazine*, July 26, 1964, pp. 30, 32.

was completely at odds with that of an older milieu in American politics, in which the old-fashioned, stem-winding exaggerated oratory had been considered a staple both at the rural hustings and in the beery camaraderie of the city machines.

The practicality of Kennedy's temperament and the rationality of his style did not, however, achieve their full effectiveness in terms of the specific accomplishments of his administration. Partially, he was inhibited by the small popular margin of his victory in 1960 and would undoubtedly have moved with a freer hand after the stronger mandate he would probably have received in 1964. More significantly, however, he was confronted by the ingrained conservatism of Congress, a Congress whose composition has not yet been affected by the sharp scrutiny of the Supreme Court, a Congress still immersed in the patterns of thought and the folkways of a previous era. Yet it was during his administration that even this character of Congress was undergoing a change that would become more apparent during the administration of his successor.

In 1960 Lyndon Johnson seemed to typify the small town as much as Kennedy did the city and the suburbs. The influences of his background—southern, western, and rural—which cast him in a provincial role on the national scene made him at the same time a happy choice as majority leader in a Senate with heavy southern, western, and rural characteristics. The Lyndon Johnson, however, who emerged from the shadows of the country's tragedy in 1963 had become a national leader by transcending his background. Indeed, the very characteristics that previously had seemed to limit the scope of his national appeal became the ones which had cast him as a great symbolic figure in a time of transition, the individual who could assimilate far-reaching social and economic reform in terms of the politically familiar, who could fulfill the new demands of an urban society without severing the ties of his rural roots, and who could mesh the Negroes' goal of equality within the frame of his own southern heritage.

Reaction: Phase Three

The early 1960's, thus, was a period of rapid ascension toward the goal of a new political system based upon both a realistic grasp of the modern country and a basic equality of individuals, rich and poor, white and black, rural and urban, and of western European and eastern European descent. The nineteenth century had cast its shadow almost six decades beyond its time. Only in 1961 did a president assume command, born in this century and committed to its urban way of life.

The new breeze of the 1960's brought long-delayed changes with marked rapidity, and the depth of the liberal wave these changes represented provoked a defensive counterattack by the conservative forces as they realized that their very means of defense was being threatened. This counterattack was waged on two fronts. The first method was to utilize the conservative strongholds in Congress and the state legislatures to pass laws and amendments that would check the Supreme Court, especially on the subject of legislative reapportionment. The second approach was political rather than legal since its purpose was to combine all the forces of discontent against the prevailing tide of change and thus secure enough popular support to win over the leading engine of change itself, the presidency.

The move to circumvent the Supreme Court, which we shall examine in a later chapter, was a new phenomenon only in respect to its conservative sponsors. The offensive, however, launched against the chief opposition fort of the presidency was in many respects a novel one. Such an attack seemed foolhardy because the presidency had been indelibly imprinted with an urban liberal character. Previously when the Republicans had attempted to win the presidency, they had always proceeded under the command of their liberal wing. In 1964, however, the liberal Republicans were unable to prevent Senator Barry Goldwater's nomination, despite its invitation to certain defeat, because of the organization and dedication of his followers. In addition, he had the single undeniable strength of setting out starkly and clearly the full implications of the conservative political philosophy from which the liberals had refused to divorce themselves. As noted before, however, when these liberals painted their political landscape, they muted and softened the harshness of its conservatism by liberal halftones and delicate shadings. When Goldwater eliminated these subtleties and reservations from his picture, the object stood out, clear and sharp.

The liberals felt that the result was really a caricature of their own work, and yet the similarity was too striking for comfort. When Goldwater would ingenuously ask in what ways his views fundamentally differed from theirs, they were trapped in their own ideological wooliness.

With the conservative wing of the Republican party in control, there would not have been even the shadow of a presidential contest in 1964 if the only issue at stake were the maintenance of the existing moderate welfare state. The race issue, however, raised a new dimension to modern American politics. It presented the hope of a full-scale formal conservative alliance against all aspects of the new tide by allowing the southern conservatives to combine with their northern counterparts—as they had in actual congressional practice. This issue, moreover, raised visions of a new solid South—but for the Republican party. This historic transposal was to be achieved by the combination of the two southern conservative strains often at odds with each other: the first was the newly expanding urban managerial and engineering class, affluent, and already the most significant factor in the Republican southern revival; the second was the strongly racist white rural population of the deep South, historically wary of association with the Republican party and yet possessing the strongest inclinations to vote for a third party.

Even this new accretion of southern strength to the traditional Republican forces would still not have been enough to carry hope of national victory. The impact of the race issue, however, was not to be limited to the South but was also likely to attract the "backlash vote" in the North. This vote referred primarily to some of the members of the ethnic minorities in the cities, who were traditionally Democratic because of their support of the New Deal's economic policies, yet who might have been tempted to bolt the party because of their hostile feelings toward the Negroes' impingement on their lives.

The presidential election of 1964 was thus an important one in American history and may even rank as one of the turning points of our political development. A last-ditch defense to check the liberal tide was attempted by bringing together all groups opposed to its modern trend, all segments which had something to fear from a realistic appraisal of the country's problems. It thus raised the possibility of a fundamental realignment of political lines comparable to those achieved in the presidential elections of 1860, 1896, and 1932. Its decisive failure emphasized the emergence of a new political system out of the dissolution of the old, and the successes of the liberals in the wake of this defeat gave additional support to their domination. This was not the first time, as we have seen, when the efforts of those who wanted to halt change had the opposite effect of hastening it.

Thus, we have traced American political history to show the dynamism of our politics in the decades of fundamental transition from one political system to another. We shall now examine how a basic tension operated within and between our political institutions, and the effects of social and economic change upon their character and role.

Chapter IV

Representation and
the Legislature

Many features of the American constitutional structure, such as federalism and the separation of powers, supported the operation of the political system established at the turn of the century and aided in the fulfillment of its principles. The heart of the system, however, lay in Congress and the state legislatures, and the impairment of the representational process was the key to the conservative structure.

This should not be surprising because the system was designed to evade a confrontation with the changing reality of American society. Since the function of representation is to reflect the country, a distortion of the process was necessary for a static conservative system to be maintained. Since this purpose was seldom explicitly stated, we will recognize how the antimajoritarian theories of Madison and Calhoun were applied in practice to justify the method of representation. We will later observe how the whole congressional power structure developed from this base and exaggerated its unequal character, thus forming a legislative world heavily insulated from the currents of the real country. We can therefore appreciate why one of the culminating points in the dissolution of the old system came with the attack on the prevailing method of legislative apportionment.

This distortion of representation was not a wholly conscious, deliberate process since it also reflected the fact that a system of representation based upon geography has certain innate disadvantages in representing a modern, industrial, urban society. We should remember that the essential purpose of such a system is to bridge the gap between the real world and the political world by allowing the legislature to be a picture, in miniature, of the whole country (and this principle holds for a state as well). This picture, however, is not a photograph because there can be no exact likeness of a nation's population. A nation embraces such a multiplicity of interests that to represent them all in the legislature would be clearly impossible. The best that can be achieved is a partial representation, a representation of only certain characteristics. We do better, therefore, to compare the legislature not to a photograph, but to a painting since certain qualities are abstracted from the rest, and these form the basis of representation. Thus no system of representation can be exact; no matter how satisfactory it may appear, it can be only a partial representation.

The fundamental questions we must ask are: "What characteristics of the population are most important—so important that they should be represented in a legislature? What system of classification is most useful for the country?" There are two basic alternatives: a system, such as used in the United States and Great Britain, that divides the country *geographically*, with each legislator representing a group of persons all living in the same area; or one, such as is generally used in European parliamentary governments, that separates the population *politically*, with each legislator representing a group of persons all sharing the same political orientation in a particular geographical area. The most common form of the first is called the single-member constituency system; the second is known as the proportional representation system.

The advocates of proportional representation argue that their system is fairer because it strives to reflect each shade of political opinion according to its popular strength in the country. Thus, in its usual application, a party that secures 40 per cent of the popular vote gains approximately 40 per cent of the legislative seats. In this way, no vote is wasted, and a voter for one party has equal electoral weight with a voter for another. Contrast this, the argument goes, with the inequities possible in the single-member constituency system. In a district won by a party securing 55 per cent of the vote, the 45 per cent who favored the opposition seem to have wasted their votes because they are not represented by a man of their political views. It is easily seen, moreover, that if this 45 per cent minority has counterparts in many other districts, a significant portion of the total community could be deprived of its rightful political influence.

Defenders of the single-member constituency system acknowledge the virtues of proportional representation, but protest that the system's advantages are purchased at too high a price. They argue that proportional representation, by trying to reflect accurately the diversity of political views, tends to accentuate these divisions, even to increase them; it thus encourages a multiplicity of parties, a situation that can lead to ineffective and weak governments based upon unwieldy, fragile coalitions. Under a single-member constituency system, however, minor parties tend to be snuffed out, their political views finding some niche within one of the two major parties. Thus the single-member constituency system, although it gives a rougher depiction of political forces than the subtler rendering of proportional representation, results in stronger, more stable governments based on the support of single parties. Abstract theory, therefore, must be sacrificed for practical wisdom. This emphasis upon practicality receives support from the fact that the single-member constituency system is used in two of the most successful democracies, the United States and Great Britain.

Proportional representation's failure to square theory with reality is further revealed when the system is attacked for dividing a country into abstract groups. In the hapless German Republic after World War I, for example, it was even possible for a party, not securing enough votes for a seat in one geographical area, to have them combined with similar loose party votes throughout the country to match the required total. Representation was thus based on artificial units, composed of persons with the same political views, but otherwise largely strangers to each other, since they had practically no other shared experience or bond of unity. The legislature, in short, was wrenched from the country's true social and economic life. Critics of proportional representation have charged it with a leading responsibility for the failure of German democracy and thus for paving the way for Hitlerite totalitarianism.[1]

[1] Ferdinand A. Hermens, *The Representative Republic* (Notre Dame: University of Notre Dame Press, 1958), ch. XV. An even fuller attack on

The single-member constituency, on the other hand, is defended because it is something real and tangible, a geographical area. One can point to a map and say: "This district, with its people and its interests, is represented by Congressman X." There is nothing abstract or theoretical about his constituency. It can be seen; it can be visited. A legislature based on such constituencies represents, by this view, the real country, a country of persons grouped around tangible interests.

It is not proposed here to enter this debate by arguing the advantages of one method of representation over another. The nature of the controversy is seriously misconstrued, however, if it is considered one between reality and abstraction. As we have seen, every representational system is an abstraction, and the alternative systems we have been discussing must both be so regarded.

The proponents of the single-member constituency system, in failing to acknowledge this, are not aware that their basic assumption is the primacy of geography, that physical location is the strongest political link between human beings. In a modern, industrial, urban society, it seems highly doubtful that man can be considered primarily a geographical animal. Increasingly, the evidence is that a legislative system which reflects the country as a pattern of geographical units conveys a markedly distorted image of the people and their vital interests.

In an earlier period, a country's social structure was much more attuned to geography. The concept of district representation originated in England as a purely practical instrument of government and not as the product of an esoteric political theory. The sovereign needed funds and this was the best method of insuring them. Since this was its purpose, there was never any question that the representative system was keyed to the true social and economic power of the country. As a modern study of reapportionment notes:

Representative government in England was conceived at a time when nearly all wealth was measured by land. It was natural, therefore, for the first representatives to the King's Council or Parliament to be selected on the basis of land holdings, since it was from such land

proportional representation is found in a previous work by Hermens, *Democracy or Anarchy? A Study of Proportional Representation* (Notre Dame: University of Notre Dame Press, 1941).

that the king hoped to attain royal revenues. As commerce grew, the king found it expedient to grant charters to cities and towns. Such charters, in addition to dealing with taxing powers of the king, usually granted the town representation in Parliament.[2]

The same realistic basis of representation obtained when the system took root and flourished in America. One of the main causes of the Revolutionary War was "taxation without representation." Within the rural setting of our country at the time, the concept of a representative of a district—a single true community with one particular interest—was realistic. Moreover, the single-member district was the most logical and practical form of representation because localism, as James Willard Hurst pointed out, "was a natural accommodation to a frontier country of great distance and poor communications."[3] Furthermore, since the population was widely diffused with only a few areas of relatively moderate concentration, there was no great disparity between one district and another. Anomalies of representation were easily tolerated because they were not significant in comparison with their character in later years.

With the acceleration of industrialization and urbanization from the 1880's and 1890's, this favorable setting for geographic representation was lost. Agriculture became an increasingly less important part of the nation's wealth, and the more dominant industries were difficult to fit into the traditional form of representation. Economic groupings in the twentieth century transcended local, state, and even regional lines to become nationwide in scope. The inhabitants of the city were at a particular disadvantage because their interests were so varied and complex.

The significance of district representation was further diluted by the limited contact and few shared interests a city dweller has with his neighbor. Decades ago in the average large city, the concept of a neighborhood had a real significance when immigrants clustered together in the ghettoes of their particular nationality. With the second and third generations of the immigrant families, these residential patterns have been largely broken or their

[2] Advisory Commission on Intergovernmental Relations, *Apportionment of State Legislatures*, (Washington, D.C.: 1962), p. 5.

[3] James Willard Hurst, *The Growth of American Law: The Law Makers* (Boston: Little, Brown, 1950), p. 39.

character has been fundamentally changed by the dissolution of the former ties of identity. One of the casualties of this trend has been a loss of a true neighborhood feeling. Indeed, the very word *neighbor* has a rustic ring out of tune with the realities of life in the modern city. The notice for the military draft which young men have received from a committee of their "friends and neighbors" has seemed ironically inappropriate for the present day.[4]

In the large, impersonalized modern city, therefore, the legislator was as much a representative of an artificial entity as any elected under proportional representation. James Willard Hurst, in noting the irrelevancy of the single-member constituency in modern American industrial society, said:

If the single member geographic district continued unchanged, the facts that shaped the balance of power in United States society did not. The contrast had profound effect upon the working significance of our representative system. After the 1880's, the United States ceased to be a chiefly rural and small-town country and became a nation mainly urban and metropolitan. This meant factors that reduced the meaning of the locality in urban areas as the unit of representation. Life in the metropolis was more impersonal and self-centered; it sharpened the contrasts in class position. . . .

. . . . .

Another combination of factors that reduced the representative meaning of the locality was, (1) the dominance of regional, sectional, and national markets, (2) the concentration of financial and industrial power, (3) the increasing sensitiveness of all parts of the economy to what went on in any one part of it. The interests for which men especially seek political expression are their concern with how they make their living, how they get some measure of economic security, and how they win and hold self-respect by some conviction that their lives have meaning in the larger pattern of the society. These interests of men had less and less relation to the fact of where they lived, especially after 1870.[5]

Only when we recognize the scope of the problem of attaining a significant representation for city dwellers can we appreciate the effect of the legislative gerrymander. If an adequate system of

[4] See Jane Jacobs' concept of the neighborhood in *The Life and Death of Great American Cities* (New York: Random House, 1961), esp. Part I.

[5] Hurst, *op. cit.*, pp. 40–41.

urban representation was difficult to secure with the best of intentions, it was practically impossible when they were lacking altogether. If a compact square block of a city can be considered an artificial unit, what can we say of urban districts which have hardly even territory in common? For example, what does a Brooklyn congressman represent when his district is so fashioned that it is practically impossible for him to walk three consecutive blocks without stepping over its boundaries? A similar question might be asked of the congressman from New York's 16th District which includes "all of Staten Island, which lies west of Brooklyn, and a small enclave on the *opposite* (*southeastern*) *side* of Brooklyn." [6] Former Mayor Wagner commented that its future candidates "won't run for office, they'll have to swim." [7] The fantastic shape of these gerrymanders, which allowed a legislative majority to remain in power, gave mute testimony to the ineffectiveness of the districts as instruments of true representation.

Malapportionment

The device of malapportionment rendered local representation still more irrelevant to the character of modern society. At the same time, it heightened the authority of the antimajoritarian theories of Madison and Calhoun by applying their precepts (see Chapter II, pp. 21–24). This was possible because it required but a short mental transition to move from an accent on locality to the view that the area, as such, was represented in the legislature, and only secondarily the people living in it. Once this was assumed, the contention was then presented that *every* district, regardless of population, deserved representation. Nothing better exhibits the suffusion of our political life with localism than the ease with which this line of reasoning could be accepted as obvious common sense. Note, for example, how convincing a defense of malapportionment Noel Perrin, a scholar from the humanities, made when it came under attack in the 1960's:

[6] David Wells, *Legislative Representation in New York State* (New York: International Ladies Garment Workers' Union, 1963), p. 26.

[7] William J. Keefe and Morris S. Ogul, *The American Legislative Process: Congress and the States* (Englewood Cliffs, N.J.: Prentice-Hall, 1964), p. 84.

What the case for country votes comes to is this. City legislators represent the people of their cities, and the cities themselves. They speak for men and the works of men. Rural legislators represent the small populations of their country districts—and they also speak for their townships and counties, for the land itself. There is quite a difference. For instance, each of the twenty-five state senators from New York City represents about 312,000 people and about 12.6 square miles of land, most of it buried under pavements and buildings. The one state senator who sits for Delaware, Greene, Sullivan, and Ulster Counties represents fewer people—only 240,000—but also more land—4,250 square miles of it. He speaks for something over two hundred towns and villages, scattered over an area a quarter the size of Switzerland. All their diverse interests he must bear in mind. Insofar as anyone does in the State Senate, he also speaks for some hundreds of rural valleys, and for a thousand square miles of mountains, filled with wild-life, waterfalls, and forests. All of this he must look out for.[8]

If land is to be represented as land, there is really no limit as to how few people can live in a district. A city of 4,000,000 can be equaled in the state legislature by one of 400,000. The same principle of equality could be applied to areas of 40,000, or 4,000, or 400, or 40—and Vermont actually did have a legislative district of 38 persons for its lower house.[9]

Furthermore, there is no logical reason for an absolute minimum. What if the district should lose all of its inhabitants? Does it not still deserve representation if area is the prime criterion? Practical men who might dismiss such an eventuality as impossible should remember that at one time in Great Britain, such an area with a phantom population actually existed. The House of Commons, before the Great Reform Bill of 1832, was marked by the grossest form of malapportionment. Some dynamic populous cities had no representation whatsoever; at the same time, rural areas, which had been given two seats in the Commons centuries before, still retained them despite a heavy loss in population. The classic specimen of this, the worst of the "rotten boroughs," as they were called, was Old Sarum, which had over the years de-

[8] Noel Perrin, "In Defense of Country Votes," *Yale Review*, LII (Autumn, 1962), 23–24.

[9] Advisory Commission on Intergovernmental Relations, *op. cit.*, Appendix B.

generated into a swamp and had no permanent residents. Despite the rotten boroughs, the defenders of the system felt that their "living," "practical" form of representation was superior to any "artificial," "abstract," "theoretical" one. "True," these realists would say as the electoral canvassers pitched their tents each election year over the swamp land at Old Sarum, "our system has its anomalies and irrationalities, but it is successful. It does work."

Despite such rationalization, the British, with the Great Reform Bill, did adjust their political system to the real social and economic character of the country. This was by no means a casual or easy step for them to take because no nation treasured its eccentricities more and was more reluctant to change existing institutions merely because they did not make sense. That transition in British political history is of special interest to Americans today because we ourselves are facing the challenge of adjusting our representational system to the country's real character.

The fact that we are living through a period of change allows us, as mentioned in our first chapter, an invaluable opportunity to analyze the justifications of the declining, older political system. We can thus, while recognizing their fallaciousness and their motivation, appreciate their plausibility because we have so recently been under their intellectual sway and their authority is still binding in many quarters today.

Future historians will not be in so fortunate a position for understanding the subject of legislative malapportionment. They will certainly be able to note its scope and depth. They will, as we do with Old Sarum, pay particular attention to the grossest examples. They will note that districts had the same number of representatives in our state legislatures even though one had 200 times the population of another, or 400 times, or even almost 1,000 times.[10] They will easily realize that the cumulative result of such disparities meant that a minority of a state's population —and, at times, a small minority—controlled its legislature. Thus 8 per cent of Nevada's population secured a majority in her senate, and the same was true of 10.7 per cent of the population

[10] Paul T. David and Ralph Eisenberg, *Devaluation of the Urban and Suburban Vote* (Bureau of Public Administration, University of Virginia, 1961), p. 3.

of California and 12.3 per cent of Florida. In the lower state houses, as well, there were some glaring examples of minority control since majorities could be commanded by 11.6 per cent of Vermont's population, 12 per cent of Connecticut's, and 14.7 per cent of Florida's.[11] The more careful historians will, of course, bear in mind that these were extreme cases, but even they will attest that these examples were by no means isolated islands of inequity in a sea of fair apportionment. On the contrary, the rarities were those legislatures whose representation fairly reflected their people.[12]

Future historians, therefore, will probably have enough material at hand to present an intelligible account of our politics. They will easily discern from the statistical evidence that the pattern of malapportionment was not a haphazard one. They will observe that in practically every malapportioned state, with dreary uniformity, the rural areas were consistently overrepresented and the urban areas, underrepresented. This trend was evident even when the metropolitan population became a majority within a state—indeed, this very growth heightened the disparity, rather than mitigated it.[13] Historians will most likely be perplexed, however, by the longstanding tolerance of the urban majority of its political insubordination.

Only those historians who can reconstruct our thought patterns as well as our actions will be able to realize the coerciveness of the Madisonian theory and the subtle tyranny of geography in conditioning our view of society. As an example, we earlier noted Perrin's contention that representation of localities, no matter how small, was justified in order to reflect the diversity of inter-

[11] Advisory Commission on Intergovernmental Relations, *op. cit.*, Appendix B.

[12] Gordon E. Baker found in 1955 only seven states where the urban population was only moderately underrepresented and only two, Wisconsin and Massachusetts, with truly proportionate representation; see his *Rural Versus Urban Political Power: The Nature and Consequences of Unbalanced Representation* (Garden City, N.Y.: Doubleday, 1955), p. 17.

[13] One of the basic assumptions of this chapter is that representatives from the cities will vote differently from those from the rural areas. This assumption has been questioned by David R. Derge, whose argument has been persuasively rebutted by Richard T. Frost. See entries in the bibliography under "Representation and Apportionment."

ests in the state. The corollary to this principle was that no one city should dominate the whole state because, no matter how populous, it was but one interest (or one "faction," to use the Madisonian phraseology). The allotment of a minority of legislative seats to a city with 55 per cent of the state's population could have been defended as a reasonable proposition. But would it also have held when the city's population reached 60 per cent, or 70 per cent, or 80 per cent, or 90 per cent, or even 99 per cent? Once the principle was accepted, there was no logical reason why one point should have been chosen over another. Furthermore, the empirical evidence strongly indicated that a minority, despite its decreasing size, would cling to its majority in the legislature until its grip was released by the courts.

Such mathematical absurdities developed from considering the interests of society primarily in a geographic sense, and conceiving of the state as a cluster of geographic areas. In popular thought, nothing seemed more tangible than a geographic area, nothing more solid and real than land itself. A practical man was "down to earth," and land and its property were *real* estate.

This instinctive conception of reality played us false in apprehending the nature of the large city. A state with such a metropolis might also contain, for instance, four small towns, A, B, C, and D. Even a child could recognize that these were four separate entities, four distinct interests, because their physical separateness was a clear reality to him. It required, however, a more sophisticated degree of observation and analysis to perceive that the city was not one interest, despite its physical limits and its apparently homogeneous mass of inhabitants. With a more refined perception, the city's population would be seen as a mixture of different groups, a set of separate and diverse interests even though found within the bounds of one community. Although not physically separated, they were just as distinct as, and often more so than, the separate small towns of A, B, C, and D. We were thus confronted, as Gordon Baker has pointed out, not with *a* rural minority, but with a complex cluster of minorities in both the rural areas and in the cities.[14]

Such an analysis based on the actual social and economic structure largely weakened the theoretical justification of mal-

[14] Baker, *op. cit.*, pp. 56–59.

apportionment, as is obvious in Alexander M. Bickel's denial that the equality of the vote was a prerequisite of a democratic society. The secret of democratic consent, he declared, was less the reserve power of the majority than:

> . . . the sense shared by all that their interests were spoken for in the decision-making process, no matter how the result turned out. Government by consent requires that no segment of society should feel alienated from the institutions that govern. This means that the institutions must not merely represent a numerical majority—which is a shifting and uncertain quantity anyway—but must reflect the people in all their diversity, so that all the people may feel that their particular interests and even prejudices, that all their diverse characteristics, were brought to bear on the decision-making process.
>
> . . . . .
>
> . . . the legislature carries the burden of reflecting the diversities of population, and . . . it could not under any circumstances perform this function if it were built strictly on the one-person-one-vote principle.[15]

A similar emphasis upon diversity was found in Justice Potter Stewart's dissent in *Lucas* v. *Colorado*, where the Court's majority, under the principle of one-man, one-vote, struck down a legislative apportionment system that had been accepted by a popular majority of the electorate:

> Representative government is a process of accommodating group interests through democratic institutional arrangements. Its function is to channel the numerous opinions, interests, and abilities of the people of a State into the making of the State's public policy. Appropriate legislative apportionment, therefore, should ideally be designed to insure effective representation in the State's legislature, in cooperation with other organs of political power, of the various groups and interests making up the electorate. In practice, of course, this ideal is approximated in the particular apportionment system of any State by a realistic accommodation of the diverse and often conflicting political forces operating within the State.
>
> . . . . .
>
> The fact is, of course, that population factors must often to some degree be subordinated in devising a legislative apportionment plan which is to achieve the important goal of ensuring a fair, effective, and

[15] Alexander M. Bickel, "Reapportionment & Liberal Myths," *Commentary*, XXXV, 6 (June, 1963), 488–489.

balanced representation of the regional, social, and economic interests within a State. And the further fact is that throughout our history the apportionments of State Legislatures have reflected the strongly felt American tradition that the public interest is composed of many diverse interests, and that in the long run it can better be expressed by a medley of component voices than by the majority's monolithic command.[16]

Yet how could we achieve this valued diversity, this "medley of component voices"? If all interests—even all substantial interests—were to be represented in the legislature, then this rule should have been followed for those making up the urban "majority" as well as the rural "minority." Since this was not the case, the extra weight given to people living in the rural areas did not protect "a minority," but rather granted the minorities in the rural areas a strong advantage over those in the cities. In effect, they controlled the state in conjunction with a few allied urban minorities even though both groups made up at times only a small percentage of the population. The façade of minority protection was removed since certain minorities were obviously put at a severe handicap commensurate with the marked advantage given others. There was, thus, little true protection of minorities in general, only the placing of the reins of power in the hands of the favored few.

The philosophical assumptions of the defenders of malapportionment were, therefore, based upon a fundamental contradiction and were vulnerable to any sustained logical analysis. If a working definition of democracy combined the concepts of majority rule and minority rights, the defenders of malapportionment refused to acknowledge that the advantages given the minority by the system of apportionment went beyond the limits of minority protection to minority rule, thereby negating the essence of democracy itself.

There was no escape from this theoretical predicament for these "democratic" believers in elite rule. Arguments about the wisdom of minorities and the waywardness of majorities were beside the point. Acquiescence to majorities is unquestionably a gamble because they are not infallibly correct or wise—no more

[16] *Lucas* v. *Colorado*, 377 U.S. 713, 749, 751 (1964), dissenting opinion.

than are minorities—but it is a gamble at the heart of democracy.

With such feeble philosophical support behind malapportionment, its demise was predictable from the moment the Supreme Court stated in 1962 that it would examine the subject. The issue seemed to be settled by the very act of raising it to public scrutiny and debate. The ensuing debate, moreover, was a thin and limited one, hardly appropriate to the theme of a major transformation of political power whose impact would be felt by every citizen for generations. There was no effective rebuttal to Chief Justice Earl Warren's flat, matter-of-fact pronouncements: "A citizen, a qualified voter, is no more nor no less so because he lives in the city or on the farm," and "Logically, in a society ostensibly grounded on representative government, it would seem reasonable that a majority of the people of a State could elect a majority of that State's legislators." [17]

The supporters of malapportionment were unable to marshal a coherent defense because they could not fall back on an explicit espousal of minority rule. Such a tactic would have detached them from the principles of democracy and the American tradition.

In contrast to the frustrating philosophical silence of American conservatives in the defense of their favored system of apportionment, there has always been from the days of Plato a strong tradition in Western political thought and practice which has upheld minority rule over the majority. The foundation of this elitist concept was the belief that a minority was superior in political wisdom or virtue to the majority. The interests of numbers were, therefore, balanced and usually outweighed by the premium put on certain favored characteristics the minority was believed to possess. These varied in particular circumstances, but all were similar in presenting rational grounds for justifying a special status. In some societies, the distinction was an aristocratic one, with one group accorded its position by virtue of lineage and tradition of service. In other countries, the distinction was oligarchical and the preferred position was based on the assumption that a person who is richer than his fellows has either greater abilities or a larger stake in the community to protect.

[17] *Reynolds* v. *Sims,* 377 U.S. 533, 568, 565 (1964).

The forms of weighing wealth in the operation of the franchise were many and varied. Usually this form of distinction was applied through a property qualification for voting. This was found in some of our early state constitutions and was used in Great Britain for the greater part of the nineteenth century. Indeed, in the heyday of its operation in Great Britain, the principle was actually doubly applied since by the plural vote system, an individual could vote in each constituency where he owned the prescribed amount of property. One unusual variant of this technique was the three-part franchise used in Prussia prior to World War I. By this system, the very few who possessed one-third of the wealth held one-third of the voting power; those with the middle third of the wealth also had their commensurate one-third of the voting strength; finally, the majority of the people who shared the bottom third of the wealth were left with the remaining third of the vote.

Still other societies granted an electoral bonus because of education on the happy thought that there was a direct correlation between education and intelligence. One of the features of the British plural vote system was a number of university constituencies, composed of persons who had received an M.A. from these institutions.

What was common to all these systems was that minorities were given a special distinction because their attributes were highly valued by their society. One can disagree with the contention that wealth, birth, training, intelligence, or education deserves extra weight in the political process, and yet recognize that it is a debatable thesis, which cannot be dismissed out of hand as patently stupid or irrational.

In the United States, on the other hand, the system of malapportionment had little in common with this rich elitist tradition. Political power had been distributed in an apparently irrational and haphazard manner. Indeed, malapportionment in practice not only neglected the traditional criteria of eminence, but was often a travesty upon them when the least educated, the least wealthy, and the least productive areas of the state held political control.[18]

[18] For the low standard of income, education, and health in the rural areas, see A. Whitney Griswold, *Farming and Democracy* (New York:

When forced to justify why the residents of one congressional district should have had four times the power in the House of Representatives of those in another and why the inhabitants of one district in a state should have had 1000 times more power in a legislative house than those of another, American conservatives were doubly tongue-tied. They could not acknowledge their adherence to the principle of minority rule and they could not openly state why one minority deserved a special position over another.

With each succeeding decade after 1910, moreover, the disparity of legislative representation increased.[19] Thus, what was represented in the legislatures was not the contemporary states but rather those of a generation or two earlier. As E. E. Schatt-schneider has written:

Unfortunately, the relocation of population has left the state legislatures high and dry as spokesmen for older patterns of population distribution. While the American people have been on the move, the state legislatures have fallen into the hands of the folks they left behind.[20]

Thus there was no way by which the majority could act with political effectiveness since, as a general rule, the greater the population in a particular area, the less impact each of its members had in the legislature. This situation frustrated the legitimate demands of people who, in moving to the city, expanded and intensified its problems, such as housing, education, health, traffic, and crime. Ironically, however, the mechanics of apportionment guaranteed that the very shift of population which increased these problems would simultaneously impede their solution.

State funds allotted to the city were not commensurate to its

Harcourt, Brace and World, 1948), pp. 6, 178–179. See also *Advisory Commission on Governmental Relations, op. cit.*, appendices G and H, which show in state by state listing that, except for the New England states, the urban areas rank almost consistently higher in education and income than the rural ones.

[19] "Rural Overrepresentation Acute in State Legislatures" *Congressional Quarterly Weekly Report*, XX, 5 (February 2, 1962), 170. Study based on David and Eisenberg, *op. cit.*

[20] E.E. Schattschneider, "Urbanization and Reapportionment," in "A Symposium on *Baker* v. *Carr,*" *Yale Law Journal*, LXXII, 1 (November, 1962), 110.

needs because they had naturally been divided less according to population than to legislative strength.[21] There is, of course, no iron rule that governmental expenditures should be made in exact proportion to the number of persons in a particular area or industry. Political wisdom might have unquestionably dictated that at certain times it would be in the long-range interest of the state to encourage a particular minority group or section beyond the point that the number of individuals involved, by themselves, would seem to warrant. Such selectivity and discriminating judgment were generally lacking in the blanket bounties given the rural areas. The urban population felt particularly short-changed because it believed that it deserved an even greater slice of the state's financial pie than its share of the population because its very concentration of people created problems proportionally greater than its number indicated. Thus, Walter Lippmann has vigorously complained that the public needs of the city dwellers have not been adequately met—even though this failure stems in great measure from the application of the political principles he has favored, the protection of "minority" rights against majority rule:

When a community grows from, let us say, 10,000 inhabitants to 100,000, the cost of the public services required is bound to go up more than 10 times. For the larger community requires extensive facilities—as for example—wider roads and underpasses—which the small town does not have to have at all.[22]

The difficulty, therefore, of a legislature's realistically reflecting the character of an urban industrial society has been aggravated by the impairment of representation fostered by the old political system. As a result, the legislatures, with their obstructed contact with the community, have responded inadequately to its problems.

[21] Baker, *op. cit.*, pp. 33–34.
[22] From a 1958 Lippmann column reproduced in Clinton Rossiter and James Lare, eds., *The Essential Lippmann: A Political Philosophy for Liberal Democracy* (New York: Random House, 1963), pp. 362–363.

The House of Representatives

Although we have primarily emphasized the impact of this process upon the state legislatures, we should bear in mind that it had national repercussions as well. Since state legislatures drew the lines for their states' congressional districts, the House of Representatives did not truly represent divisions of the country's population even though the states themselves were represented in it according to their own popular strength. Rather, the rural, small-town character of an older America was reflected as in the state legislatures, even though to a less pronounced degree.

The pattern of rural overrepresentation is readily ascertained. Herbert Wechsler has pointed out that, whereas, after 1950, the farms plus the towns and cities with under 10,000 people had 51 per cent of the country's population, they were dominant in 265 of the 435 congressional districts, 61 per cent of the total.[23] Senator Paul Douglas showed that the average seat in the House in 1956 should have represented 350,000 people. When he examined the districts over this average, he dicovered that they were practically all urban ones: "Of the 27 districts, not including Congressmen at large, with populations of over 450,000, all but 1 are urban districts, and almost all of the 52 districts with populations between 400,000 and 500,000 are urban districts." [24] Gordon Baker wrote similarly for the same period that "the nation's thirteen largest districts, all of them urban and each containing over 500,000 inhabitants, total enough population collectively for approximately twenty-two congressmen instead of thirteen." [25]

More recent statistical analyses of congressional representation have indicated that possibly the cities are not now as underrepresented as these previous studies claimed. This divergence of

[23] Herbert Wechsler, "The Political Safeguards of Federalism: The Role of the States in the Composition and Selection of the National Government," in Arthur W. MacMahon, ed., *Federalism: Mature and Emergent* (Garden City, N.Y.: Doubleday, 1955), p. 103.

[24] Senator Paul Douglas, speech in Senate, March 26, 1956, *Congressional Record*, Vol. 102, pt. 4 (Washington, D.C.: U.S. Government Printing Office, 1956), pp. 5543–5544.

[25] Baker, *op. cit.*, p. 44.

view, however, does not in fact lessen the importance of malapportionment nor does it render the House a more valid reflector of the country. This change resulted primarily from the population loss of the cities in recent years to the suburbs, which, because of their impressive increase in population, have now become the areas most underrepresented in Congress. Therefore, as a geographical area loses population, each inhabitant remaining gains political power correspondingly. The cities have been gaining in legislative strength as they have been losing population. The rural areas still retain their favored position because they have still been fortunate, in political terms, to be losing population. If a new area were ever to develop as a residential haven for fleeing suburbanites, it would then become the most malapportioned area, and the suburbs, like the cities today, would gain political ground proportionally.

Observers who do not appreciate the importance of this basic character of representation have expressed the opinion that a fairly apportioned House of Representatives, with a substantial increase in suburban legislators, might become even less responsive to the needs of an urban society than they are at present.[26] Such views are not without tangible support. No one can overlook the many points of friction between the cities and the suburbs or the usual political alliance of the rural areas with the suburbs. Nevertheless, the distinction between the suburbs and the city is of a different order from the distinction between the city and the rural areas. The number of persons affected by city problems comprises many more than just those persons living in the cities. If a person spends his whole working day in the city—and some parts of his leisure time as well—he may be considered as much a product of urban civilization as one who lives there a full twenty-four-hour day. In many instances, city dwellers and suburbanites share the same problems, although they may per-

[26] See "On Urban-Rural Representation; Suburban Areas Most Unrepresented in House," *Congressional Quarterly*, February 2, 1962, pp. 153–157, and Andrew Hacker, *Congressional Districting: The Issue of Equal Representation*, rev. ed. (Washington, D.C.: The Brookings Institution, 1964), pp. 88–99. For skepticism about the suburbs in general supporting the cities in the legislatures, see Marilyn Gittell, letter to *The New York Times*, July 1, 1964, editorial page. For a partial rebuttal to arguments of this nature, see Schattschneider, *op. cit.*, p. 11.

ceive them from differing points of view. The long-range trend will probably be toward harmony between them because the suburbanite cannot escape the city. The rural dweller can damn the Industrial Revolution and turn his back on the city; the suburbanite cannot.

The Senate

The impairment of the representational function in the House was a matter of concern because that body was expressly designed to represent numbers. So sharp has been this distortion in the House that in recent years its sister chamber, the Senate, has been more closely attuned to the country's economic and social character. Such a comparison is a pointed reflection upon the House because the Senate, unlike the House, makes no pretense at representing numbers and its membership, based upon an unamendable part of the Constitution, cannot be adjusted to changing national tides.

This comparison, however, should not obscure the effect on our politics of the Senate's equality of state representation. Although this feature is taught every American school child, its implications have seldom been recognized by the general public. Most persons are usually caught off their guard when confronted by the mathematical starkness of the great differential of political power held by the inhabitants of the various states of the Union. In 1940, New York State, the most populous, had more than 120 times more people than Nevada, the least populous. Equality of state representation meant that a citizen of Nevada had more than 120 times the power in the Senate of a citizen of New York. By 1960, the gap was somewhat bridged with New York, still clinging to its front rank, having almost 75 times the population of Alaska, the most sparsely settled state.[27] The result of such disproportions is best grasped when we group states together. Thus, in 1940, the eight mountain states with 3.6 per cent of the national vote had the same strength in the Senate as eight other

[27] "United States Population (Official Census), 1890–1960," reproduced in *The World Almanac, 1966, and Book of Facts* (New York: *New York World-Telegram and the Sun*, 1966), p. 325.

states with 50.5 percent of the vote.[28] By the 1950's, the disparity may even have worsened since "the eight largest states with 54 per cent of the voters" were matched by the "eight smallest with less than 3 per cent of the voters." [29] As a result, Senator Paul H. Douglas pointed out to his colleagues, "one-sixth of the population therefore have half of the Senators and one-half of the population have one-sixth of the Senators." [30] One can thus sympathize with his charge, "In the Senate, the small States are certainly in the saddle. They are booted and spurred and we of the large States are saddled and bridled." [31]

The defenders of the Senate believe this judgment to be unjustified and are little impressed with the supporting statistics. Although they admit the possibility that the small states could combine their senatorial strength against the large ones, they dismiss it as a theoretical phantom because the actual divisions in the Senate are based on lines of interest which have little correlation to population. Thus Lindsay Rogers, who acknowledged in the 1920's that the Senate was "probably the worst rotten borough institution in the world"—a distinction it has since lost to some of the state legislatures—nevertheless stated: "An examination of the Senate votes on the major battles in Congress . . . discloses that the average population of states opposed has not differed greatly from the average population of states in favor. There are no traces of a combination of small states." [32]

Similarly Alexander Bickel objects to the unreality not only of the majoritarian critique of the Senate, but also of other specters of minority rule in our country:

. . . the first wisdom is to look at the reality of our political arrangements, the reality of our allocations of power to govern, and not at paper provisions and statistical nightmares. What does it mean to juggle ratios or to bewail the fact that 20 per cent of a state's population can elect a majority of its legislature, X per cent of the population

[28] George B. Galloway, *The Legislative Process in Congress* (New York: Crowell, 1953), p. 270.

[29] Robert Dahl, *A Preface to Democratic Theory* (Chicago: University of Chicago Press, 1956), p. 116.

[30] Douglas, *op. cit.*, p. 5537.   [31] *Ibid.*, pp. 5537–5538.

[32] Lindsay Rogers, *The American Senate* (New York: Knopf, 1926), pp. 91, 98–99.

of the United States can elect the President, and X—10 per cent can elect the Senate? These are not facts; such things never happen.[33]

One might answer the preceding question that it means a great deal for in such legislative mathematics is the very stuff of power—as many conservatives will tacitly testify by their zeal in maintaining these meaningless ratios. We will also see later in discussing the filibuster that the population of a state can be a factor in determining a senator's vote. More to the point, however, is the argument that senators reflect the true character of the country because they represent people not as abstract individuals but in their most meaningful roles in modern society, as members of concrete economic and social interest groups. The Senate, therefore, with its equality of state representation, allows a voice for these groups that would otherwise be muffled because of their size. The beet-sugar interest, the copper interest, the silver interest—or, more explicitly, the persons involved in the production of beet sugar and in the mining of copper and silver —can exert their weight and have their demands accommodated in the political process.

Such a description of the Senate also seems to be answering the charge made earlier that the system of district representation is inadequate in the modern technological society because it does not represent persons in their most important roles but in one of their least important, as residents of an area. The Senate may, thus, be considered by this view as a realistic balancing force to the distortions of the House.

Upon examination, however, this defense of state equality in the Senate proves a dubious justification. Interests are unquestionably represented in the Senate, but in such a capricious manner that the system fails in its supposed function of representing realistically the social and economic forces of the country. The Senate does not prove to be an antidote to the distortions caused by the geographical emphasis of district representation. On the contrary, these biases and distortions are projected on a greater scale because the states are, in essence, large districts themselves.

To consider the Senate as a true reflector of the social and

[33] Bickel, *op. cit.*, p. 489.

economic interests of the country, one is forced to accept the assumption that there is a correlation between economic interests and state lines. Such an assumption was reasonable in the late eighteenth and early nineteenth centuries, when the country was primarily agricultural. In a modern industrial economy, however, with a dense concentration of diverse interests, it is almost completely untenable. By the pure accident of geography, one state may have a great number of economic interests within its boundaries; another, but one. Obviously, the latter interest has a much greater voice in the Senate than its fellows because it has the undivided attention of two senators. Furthermore, in a state with a number of diverse interests, the senators may be primarily concerned with the protection of only the dominant one. Thereby, the minority representation of the Senate becomes a questionable protection for the particular minorities in that state. The Negroes in the South are only the most glaring example.[34]

Furthermore, the refusal of economic interests to conform to state lines has still another marked injustice. If states are associated with a differing number of interests, then interests are very likely to be found in a differing number of states. Thus, some interests may be situated entirely within the boundary lines of one state, or, at best, two or three; others may stretch over a great many. The number of persons, however, involved in each category may be virtually the same.

Authorities are not in agreement as to which interest is the most overrepresented in the Senate. A good case can be made for the choice of sugar production or silver mining. John Gunther comments on the dispersion of the sugar interests and their resultant political power:

Only 3 per cent of American farmers grow sugar beet and cane; the entire processing industry employs no more than twenty-five thousand people. But sugar is spread through many states—beets grow in seventeen, cane in two—which gives it thirty-eight senators. . . .[35]

The silver-mining industry is another gross example because its six states are among the most sparsely populated in our country. Nevertheless, twelve members speak for the silver interest in

[34] Dahl, *op. cit.*, pp. 113–118.
[35] John Gunther, *Inside U.S.A.*, rev. ed. (New York: Harper and Row, 1951), p. 241.

the Senate. Equality of state representation, it is true, is supposed to guarantee a voice for minorities. The silver senators, however, have more of a roar than a voice, and the sugar senators, as Gunther writes, "can certainly make a noise."

The view that this disproportion does not really matter as long as there is some form of representation for various interests is clearly erroneous since it can easily be discerned that such power carries a great deal of influence in the political process. The privileged position of silver in our political system is a classic example. Arthur Schlesinger, Jr., in a work highly favorable to the New Deal, was critical of Roosevelt's acquiescence to this formidable power in his silver policy:

Roosevelt surrendered to political blackmail on the part of the silver bloc. He had reason to fear that a silver filibuster might hurt his legislative program, or that a silver veto might damage congressional prospects in the fall [of 1934]. In capitulating, he committed the government to the unlimited purchase of silver at artificial prices until government silver holdings reached a value equal to one-third of government gold reserves. The Silver Purchase Act, in short, assured the producers of silver a lavish subsidy, while the government received in exchange growing stocks of a metal which it did not need and for which it had no use.

The silver policy represented the most remarkable—as well as the least remarked—special-interest triumph of the period. A minor industry, employing in 1939 less than five thousand persons, the silver industry, in effect, held the government to ransom, extorting nearly a billion and a half dollars in the fifteen years after 1934—a sum considerably larger than that paid by the government to support farm prices over the same period. The silver acquired under the legislation played little part in the American monetary system and the American silver policy only complicated the monetary problems of countries, like China and Mexico, where silver constituted part of the circulating medium. No legislation passed in New Deal years had less excuse. "Our silver program," Morgenthau confessed in 1935, "is the only monetary fiscal policy that I cannot explain or justify." [36]

The Senate, therefore, cannot be defended as the arena in which minority economic interests have a voice in the political process. It does give some of these interests extraordinary power

[36] Arthur Schlesinger, Jr., *The Coming of the New Deal* (Boston: Houghton Mifflin, 1959), pp. 251–252.

—but at the expense of others. Those interests are the fortunate ones, Robert Dahl points out, which are geographically concentrated in sparsely settled states:

. . . equal representation of geographical units overrepresents some minorities concentrated in sparse areas but underrepresents those concentrated in heavily populated areas. Moreover, to the extent that a minority is not geographically concentrated, it receives no protection per se from equal state representation. Why, then, this special tenderness toward minorities concentrated geographically in sparse areas? [37]

To the degree that the Senate emphasizes geographical concentration, it is affected by chance and irrationality; to the degree that it emphasizes sparse population, it continues and exaggerates the bias we have already seen in the state legislatures and in the House of Representatives. Thus, despite the claims of its adherents, the Senate's representation of American society bears only the crudest resemblance to its actual features.

This reflection has been further distorted by the prominent role in the Senate's operation of one-industry states. As a general rule, if a state limits itself to one dominant industry, there is a greater likelihood of its having a stagnant and static economy than a state with a greater degree of diversity. The growth of new industries is almost an inevitable result of an expanding vital economy. The political system of representation in the Senate, therefore, tends to assure that these new economic and social forces will be underrepresented.

The proverbial man from Mars, in picturing the United States from observing its Senate, would credit it with a moderate amount of manufacturing, but with great agricultural, mining, and grazing industries. The Senate, therefore, really represents a country with different characteristics from our own.

Congressional Practice and Power

This unrepresentative nature of the legislatures is but one factor in their inability to reflect the needs of the actual society. Legislative practice tends to accentuate and aggravate the disparity between the political world and the real world instead of

[37] Dahl, *op cit.*, pp. 115–116.

bridging the gap. The world of Congress, therefore, is primarily marked by the spirit and ethos of the countryside and small town, the America of half a century ago.

One reason for this character of Congress is that its operation as well as its composition emphasizes localism. Many legislators are primarily concerned with the interests of their constituency and immersed in their "messenger boy" function between their voters and the administrative apparatus. Consequently, they often develop a parochial attitude which blurs an insight into national problems and inhibits the attainment of enough cohesion and discipline for a meaningful legislative party system.

Geographical considerations play a prominent role in appointments to committees. On some committees, the attempt is made to secure representation of all the country's major regions, with each region holding, in effect, a permanent seat; in other committees, a state may have a similar status with a vacancy from that state being filled by another member of its congressional contingent. In addition, the prevailing rule in Congress is that a committee which primarily deals with a particular industry will contain, whenever possible, a majority—and, at times, an overwhelming one—of members from states involved with it. With the House Agriculture Committee, this specialization is carried one step further since its membership not only comes almost wholly from farming states, but also is composed to represent the various types of crops.[38]

This emphasis upon localism in the operation of Congress is unquestionably valuable in giving the individual citizen, at times, a direct relationship to government, in assuring the protection of certain interests, and in securing a broad consensus of diverse geographical areas. The advantages, however, are more than counterbalanced by the reinforcement of the special position in Congress of minority interests favored by geography. The manner of assuring a broad consensus is partly illusory because it concentrates upon individuals as producers rather than in any other capacity. As a result, the political influence of the cities and suburbs is further depressed.

[38] Charles O. Jones, "Representation in Congress: The Case of the House Agriculture Committee," *American Political Science Review*, LV, 2 (June, 1961), 358–361.

The heaviest toll of legislative localism is in the diminution of a national viewpoint in one of the most important segments of the national government. In discussing federalism, we shall see the question raised as to whether there is a significant relationship between the national government and the state governments when the "national" government is so much the creature of the states. Before a congressman on a committee can be criticized for lacking a national perspective, we should recognize that his assignment, as well as his election, was intimately tied to local considerations. Although congressmen do transcend these limitations, the flouting of the basic spirit of an institution cannot understandably be expected as a common occurrence. Thus, as the country's population moves into metropolitan areas and as its culture and economy become increasingly nationalized, the operating rules of Congress continue to follow the localistic patterns of an older America.

The seniority system is probably the practice of Congress which is most responsible for its character. Seniority is king, and it determines a man's power position throughout his career in either house. Other factors may be of some influence, but there is little real usurpation of the dominant power of seniority. A legislator's seniority ranking within his party is a heavy determinant as to which committee he will be appointed to, and it is, for all practical purposes, the sole criterion for committee chairmanship.[39] Since these chairmanships or places on choice committees are positions of great power in the operative structure of Congress, the most important attribute of legislative influence is the winning of elections. "No other major Western democracy," James MacGregor Burns has written, "rewards its politicians with so much power for so little relevant accomplishment." [40]

The premium which the seniority system puts upon electoral success has an impact far more important than the effect upon an

[39] George Goodwin, Jr., "The Seniority System in Congress," *American Political Science Review*, LIII, 2 (June, 1959), 412–436. A significant limitation upon the influence of seniority upon committee appointments was the practice established for the Senate when Lyndon Johnson was Majority Leader: that each Democratic Senator, no matter how junior, should be given at least one major committee post.

[40] James MacGregor Burns, *The Deadlock of Democracy: Four-Party Politics in America* (Englewood Cliffs, N.J.: Prentice-Hall, 1963), p. 244.

individual congressman's career. The system, which had meaning in an earlier period when it accurately reflected the old sectional system of politics, gives an enormous advantage to the one-party states and to the one-party legislative districts.[41] As a general rule, these tend to be the areas not only with less population than the others, but also with a population more static and more rural. Lewis Froman, Jr., has pointed out that in 1960 the mean population of the 22 one-party and modified one-party states was 3,186,-590, of which the mean urban proportion was 53 per cent. The 26 two-party states, on the other hand, had a mean population of 4,138,281, and their mean urban percentage was 69.4 per cent.[42] This correlation is not at all accidental. The very fact that the areas are static and not touched by new industrial, social, and economic forces is the primary factor in allowing the dominant party to maintain control. Even the chief reservations to this generalization, some urban one-party districts, are often static and indeed losing population. The operating rule of Congress, therefore, has become that the smaller an area's population is and the less involved it is in the changes that affect the rest of the country, the greater its influence in legislating for our modern needs. Conversely, those areas most affected by the dynamic social and economic pressures of our time and most concerned with its problems are given a lessened role in the legislative process.

The effects of the seniority system are most clearly seen in the details of its actual operation. In 1952, for example, more than a quarter of the 160 members of the House of Representatives who had served ten years or more were from the South. As a result, there were southern chairmen in 11 of the 19 standing committees. An analysis of Congress in 1964 showed that although only 38 per cent of the Democratic members came from the South, they, nevertheless, accounted for "53 per cent of the chairmanships of the 17 major standing committees, 53 per cent

[41] Schattschneider, *op. cit.*, pp. 11–12.

[42] Lewis A. Froman, Jr., *People and Politics: An Analysis of the American Political System* (Englewood Cliffs, N.J.: Prentice–Hall, 1962), p. 85. Indications are, however, that in the House, the noncompetitive districts are becoming less rural and southern than previously. Raymond E. Wolfinger and Joan Heifetz, "Safe Seats, Seniority, and Power in Congress," *American Political Science Review*, LIX, 2 (June, 1965), 346–347.

of the chairmen of all these 17 committees' subcommittees; and 49 per cent of all the representatives who hold the first three positions (chairman and first and second ranking majority members) on each of the 17 committees." [43] Furthermore, in one session of the House, the more urban half of our congressional districts had slightly more than one-third as many committee chairmen as the less urban half. [44]

Even more enlightening than these statistics are the specific home areas of leaders of the House of Representatives. In 1955, only 2 out of 38 prominent leaders of the House were from large cities, one from New York and one from Chicago; by 1963, the proportion was 4 out of 40. [45] In 1961, the committee chairmen and ranking members came from "Millidgeville, Melvin, Canton (Ill.), Ogelsby, Rensselaer (Ind.), Alton, Exira, North Attleboro, Allegan, Tyler, Eisberry, Center Ossipee, Rumson, Malone, Auburn, Lyndhurst, Mahoney City, Lubbock, Texarkana, Bonham, Broad Run, Wenatchee, and Mercer." [46] It is thus obvious that the most influential men in the House of Representatives do not as a general rule come from the areas of greatest concentration of population. This observation does not imply that the legislators coming from these areas are in any way less able, less conscientious, or less intelligent than those coming from the metropolitan regions. It only means that their villages and towns are obviously less affected by the problems that they are called upon to solve.

If we look at the operation of the seniority system in the Senate, the results are quite similar. The one-party states are in a position of control and these are not, as pointed out before, the more populous, the more urban, or the more dynamic states. [47]

[43] Galloway, *op. cit.*, p. 367; Wolfinger and Heifetz, *op. cit.*, pp. 338–339.

[44] Burns, *The Deadlock of Democracy*, p. 245.

[45] Baker, *op. cit.*, p. 49; *Official Congressional Directory for the Use of the United States Congress* (Washington, D.C.: U.S. Government Printing Office, 1963), 88th Cong., 1st sess., pp. 251ff.

[46] Schattschneider, *op. cit.*, p. 12.

[47] This conclusion is somewhat at odds with George Goodwin's contention that the seniority system has been overrated as a force that has kept the more urban and more dynamic areas of the country from their proper share of congressional power. However, his own statements, as well as his re-

The most influential senators, therefore, generally come from the deep South, the border states, the northern tier of New England, the dust bowl layer of the Midwest, and the mountain states. In 1952, for example, of the 26 senators with the longest continuous service, 8 were from the South, 8 from the mountain states, 5 from New England, 4 from the north-central states, and 1 from a border state.[48] Similarly, in 1963, the list of the seniority ranking of the senators by states began in this order: Arizona, Georgia, Virginia, Louisiana, Alabama, Vermont, Mississippi, Arkansas, Washington, Arkansas, Iowa, South Carolina, Oregon, Massachusetts, North Dakota, Florida, Virginia, Alabama, Delaware, and Mississippi. The translation of this seniority ranking to actual committee chairmanships yields the expected results. Ten out of the 16 committee chairmen in 1963 came from the southern states and three from the mountain ones. The most populous state represented by a chairman was Michigan.[49] When the Republicans have controlled the Senate, there has been a greater representation of populous, industrialized states among the chairmanships than when it has been under Democratic rule. The Republicans, however, have held congressional majorities for only four years since the election of Franklin Roosevelt.

---

search, do not strongly justify his opinion. This discrepancy is partially caused by the limits of his inquiry, from 1947 through 1958, covering the 80th through the 85th Congresses, 4 of which were Democratic and 2 of which were Republican. This period can be contrasted to a much larger one, between 1933 through 1966, when there were 15 Democratic Congresses and the same 2 Republican ones. Although Goodwin notes the more regressive nature of the states of the Democratic chairmen, the significance of this fact is lessened by the narrow scope of his subject. He also tends to present a misleading impression of the backgrounds of the House chairmen by emphasizing that many of their states were urban and progressive. However, as he himself admits, the character of their districts is a more direct influence upon them than that of their states. Thus, a Republican chairman from an urban, progressive state like New York or Illinois can represent areas as rural and stagnant as any from less favored states. See "The Seniority System in Congress," *American Political Science Review*, LIII, 2 (June, 1959), 412–436.

For the linkage between safe seats, rural areas, seniority and Congressional power, see Wolfinger and Heifetz, *op. cit.*, pp. 337–349 and "On Urban-Rural Representation. . . ," *op. cit.*, p. 155.

[48] Galloway, *op. cit.*, p. 366.

[49] *Official Congressional Directory*, pp. 222, 239–247.

When the seniority system operates in placing men upon committees, its effect is similar. As a general rule, the more important the committee, the more likely there will be an overrepresentation of the less dynamic and less populous states and districts. In the House of Representatives, the Rules Committee, which plays a crucial role in guiding bills through the legislative process and in determining their success, exemplifies this characteristic. Since the mid-1930's, the committee's membership has consisted of a stable majority composed of conservative Republicans and southern Democrats, both of which tend to come from overrepresented, rural, safe, one-party districts. This conservative domination of the committee has thus been a constant fact of political life despite the fluctuation of electoral tides. The committee's unrepresentative character stood out most starkly in the New Deal period when President Roosevelt, in order to protect his program, successfully eliminated its chairman, John O'Connor of New York, in his one true victory in the "purge" campaign of the 1937 Democratic primary. President Truman used the same device to eliminate another conservative member, Roger Slaughter of Missouri, in order to defend his Fair Deal program. In 1961, an attempt was made to eliminate, or at least temper, its innate obstructiveness by enlarging the committee from 12 to 15 members; in 1963, this change was made permanent.

Another center of power in the House is the Ways and Means Committee. Its importance, too, is underlined by the seniority of its members. "Ways and Means assignments from both parties," Douglass Cater wrote in 1962, "generally go to the senior and the safe." The majority of its Republicans are usually from rural, safe, one-party districts, while the southerners, border state men, and representatives from urban one-party districts dominate the Democratic side. This Democratic contingent is of particular importance because its members, together with the Speaker and the Majority floor leader, compose the Democratic Committee on Committees of the House. Its conservatism and its rural and small town inclinations can, therefore, be felt not only in the field of taxation, but in all other areas as well through its power of appointment to other committees.[50]

[50] Douglass Cater, "The Ways and Means of Wilbur Mills," *The Reporter*, XXVI, 7 (March 24, 1962), 25; Nicholas A. Masters, "Committee

The Senate also has as great a genius for overrepresenting in its positions of power the most unrepresentative areas of the country. This characteristic was placed in sharp focus by a number of speeches on the Senate floor in February, 1963, by Senator Joseph Clark of Pennsylvania. The collection of these speeches is appropriately titled *The Senate Establishment*, because it was Clark's contention that there actually is such a power group and that it has a stranglehold upon the most important committees primarily through operation of the seniority system.[51] This system not only facilitates the inclusion of senior men on the choice committees, but also tends to guarantee that the truly prized committees, such as Foreign Relations and Appropriations, will be composed largely of chairmen of other committees, thereby compounding their power.[52]

Senator Clark was particularly concerned with his own Democratic party since in 1963 it not only had a nominal majority in the Senate, but a full two-thirds of the membership. Although the majority of these 67 Democratic senators were liberal (a minimum of 40 by Clark's estimate) and nonsouthern (44), it was the southern and the conservative character of the one-party Democratic states that was in actual control. Senator Clark made a special analysis of the composition of the Democratic Steering Committee, not only as an example of the process, but also as one of its key causes since it assigns the Democratic members to their committees. On the 15-man committee, there were 7 southerners and 2 additional members of the conservative Establishment. Thus, there was a majority of conservatives, almost all of them southerners, despite the fact that both conservatives and southerners were minorities within the Democratic senatorial delegation.[53]

The situation is ironic when there is a strong liberal Democratic tide in the country since the accretion of the new Democratic recruits from the North and the West only serves to bring in or maintain the southern-conservative power group whose

Assignments in the House of Representatives," *American Political Science Review*, LV, 2 (June, 1961), 345–357, esp. p. 347.

[51] Joseph S. Clark (and other senators), *The Senate Establishment* (New York: Hill and Wang, 1963).

[52] Donald R. Matthews, *U.S. Senators and Their World* (New York: Vintage Books, 1960), p. 151.

[53] Clark, *op. cit.*, pp. 32–35, 105–106.

members already have seniority. The political tide sweeping the country in no way affects their particular seats, and, indeed, their very insulation allows them to benefit from it.

One can readily understand why observers of congressional behavior insist that, in such an institutional setting, the rules of procedure are not neutral but rather work to the distinct advantage of the entrenched power group. William J. Keefe and Morris S. Ogul have written:

Legislative rules are significant because the methods used to reach decisions often shape the decisions themselves; procedure and policy, in other words, are often interlaced. This fact accounts for the controversy inherent in all rules of procedure. Never wholly neutral, rules benefit some groups and disadvantage others. They are, commonly, one of the many faces of minority power.[54]

It is thus particularly appropriate that the major stumbling block to liberal legislation is the House Rules Committee. In fulfilling its formal function of granting the necessary rules by which bills are handled on the floor, it can largely determine their ultimate fate. It can decide what parts of the bill will be amendable and how much debate there will be; it can pressure the committee presenting the bill to meet its demands on particular provisions; and it can even refuse to allow a bill to come to the floor—all of these powers it wields under the authority of the rule-making function.[55]

Senior legislators generally benefit from the permanent rules of Congressional debate because their years of service have given them the opportunity to master their intricate detail. One should also credit the admitted acumen in their use by the power group, especially its southern members. Even their opponents have stood in awe at the sheer craftsmanship of Smith of Virginia, Barden of North Carolina, and Eastland of Mississippi. As a result of their efforts, liberals seemed to be continually meeting parliamentary hurdles manned by their opponents. Undeniably, there were liberal products of this legislative process, but they always bore

---

[54] Keefe and Ogul, *op. cit.*, pp. 45–46; see also David Truman, *The Governmental Process: Political Interests and Public Opinion* (New York: Knopf, 1964), p. 330.

[55] For the operation of the House Rules Committee, see references in the bibliography under "Congress."

the marks of the race they were forced to run. The very rules, however, which obstructed their path, greased the flow of conservative bills to final passage. Howard Shuman's analysis of the progress toward civil rights legislation in 1956 and 1957 demonstrates a particularly outstanding example of such a pattern.[56]

In 1956, as he points out, the Senate liberals were outmaneuvered because, as their leader left the Senate floor to pick up the civil rights bill which had already passed the House of Representatives, the bill itself was already being sent by messenger to the floor and was given to the southern presiding officer. The bill was read quickly the necessary two times before being sent for consideration by committee, the Judiciary Committee, which under the chairmanship of Senator Eastland had been the graveyard of civil rights legislation. Eastland had at hand a number of parliamentary devices by which he was able to maintain this record of death for all civil rights bills, and he would use the one most appropriate for the occasion. He could be punctilious about not calling meetings when technically they conflicted with Senate sessions; he could recognize speakers who would eat up the limited amount of committee time. In addition, in a number of instances, there could be no meeting because a quorum was not available.

Understandably, the liberals attempted to file a petition to discharge the bill from the committee. Such a petition, however, could be introduced only in the morning hour, except by unanimous consent. Although the petition was brought up in the morning hour, Senator George of Georgia insisted that unanimous consent was, nevertheless, required because the new day had not officially begun since the Senate had only recessed the previous evening. As Shuman dryly reported, "the Senate . . . , in fact, had not adjourned since the evening of July 13, i.e., 10 days previously. Although the date was then July 24, the legislative day was July 16, and thus technically, there was no morning hour." The petition was finally filed—but only on the last day of the session, when it was, of course, too late to accomplish anything. Indeed, the method of discharging a bill by petition, as

[56] Howard E. Shuman, "Senate Rules and the Civil Rights Bill: A Case Study," *American Political Science Review*, LI, 4 (December, 1957), 955–975.

Shuman has pointed out, required nine separate steps, which would have taken a minimum of five to eight weeks. The next year, the liberals bypassed the Judiciary Committee by using still another parliamentary route and they secured passage of a civil rights bill. This occurred, however, only after the measure had been weakened by the southerners' threat to use their ultimate weapon among the Senate rules, the filibuster.

The Filibuster

The filibuster justifiably has a prominent position in the cluster of rules by which a powerful minority can check a majority. It achieves this distinction because, by its operation, a Senate minority can prevent a measure from even coming to a vote. It can be broken through by use of the cloture rule, which terminates debate, but this can be applied only by the vote of two-thirds of the senators present. Although primarily a reserve weapon and much less used in practice than many other rules, it represents, in extreme form, the character of a legislative world that has lost contact with the greater part of the society it is supposed to represent. Thus, its defense deserves examination because, in carrying out the implications of the Madisonian theory, it is in essence a defense not only of Congress, but of the whole prevailing political system.

The filibuster was—and, indeed, still is—primarily justified as a guarantee of constitutional democracy and individual liberty. It performs this role by allowing a significant minority, on an issue of absolute importance to its interests, to protect itself by halting the majority. In defending its rights, the minority benefits the country as a whole because careful consideration is secured before a significant step is undertaken by a majority, which may be a temporary, shortsighted one.

Despite the plausibility of this defense, the filibuster has proven in practice an unreliable and dubious guarantee of constitutional democracy and individual liberty. Has the filibuster actually protected minorities? In certain instances, it obviously has. As we have seen in our analysis of representation and malapportionment, however, minority protection under the old political system generally meant protection for certain minorities—

and at the expense of others. One might, for purposes of argument, accept Walter Lippmann's assumption in its defense that "only a minority with deep convictions facing a majority with weak convictions can under present rules conduct a filibuster." [57] What happens, however, if the issue does not resolve itself so neatly that a concerned minority faces an apathetic majority? What occurs if two minorities, rather than one, have vital interests on the opposite sides of a particular subject? In such circumstances, what becomes of the protection of *the* minority when a filibuster occurs?

This suggestion of two competing minorities is more than a logical possibility; it was the actual situation on the most important subject affected by the filibuster, civil rights. Earlier this century, it is true, the majority-minority conception could have been upheld as a reasonable depiction of reality. At that time, a determined white South dealt in its own fashion with its politically impotent Negro population, while the rest of the country stood by, apathetic and unconcerned. In recent decades, a profound change has occurred in race relations. Nevertheless, a vitally concerned Negro minority, allied with a sympathetic majority, found it difficult until 1964 to break through the filibuster because of our theoretical attachment to minority rights.

We can discern how the Negro minority was effectively checked when we examine the attempts to impose cloture. We must first remember that the one-third of the senators plus one who can squash the application of cloture can represent much less than one-third of the people. Senator Paul Douglas pointed out in 1956 that "the Senators from the 17 smallest states with a total population of only 12.1 million, or only 8 per cent of the population, . . . [could theoretically] exercise a veto over legislation desired by the other 92 per cent of the population." [58]

The defenders of the Senate, as noted earlier, consider such statistics as meaningless, and the advocates of the filibuster, in particular, believe that they are divorced from the realities of Senate divisions. In observing the voting pattern of the Senate on cloture, however, these dangers are not quite so theoretical and

---

[57] From a 1938 Lippmann column reproduced in Rossiter and Lare, *op. cit.*, p. 219.

[58] Douglas, *op. cit.*, p. 5538.

imaginary. Although it would be farfetched to portray the division as one between the large and the small states, there is a significant blending of state interest with population. In two separate senatorial roll calls in 1961 and 1962 on the filibuster, one to liberalize the cloture rule and the other to invoke it, a small majority voted on the prosouthern side. In each instance, however, the number of persons in the states represented by a majority of the Senate was only a minority of the country's population.[59] The correlation between population and voting is even greater than here indicated because all calculations are based upon census figures which cannot be accepted at face value for purposes of comparison because of the systematic disfranchisement of a heavy portion of the Negroes in the southern states. When we estimate, therefore, that the senators against the invocation of cloture represented 40 per cent of the population, we

[59] On the key roll-call in 1961, by which the Senate sent the question of revising the cloture rule back to the Rules Committee, the vote, pairings included, was 50 (32 Democrats and 18 Republicans) for the motion and 46 (31 Democrats and 15 Republicans) against it. The assumption was correctly made that this step practically killed the chances of civil rights legislation in that Congressional session. *New York Times,* January 12, 1961. If we tabulate the presidential electoral votes of the senators' states—a system weighted to the advantage of the less populated states—we find 18 states with 165 electoral votes as registered for the motion, 16 states with 245 electoral votes against it, while 16 states with 101 votes were split. If we apportion the electoral votes of these divided states evenly, our final count is 215½ electoral votes for and 295½ against a motion which had secured a majority vote in the Senate.

In May, 1962, an attempt to invoke cloture was defeated by a vote, pairings included, of 54 to 45. *New York Times,* May 10, 1962. Here, too, the majority of the Senate did not reflect the popular majority as could be determined from the vote. If we add the population of the states whose senators voted for the invocation of cloture (and add one-half the population of those which split), the total 109,043,988, almost 61 per cent of the country's total population (1960 census) of 179,323,175. (In reality, the total population of these states could have included the full population of Washington, since the only senator not recorded was its Warren Magnuson, considered a civil rights supporter. This would boost the population of these states to 110,470,595 and render it closer to 62 per cent than 61 per cent of the country's population.) More significantly, as the text points out, the percentage should be considerably higher because the total population of the southern states is counted as their senators voted.

must scale down that percentage significantly because the southern Negroes were included in the original estimate.

The degree of correlation between the filibuster votes and the population is based primarily on the tendency of the senators from the large urban northern states to support civil rights legislation and the procedural rules that facilitate its passage. Although the votes of the senators from the least populated states were dispersed on this issue, a greater number than anticipated had sided with the southerners, and their motivation sheds light on the nature of the filibuster.

Arthur Krock, a man imbued with a keen and sympathetic understanding of the southern and small-state senators, perceptively pointed out in 1962 that the vote that year for applying cloture was no true reflection of the views of the members of the Senate on civil rights legislation. He explained that some of the small-state senators who were sympathetic (or claimed to be sympathetic) to such laws nevertheless felt that they could not vote for cloture because that would be an attack upon a cherished minority protection against the majoritarian interests of the population of the large states. They believed, therefore, that as representatives of states with small populations, they had a vested interest in maintaining minority protections in the legislative process.[60]

Thus, practically each senatorial session would witness the drawing of a closed circle that effectively shut the southern Negro off from his civil rights. The operation would begin at the opening of the session when, as in 1959 and 1961, the argument was presented that a loosening of the cloture rule would be a violation of minority protections. This could not be condoned because of the civil rights issue since such legislation, it was claimed, could be passed even with the existing cloture rule. The southern senators were, therefore, successful because this pattern of argument won over enough small-state senators in addition to those with a basic conservative predisposition for established procedural rules and traditions.

Later in the session, such as in 1962, when the actual cloture procedure was ready to be invoked, a number of senators from

[60] Arthur Krock, "In the Nation," *New York Times*, May 15, 1962.

the small states, as Krock showed, were convinced by a similar line of reasoning and were, therefore, reluctant to set a precedent against a filibuster. The procedural issue was of vital importance to the small states, and the substantive issue to the southern states. By the rules and composition of the Senate, the combination had proven almost impregnable.

Only when the countervailing forces in the other parts of the political system exerted pressure on the Senate and when the outlines of a determined national majority could not be mistaken was cloture successful in 1964 and 1965. Even at that late date, however, the cloture drive by the civil rights advocates might still have been a few votes shy if the precedent had not already been set in 1962 when it had been imposed to end the liberal filibuster against the establishment of a satellite communications corporation. Although some liberals unquestionably compromised with their principles in utilizing for their own objectives the very target of their consistent legislative efforts, those conservatives who, for the first time in their senatorial careers, voted to impose cloture or abstained lost their main theoretical justification on all future cloture votes.

Thus, the civil rights issue belied the idea of the filibuster as an effective protection of minorities. The main result of its operation had been the maintenance of the racial segregation pattern in the South. The defenders of the filibuster were forced to admit that the nation could not aid a long-suffering minority, one that has endured lynching, privation, and the most invidious forms of racial discrimination. They had been lured into this position because they limited the concept of a majority-minority relationship to but one example, that of a national majority to a southern minority—and, in fact, a southern white minority. Within this abstract and legalistic framework, the defenders of the filibuster had lost contact with the real world of race relations and could thus paradoxically refuse to protect the Negro in order to preserve minority rights.

The World of the Legislators

As we observe the intricacies of congressional behavior, we become increasingly aware of contact with a particular way of life with its own standards and mores. When Donald R. Matthews entitled his work on the Senate *U.S. Senators and Their World*, he was not indulging in a meaningless attempt at imagery, but was rather recognizing the basic assumption of legislative analysis, that the legislative world is a real one to its participants. It is in this world that the law-maker lives each day. Its separate insulated nature heightens its distorted image of the outside world because the very reality of the environment prevents the congressman from appreciating this distortion.

This world is, of course, not wholly unlike the outside world and there are many recognizable similarities. The fundamental legislative institutions and procedures are based upon an unquestioned solid kernel of sense. The character of this world becomes unreal, however, when these sound principles are carried to illogical lengths. Both the committee system and the seniority system illustrate this tendency since, despite their limitations, they can be justified in theory. A large legislative body should have a division of labor to insure that its members can secure some degree of expertise in specific fields in order to make laws for a complex society and to oversee the operation of the bureaucracy. Thus, the members of the House of Representatives believe they are a more efficient body than the more prestigious and publicized Senate because their larger size can allow a more intensive and refined specialization for individual members.

Similarly, the seniority system is based upon the common respect accorded age and experience. Its defenders rightfully insist that experience deserves recognition. This judgment, however, was caricatured by the absolute rigidity of Congress' adherence to seniority, since the nectar of wisdom and experience has been at times diluted by mediocrity, senility, and eccentricity.

The prime values of the legislative world are, by themselves, not particularly striking or unusual since they are rated highly outside Congress as well as inside. Almost anyone would welcome the company of an individual graced with the qualities of a good senator, a member of the Inner Club, as drawn by William S. White:

A credible emanation of ultimate good faith in what he is about, one of the main criteria of good faith being the absence of petty exhibitionism. An understanding acceptance of the requirement of compromise, and therefore a willingness to abide dissent. A concentration upon the coherent and important and an avoidance of the diffuse and the doubtful. A deep skill in sensing what may and may not be done. A gift if not for friendship at least for amicable association with other minds and with the interests of others.[61]

These standards are not limited to the Senate, but apply to the House of Representatives as well. Nicholas Masters has pointed out that the most important criterion of a candidate for a major House committee is whether he is a "responsible" legislator, defined as one who is a moderate and a gradualist and has "a basic and fundamental respect for the legislative process" as well as "the respect of his fellow legislators." [62]

In the same vein, Richard Fenno, Jr., stated that selections to the important House Appropriations Committee are influenced by consideration of the nominees' inclinations toward responsibility and cooperation. An individual is chosen, he was told, because he is, "the kind of man you can deal with" or "a fellow who is well-balanced and won't go off half-cocked on things." [63]

This composite portrait of the legislator is unquestionably a complimentary one emphasizing the qualities which lead to the harmony and moderation of a congressional consensus. Disquieting shadows emerge, however. The man who is primarily valued because he realizes "what may and may not be done" in the legislature may not be so sensitive in grasping the country's needs. The heavy concentration upon institutional values encourages the distortion of the congressional perspective. Thus, in considering the avoidance of extreme positions, it should be realized that what may be termed moderate or responsible within Congress can often readily be rated conservative without. Citizens, for example, opposed to the extraordinarily generous income tax provisions for oil-producers, possibly the largest loophole in a tax system fairly riddled with them, generally fail to appreciate that within the environment of the House Ways and Means Commit-

[61] William S. White, *Citadel: The Story of the U.S. Senate* (New York: Harper and Row, 1957), p. 117.

[62] Masters, *op. cit.*, p. 352.

[63] Richard F. Fenno, Jr., "The House Appropriations Committee as a Political System: The Problem of Integration," *American Political Science Review*, LVI, 2 (June, 1962), 313.

tee, an advocate for their change might easily be considered a radical or a person who tends to "go off half-cocked on things."

The legislative world, therefore, although a distorted one, is, nevertheless, a real one, and this reality has proven a fundamental hindrance to any change in the system. When Senator Clark made his attack upon the Senate Establishment, it was less the substance of his indictment which was remarkable than the fact that a senator was presenting it. The members of the Establishment were not shadowy public figures to him, but flesh and blood individuals with whom he had been working in close association.

At the state level, the reality of legislative life has similarly inhibited reform. Malapportionment and gerrymandering, for example, have been the justifiable targets of much criticism. The critics have often failed to appreciate, however, that it is inordinately difficult for a legislature to change the very system by which it was elected to office. An urban legislator can, as a liberal, perceive the tangible advantages of reapportionment; as a human being, however, he can also see that the legislator to be apportioned out of his seat is his own colleague in the next aisle.[64] Schattschneider has memorably described the problem: "Our experience with legislative reapportionment by the legislatures themselves proves that it is a little like do-it-yourself surgery, a painful job that is apt to be done badly." [65] These legislators fully appreciate the observation of the British historian, H. R. Trevor-Roper: "To reform is a frustrating task; to be reformed is maddening." [66]

The legislative world is never more real to the individual legislator than when it rewards or punishes. We have emphasized the character and position of the power group because their values become those of the whole legislative world. A member may question these standards, even defy them. He does this, however, in full realization that he is moving against the spirit of his institution. It was Sam Rayburn who culled from the experience of

[64] Malcolm E. Jewell, "Political Patterns in Reapportionment" in Malcolm E. Jewell, ed., *The Politics of Reapportionment* (New York: Atherton Press, Prentice-Hall, 1962), p. 28.

[65] Schattschneider, *op. cit.*, p. 12.

[66] H.R. Trevor-Roper, *Men and Events: Historical Essays* (New York: Harper and Row, 1957), p. 69.

many years as Speaker of the House (a longer tenure than any other) the sage advice of conformity: "If you want to get along, go along."

On the vote for a change in the cloture rule in January, 1959, freshmen senators were quickly introduced to this aspect of the legislative world. Since this vote on whether to accept the compromise fashioned by Lyndon Johnson or the stronger version desired by the northern liberals was upon the basic operating rules of the Senate, it took precedence over practically all other pieces of business, such as the placement of freshmen senators on committees. Thus each of these senators was painfully aware of what was personally at stake in agreeing or disagreeing with his party leadership, and some of their votes proved essential to the success of Johnson's maneuver. The committee assignments that were eventually made did follow his enlightened policy that every senator, no matter how junior, should be given a seat on at least one major committee. There are, however, different gradations of major committees, and there was a correlation between the desirability of a committee seat and a man's vote on the rules.[67]

In his attack on the Senate Establishment in 1963, Senator Clark charged that the senators who had voted that year with the party leadership against a change in the cloture rules generally received the committee post they desired and that those who were for a change did not.[68] Needless to say, Clark, in raising the issue of the power group's use of the carrot and the whip, was an obvious candidate for a few lashes himself. Senator Douglas of Illinois, in praising Clark's courage, said that he would undoubtedly be told in the future: "The legislation you favor will not go through. The dam your constituents want will not be built. The river improvements your constituents want will not be built." [69]

The values of the power group are also reflected in the esteem and respect in which a senator is held by his peers. One of the

[67] Daniel M. Berman, *In Congress Assembled: The Legislative Process in the National Government* (New York: Macmillan, 1964), p. 145; Rondal G. Downing and Jack W. Peltason. "Prelude to Election Year: The First Session of the 86th Congress," Earl Latham, ed. *American Government Annual,* 1960–1961 (New York: Holt, Rinehart and Winston, 1960), pp. 66–69, 73.

[68] Clark, *op. cit.,* pp. 99–103, esp. p. 100.   [69] *Ibid.,* p. 131.

most remarkable insights gained from William White's authoritative and sympathetic description of the Senate was that the prestige and influence of a senator within the chamber have little relation to his reputation on the outside. Thus, some of the most famous and respected senators in recent years, like Lehman and Vandenberg, were not acknowledged as such by their colleagues. On the other hand, senators such as Payne of Maine and Johnson of Colorado, although they were hardly known outside their own states and although their qualities of statesmanship were not readily discernible to outside observers, were men highly regarded and influential in the Senate.[70]

Although we have primarily conceived of the legislative world as encompassing both the Senate and the House, we should remember that they are distinct. Indeed, one of the most amusing—and alarming—events in recent congressional history was the collision of both legislative worlds in 1962. At that time, the House Appropriations Committee, under the chairmanship of eighty-three-year-old Clarence Cannon, and the Senate Appropriations Committee, headed by eighty-four-year-old Carl Hayden, could not get together for months because they were unable to agree on the question as to whether half of their joint conferences should be held in one chamber and half in the other. The country watched with a curious fascination this adamant stand on legislative dignity and amour propre, which created an impasse whereby the government was stalled in paying its necessary appropriations. Tom Wicker, in describing the spectacle of this battle between the two aged warriors and their cohorts, wrote:

> Their collision, on matters that to most Americans could have seemed little more important than last week's comic strips, dramatized a question that thoughtful observers in Washington long have asked:
>
> Is Congress approaching the limits of that adaptability to changing circumstances that has been the genius of the American system of government?[71]

"The House without Windows" and Plato's Cave

As this chapter has shown, the character of the legislative world is, in great degree, self-perpetuating, with little possibility

[70] White, op. cit., chs. VII and IX.

[71] Tom Wicker, "House vs. Senate," New York Times, "The News of the Week in Review," July 15, 1962, p. 9.

of significant reform except from outside pressure. This character has thus led to a fundamental difference of outlook between the participants in the law-making process and its observers and analysts, between the legislators and their critics. There has usually been an understandable tendency for persons skilled in legislative maneuvering through many years in politics to find outside criticism misinformed, and proposed reforms based on this criticism, unrealistic and impractical. Indeed, there is a natural reluctance for any "practical" man to acquiesce to—much less advocate—any fundamental change in a system by which he has achieved success. Moreover, so established has been the reputation of politicians for hardheadedness and practicality that it seems paradoxical to consider them as out of touch with reality.

The practical politician, it is true, makes what he considers realistic judgments—but his idea of what is real is conceived primarily in terms of his own world. What he overlooks is that there is more than one level of reality. The reality of which he is so proud is actually a limited one rigidly bound by the contours of the political world within which he operates. He must recognize, as well, the real world outside with its powerful economic and social pressures. The basic problem of our politics derives less from the fact that the legislator lives in a world of his own than from the extent to which his world is insulated from the world outside.

Constantin Melnik and Nathan Leites recognized this character of the legislative world when they used the title *The House without Windows* for their study of the French legislature's election of a president in the Fourth Republic.[72] They felt that the French parliament, immersed in the intricacies of complex political maneuvering, was operating as a self-contained isolated unit with no relationship to the French nation, which it was ostensibly representing.

The illuminating image of a house without windows may be too extreme as a general description of the relation of the political scene to the world outside. In truth, the latter does get reflected on the former because there is no blank wall between them, but

[72] Constantin Melnik and Nathan Leites, *The House without Windows: France Selects a President,* trans. Ralph Manheim (Evanston, Ill.: Row, Peterson, 1958).

the reflection can be a highly distorted one. The America perceived in Congress is, as we have seen, for a number of electoral and parliamentary reasons, a fundamentally different country from the one recognized outside.

If we seek guidance through political imagery, we may be safer in the hands of Plato with his fable of the cave.[73] Plato conceived of human beings as imprisoned in a cave with their backs to its opening. Hence, it was impossible for anyone in the cave to perceive directly the characteristics of the outside world. Their only reality—if we simplify Plato's image—was the shadows on the walls of the cave, the reflections of a world they could not see. Practical men, of course, accepted this reality of the shadow world and moved surefootedly in the darkness of the cave.

Imagine, wrote Plato, that one man should leave the cave and go out into the real world. He would realize, once he became accustomed to the blinding light, that the world outside was quite different from the shadow world of the cave. What would happen, however, if he should return once more to the cave and should try to describe to those inside the nature of the real world? Would they believe him? Would not those who were adept at moving in the darkness and skilled in analyzing the shadows feel that their world was the only real one? Would they not dismiss him as a foolish visionary, especially when they saw him stumbling in the darkness to which they had become accustomed? Moreover, if he should persist in his attempt to recount what he had seen, would they not eventually become angry and try to kill him—as the practical men of Athens did to the philosopher Socrates?

The episode of Plato's cave, particularly with its violent conclusion, seems a rather harsh analogy for the American legislative process. It can, however, be considered a sympathetic portrayal because it points out the ease with which a shadow world can be accepted as reality, especially by those who most pride themselves on their practicality. Since the balance of congressional

[73] This reworking and simplification of the platonic image of the cave is consciously influenced by a similar adaptation, which used the device of movies instead of shadows, in Charles P. Curtis, Jr., and Ferris Greenslet, *The Practical Cogitator or the Thinker's Anthology* (Boston: Houghton Mifflin, 1945), pp. 553–556.

composition and power is clearly with the countryside, Congress has perceived the United States in its own image as a small-town rural country rather than the industrial urban one which it really was. Thus, the strong criticism against it for not recognizing and meeting the problems of the modern world are only partially justified because the areas where these problems are occurring are not adequately represented in its chambers. The legislators, as a rule, lack neither intelligence, public spirit, nor sympathy. They are undoubtedly intellectually aware of these problems, but cannot feel them as matters of vital interest because they are not relevant to the experiences of their constituents. Considering its structure, what should possibly be considered remarkable is that Congress has done as well as it has.

There is nothing magical about political processes and we have little right to expect a legislator miraculously to transcend his milieu. As R. H. Tawney wrote: " . . . the whole complex machinery through which society expresses itself, is a mill which grinds only what is put into it, and when nothing is put into it grinds air." [74] Thus, a change in the nature of the composition of the legislature will result in a more substantial product.

By the midsixties, indications of this change were evident, and the insulated, unrepresentative character of the legislative world was being modified. In the House of Representatives, the majority-party leadership was able to ease the conservative grip on the Rules Committee as well as to moderate its power. In the Senate, the filibuster was no longer a permanent barrier against civil rights, and the ranks of southern conservative stalwarts were thinning out. In addition, the initial stages of congressional reapportionment were already foreshadowing a changed political climate. This change was achieved by the generation of countervailing political forces that balanced out the rigid conservatism of the legislatures. The remainder of this work will be concerned with the manner in which the dynamic elements of society were able to transform the political process into becoming more attuned to the nation's needs.

[74] R.H. Tawney, *The Acquisitive Society* (New York: Harcourt, Brace and World, 1920), p. 3.

Chapter V

The Countervailing Forces

The inability of the legislatures, both state and national, to represent the true character of the country has affected the operation of our political structure and the relationship of its elements. This quality of our representational system presented a latent danger to the country that could have resulted in intense frustration and an eventual constitutional crisis.

In recent crucial decades, however, we have been spared such political upheaval and have not had to pay the full cost of legislative intransigence. Primarily this has been a result of the looseness and flexibility of our political structure that has allowed the operation of a number of countervailing liberal forces. Thus, the pressures of modern life were not completely frustrated in expressing themselves since what could not be gained through the legislatures could in some measure be secured elsewhere. Not being dammed within the confines of a more rigid system, these pressures did not redouble in unhealthy intensity.

Robert Hirschfield, in describing one important aspect of this process, the role of the Supreme Court under Chief Justice Earl Warren, has perceptively noted its similarity to the attainment of a dynamic balance within the human body. The Court has acted

because the needs of the nation have required action on these problems and because the only place in our governmental system where that action could be taken has been the Supreme Court. It has in this way operated according to a principle of *organic compensation*— analogous to homeostasis in the human body—by which the inefficiency or incapacity of one organ in the body politic demands an increase in the activity of another if the society's health is to be preserved.[1]

Under the stimulus of the pressure of modern problems, the greater part of the American political structure has been in a state of dynamic flux to compensate for the inaction of its more rigid elements, particularly the state governments and the legislatures. We should thus realize that we are studying not a fixed system but rather one whose parts have in recent years drastically changed their functions and their relationship to each other. These changes have been partially obscured because the institutions have survived under their original names. We should recognize, however, that when we deal with terms such as the presidency and the federal system, our conceptions of them may be quite different from those held a generation or two ago.

Federalism

The first important change to be examined is in the concept of federalism because it is directly related to the conservative position of the legislatures. Not only have the legislatures played a prominent role in state government, but the diminution of localism, which has rendered the mode of legislative representation somewhat obsolete, has similarly changed the role of the states within the federal system and has even called into question the viability of states as separate units.

The dynamism of change has acted upon the federal system at two different levels, with one changing the balance within its parts, and the second moving toward its virtual elimination. The changing balance is to be expected since the equilibrium of any federal system is dynamic rather than static. It is constantly under pressures pushing for centralization and unification on the one hand and for localism and diversity on the other.[2] When the

[1] Robert S. Hirschfield, "Tenth Anniversary of the Warren Court," *American Government Annual, 1964–1965,* ed. Donald G. Herzberg (New York: Holt, Rinehart, and Winston, 1964), p. 118.

[2] A.V. Dicey wrote about the "very peculiar state of sentiment among the inhabitants of a country, which it is proposed to unite. They must desire union, and must not desire unity." *Introduction to the Study of the Law of the Constitution* (London: Macmillan, 1915), p. 137, quoted by Arthur W.

equilibrium is upset from either direction, the federal state is ended and is succeeded either by a centralized unitary one or by separate countries, possibly linked together in confederation. Because of the precariousness of this balance, a number of countries have failed this century in their attempt at federalism although some still retain the elements of its structure. The list of federal systems that have been established and have failed since World War II alone is a sobering one: Indonesia, the West Indian Federation, the Mali Federation, and the Federation of Rhodesia and Nyasaland. In addition, at the beginning of 1967, the federal characteristics of Nigeria, Malaysia, and the Congo seemed particularly dubious. Even the history of successful federal systems, including our own, has been marked by the tension of these conflicting pressures.

This federal tension is inevitable because the formal division of governmental powers between national and state spheres actually settles nothing since it is only an abstract formula. It begs the question as to what is national and what is state—and the answer evolves from the needs and services of a specific time. Under our system, the Supreme Court has the important function of defining the line of federal separation for each generation. Even though its performance throughout our history has not been a consistent one, when the Court has followed the lead set by its greatest member, Chief Justice John Marshall, it has treated this division as a loose and flexible guide, adjustable to the spirit of the times, rather than as a rigid barrier laid down in 1787. Especially has this proven the case with the interstate commerce clause where the Court, particularly since 1937, has supported Congress' recognition of our interrelated economy.

The American federal system has probably achieved the most flexibility through the grant-in-aid programs, by which the national government has appropriated huge sums of money to the states. While taking advantage of this largesse, the states have had misgivings about Washington's capitalizing upon their own cupidity to increase the span of its authority. They believed that the national government was successfully seducing them from the

MacMahon, "The Problems of Federalism: A Survey," in Arthur W. MacMahon, ed., *Federalism: Mature and Emergent* (Garden City, N.Y.: Doubleday, 1955), p. 60.

maintenance of their true sovereignty and the resultant protection of individual liberties.

The states have also contended that in these programs the national government has used the constitutional loophole of spending for the "general welfare" to disburse funds for activities reserved for the states. Admittedly, it does require some rather subtle reasoning to justify Congress' power to make rules for the appropriation of funds for matters about which it cannot legislate directly. The national government is, in fact, making policy by its strong influence upon state powers in those fields that fall under the broad umbrella of the "general welfare," an unusually flexible concept even in a flexible constitution.

If, however, we examine the issue from a different angle from that of governmental relationships and concentrate rather upon the content of the programs themselves, our new perspective frees us from the distortion of the conspiratorial preoccupations of the states. We are confronted instead with the hard facts of the basic nationalization of American life noted earlier. Can education, health, roads, air pollution, and the other objects of these programs be considered matters of general national welfare in the context of modern American society? Once we answer in the affirmative, the grant-in-aid program is seen not as a constitutional loophole for the entrance of expanding national control into spheres of state activity, but rather as one of the flexible devices that has allowed the Constitution to survive through many generations with different problems and differing conceptions of the general welfare. Thus, the states have failed to give due recognition to the benefits received by these programs that have allowed them to provide better services for their people, as well as to survive and play a significant role in the face of strong centralizing pressures.

The grant-in-aid programs not only show the sharp turn in our modern federal balance from localism to nationalism, but also reveal that this change reflects the interrelationship of all aspects of American life, the cultural and the social as well as the economic. Thus, it is to be expected that a federal balance originally established when men's instinctive loyalties were to their states would be altered in a period when they would think of themselves first as citizens of the whole country and would have but a shadowy, formal allegiance to their state. Moreover, this allegiance is made even more tenuous when, because of the mobility of the country's population, *their* state is not the one in which they were born. The shifting federal balance emphasizes again the point of much of our critique of the legislative system: that in the context of a modern industrialized urban society, a person's location—particularly his state—is often a secondary, peripheral characteristic rather than a primary, essential one.

Therefore, what would have been considered a completely unreasonable exercise of national authority in one historical period becomes justifiable in another because the character of the country has changed. Instances of this process, which are many, range from the minor to the most important. Qualifications for voting in both state and national elections, for example, are set by the state governments. This was a reasonable constitutional provision in 1787 in the light of state allegiance and loyalties; it was also a practical method by which the Founding Fathers could avoid the thankless and contentious task of establishing the criteria for the franchise. A curious result today, however, is that many persons have been deprived of their vote for president and vice-president of the United States solely because they have not lived in their state or district for the required period of time.[3]

The national significance of state franchise qualifications was made vividly clear with the southern states' systematic barring of Negro suffrage. This practice stimulated the formation of a national consensus for federal legislation against it. When the difficulty of implementing the civil rights bills did not insure the Negro's freedom of access to the polls, Congress passed, at President Johnson's urging, the Voting Rights Act, which provided for the suspension of literacy tests and the use of federal voter registrars in offending areas. This step has carried the nationalization of the vote almost to its logical conclusion.

The spokesmen of states most affected by this trend have claimed, as did Attorney General Patterson of Mississippi, when the Supreme Court upheld the major provisions of the Voting Rights Act, "The Court has upheld the right of Congress to prescribe voting qualifications irrespective of state laws."[4]

[3] See editorial, *The Nation*, 201 (July 5, 1965), 4–5.
[4] *New York Times*, March 8, 1966, p. 26.

These men have failed to realize, however, the flexible nature of the division between state and national powers and its responsiveness to the realities of national life. Even more significantly, they have failed to appreciate that their own obdurate insistence upon abusing their powers has been the prime factor for change in the consciousness of the American people and in the actions of Congress, which has usually been sensitive to state interests. Thus, the stubbornness of southern politicians, the strongest advocates of states' rights, has ironically resulted in a changed view of what is of national significance, not only on the subject of the franchise but on the whole gamut of civil rights as reflected in the various sections of the Civil Rights Bill of 1964. The previous federal balance has, therefore, been irreversibly upset.

There is, moreover, no apparent limit as to how far this trend will be projected. One cannot dismiss out of hand the prediction made by Attorney General Gremillion of Louisiana, on the day the Court validated the Voting Rights Act: "This is really another step in the total destruction of the rights of states to regulate their internal affairs." [5] The excesses of southern particularism have already begun to limit even the state and local basis of law enforcement and judicial proceedings. Each time a southern jury maintains a virtually spotless record of never convicting a white man for the murder of a Negro, each time the severity of the punishment for a Negro's transgression against a white man is contrasted with the slap on the wrist meted out when their roles are reversed, and each time sheriffs and police deprive people of the benefits of the law they are sworn to uphold, the fabric of local law enforcement is significantly weakened. This process will occur despite the conservative reverence for the ancient lineage of the local jury trial, the localistic desire to protect it from an increasingly powerful national government, and the liberal value put upon it as a prime support of individual liberties. The responsibility, nevertheless, is unmistakably upon the shoulders of those who have abused the processes of the law and have violated its spirit. By invoking the authority of the law, while in the act of desecrating it, they are obscuring its essence. Although the right of a man to be tried by a jury of his peers is one that has long been cherished in the Anglo-American conception of justice, it is,

[5] *Ibid.*

nevertheless, not an end in itself to which justice must be sacrificed. It is only an instrument to secure justice, and if it fails in this purpose, it deserves reexamination.

In this sphere, the southern influence is working in consonance with a remarkable change in our conception of the nature of justice. At the time the Constitution was drafted, the exercise of justice was considered primarily a state and local matter. The Founding Fathers, despite their nationalizing bent, did not, except for the Supreme Court, establish a national judiciary. They allowed future Congresses to set up such national courts as they would see fit—an option which the first Congress accepted. Even when national courts were established, most citizens still thought of them as somewhat alien institutions, distinct from the closer state courts, *their* courts. Thus, until the passage of the Fourteenth Amendment after the Civil War, the Bill of Rights, with its heavy emphasis upon the protection of the individual in criminal proceedings, was held applicable solely to the national government, not to the states. Although this limitation was partially a recognition that the state constitutions had their own bills of rights, it reflected the popular feeling that if a citizen's rights were to be abridged, it would probably be by the centralized power. Even past the middle of the twentieth century, the Supreme Court, influenced by this sentiment, was willing to tolerate a double standard of justice in which the national courts had to follow more rigorous standards than those of the states.[6]

This position of the Court, which has been largely reversed, was anachronistic because the citizen usually discovered that his basic rights and liberties were more safely guarded at the national level than by the state judiciary and law enforcement authorities. When the Supreme Court has declared a restriction of individual rights unconstitutional, the state rather than the national government has generally been the transgressor, and federal laws have hardly ever been declared invalid upon these grounds.[7]

[6] For a justification of a double standard of justice in a federal system, see Justice Frankfurter's majority opinion in *Wolf* v. *Colorado* 338 U.S. 25 (1949), particularly 31–33.

[7] Both Henry Steele Commager and Robert Dahl have noted the reluctance of the Supreme Court to declare unconstitutional Congressional legisla-

In addition, doubts have even been raised about the local nature of law enforcement. This is a noteworthy phenomenon in a country which had hardly anything resembling a national organization to deal with crime less than half a century ago. The development of the interrelated economy, which justified an increasing degree of federal regulation, has also brought in its wake interrelated criminal activity. Thus, some liberals, who have welcomed the regulation of business because of the interdependence of our national life, are in the paradoxical position of being wary of the potential limitations of freedom that may result from more power for the Federal Bureau of Investigation, even though it is largely a product of the selfsame national interdependence. There is, however, no evading the fact that the incidence of state boundary lines has proven as artificial in dividing the real world of major crime as it has that of the real world of commerce. Consequently, when southern law officials have proven derelict in their duties, they have given additional impetus toward the nationalization of another sector of governmental activities. The states and their agents, therefore, by their own actions have accelerated and intensified the very centralizing currents which they decry.

The ironic spectacle of the states acting contrary to their own long-range interests is not a new one. They conducted a somewhat similar performance in the area of supplying the basic social services of modern life to their population. The states, unquestionably, were not solely to blame for their predicament since the dimensions of these problems were clearly beyond their scope and means. The years of the Great Depression and the New Deal sharply revealed the inability of the states to handle within their borders the effects of an economic dislocation of national proportions and unmistakably pointed to the requirement of a national solution to national problems. No facet of the Supreme Court's adaptation to economic change after 1937 was more fundamental

---

tion in the field of individual liberties—although, in truth, they consider this more a reflection on the Court than the liberalism of the national government. Henry Steele Commager, *Majority Rule and Minority Rights:* (New York: Oxford University Press, 1943), pp. 47, 55, and Robert Dahl, *A Preface to Democratic Theory* (Chicago: University of Chicago Press, 1956), p. 59.

and far-reaching than its recognition of the scope of national powers and the shift in the former federal balance. Indeed, the experience of these years shook the federal system itself to its roots because the state governments could not fulfill what had hitherto been normally expected of them.

Although faced by great challenges, the states, nevertheless, aggravated an unhealthy economic and social situation by their limited grasp of the problems of a modern industrial society. The reluctance of the states to respond to these obvious needs and pressures derived largely, as we noted earlier, from the fact that the legislatures did not adequately reflect the true character of a state's population. The growing numbers of people living in the large cities and their environs, therefore, were often tempted to bypass the unsympathetic state legislatures and to secure from a national government, more attuned to the real character of the population, the programs which compensated for state inactivity. The entrance of the national government into the vacuum left by the states is an excellent example of Hirschfield's "organic compensation." The psychological health of the country was sustained because the popular frustration with the state political machinery was eased by the increasing reliance upon the national government.

The states, on the other hand, often viewed this expansion as a temporary, abnormal dislocation or as a deliberate attack against them. The suspicions of the states were shared and reinforced by those conservative elements which refused to acknowledge the character of modern social and economic change and resisted the adjustment to it by any part of the political system.

These conservative forces quite justifiably linked their interests with the desire of the states to undo the new federal system and to return to the old. The previous federal balance, it should be remembered, was an integral part of the old, conservative system that had been smashed by the combined force of the depression and the New Deal. The basis of that system had been a de facto sharing of political power, with eastern financial and industrial interests dominating the majority Republican party, the rural population controlling their states, and the white southerners maintaining a hegemony in their one-party region. The farmers and the white southerners were generally willing to forego the fruits of national political power in order to secure an apparently invulnerable supremacy in their respective areas. This supremacy, however, was meaningful only to the degree to which the states retained their power and authority. When the balance of federal power shifted from the states to the national government, state control proportionally lost its appeal as the stakes in national control rose. The power of the formerly dominant groups became less substantial in this process because other elements in society, especially the ethnic minorities and the workers in the cities and the Negroes in the South, could now secure political equality as parts of the new national majority forged by the New Deal. The changing political balance, moreover, particularly hurt the business and financial interests. The national government, generally controlled by the new dominant political coalition, was much more vigorous in its economic regulation than the states, which were often heavily influenced by large private interests. The conservatives, therefore, could hardly be expected to be tolerant of a fundamental change that had undermined their dominant position; consequently, they had good reason for joining the states in their defense against the "aggression" of the national government.

These conservatives, as noted earlier, enthusiastically expected after the Eisenhower victory of 1952 that a Republican president and Congress would reverse the political trend set by Roosevelt and the New Deal. The changing federal structure was one of their most important concerns because its many facets impinged upon practically every aspect of modern life. The Eisenhower administration seemed to respond appropriately by urging the establishment of a commission to examine the operation of the federal structure in the light of modern conditions and needs and "to study the means of achieving a sounder relationship between Federal, State, and local governments." [8] A reliable indication of the spirit of the inquiry and of the direction in which it would seek this "sounder" federal relationship was the choice of a conservative chairman, Dean Clarence Manion of Notre Dame Law School. Before the commission had finished its deliberations,

[8] Presidential message to Congress, March 30, 1953, quoted in Commission on Intergovernmental Relations, *A Report to the President for Transmittal to the Congress,* June, 1955, p. v (generally known as the Kestnbaum Report).

however, Manion embarrassed the administration by issuing a number of statements of a strong states' rightist coloration. Although their tone was hard and uncompromising, they could not be considered contrary to the sentiments expressed in the Republican presidential campaign. The men, however, who were faced by the sobering practicality of running the national government realized that Manion's approach would entail its fundamental reorganization, as well as provoke a vast upheaval of the pattern of national life. Manion eventually resigned and his place was taken by Meyer Kestnbaum, a clothing manufacturer. The commission's report was a moderate, realistic document. Although indicating ways in which the states could increase the scope of their activities, it definitely stood by the conclusion that the dominant role of the national government was a necessity of modern life and that there could be no real reversal of power. The report thus underlined the historical evidence that the national government assumed new functions because of the changing social and economic character of the country and the states' inability and unwillingness to respond to it.

THE FUTURE OF FEDERALISM

In the face of this strong nationalizing trend, what is the future of federalism in the United States? The question has even been seriously raised as to whether the federal system should be continued or whether it should be discarded as an outmoded barrier to the facing of reality. An impressive number of political scientists feel, as does Karl Loewenstein, that federalism has been at odds with "the implacable facts of socio-economic life." "As our great business concerns," George C. S. Benson has argued, "grow more specialized and conduct larger-scale operations in an age of complicated machinery, government cannot be expected to remain simple and pastoral." [9]

In considering this question, we should remember that, as in the case of legislative representation, our federal system was established for utilitarian, rather than theoretical, reasons. It was a practical compromise made necessary because a more central-

[9] Karl Loewenstein, *Political Power and the Governmental Process* (Chicago: University of Chicago Press, 1957), p. 296; George C. S. Benson, *The New Centralization* (New York: Farrar and Rinehart, 1941), p. 42.

ized political system, generally favored by a majority of the Constitutional Convention, especially by its leading figures, aroused some fears of the contingent of small states. Moreover, the Founding Fathers realized that a greater degree of centralization would probably not have received popular approval because of strong localistic and state feeling. Thus, the division of powers was a concession to the hard facts of political life and not the fulfillment of any fundamental theories.[10]

The defenders of federalism maintain, however, that the political reality of the young country, in forcing a balance between diversity and unity, stimulated the development of a most valuable political principle. Federalism was thus the means of gaining the advantages of a strong united nation while at the same time preserving the rich diversity of the thirteen states, with their differences in size, industry, wealth, climate, population, and even social system. This defense usually concludes, implicitly or explicitly, with the question: Is not the basic principle of federalism even more applicable today, since modern society is much more complex and diverse than in 1787?

Paradoxically, however, the main forces operating within this modern web of comprehensive diversity are pressing for homogeneity and conformity. Sociologists, in analyzing twentieth-century totalitarianism, have felt that the currents of industrialism and urbanism, which have freed the individual from traditional patterns of regulation and organization, have also left him vulnerable to a degree of conformity impossible to achieve under a less advanced technology and a simpler economy. Even in our own democratic society, we are readily aware that modern institutions as different as the giant corporation and national television networks, the cosmopolitan university and the large circulation magazines, the chain supermarkets and mass clothing producers, have all largely succeeded in obliterating the lines that prevented the formation of a true nation at its birth. When H. V. Kaltenborn, who had been a journalist even before the turn of the century, was asked in a television interview, "What is the main

[10] Martin Diamond, "What the Framers Meant by Federalism," in Robert Goldwin, ed., *A Nation of States: Essays on the American Federal System* (Chicago: Rand McNally, 1964), pp. 24–41. For a similar view, see Herbert J. Storing, "The Problem of Big Government," *ibid.*, p. 7.

change you have seen in this country in your years of reporting?" he answered "Unification." "He went on to elaborate," William H. Riker has recounted, "that when he was young he thought of the United States as just that, a set of states united; but now he thought of it as a nation." [11] Similarly Martin Landau, in describing this process of true nationalization, has written:

It [the United States] no longer possesses federal characteristics. . . . That nation concealed under federalism finally emerged. The United States has been for a long time now becoming the United State.[12]

This unlikely marriage between diversity and conformity derives largely from the fact that diversity today, unlike 1787, is not based primarily upon geography and has little regard for state lines. This diminution of localism has given the states a phantom-like, abstract quality similar to that of our legislatures, and has raised the same doubts about their contact with reality.

The existence of states in a federal system forces us to bear the image of the national-state dichotomy constantly in our minds and to fit all our political problems within its matrix. Thus, our first question is not the obvious: "How can this problem best be met?"; almost instinctively, rather, we ask: "How can this problem best be met within the context of the different state and national powers and authorities?," a stickier and more complex question. Many problems do not lend themselves to a state-national consideration and thus, difficult to solve under the best of circumstances, become particularly intractable in this unnatural situation. Some problems may concern one region encompassing a number of states; others may best be treated by a direct relationship between the cities and the national government. The problems of metropolitan areas, of particular importance with the spread of the suburbs, may affect parts of a number of states and create a community of interest that has little correlation with state lines. With the development of the New York metropolitan area, for example, an inhabitant of New York City has much less

[11] William H. Riker, *Federalism: Origin, Operation, Significance* (Boston: Little, Brown, 1964), p. 105.

[12] Martin Landau, *"Baker v. Carr* and the Ghost of Federalism," in Glendon Schubert, ed., *Reapportionment* (New York: Scribner's, 1965), p. 246.

in common with a New York State resident from the Adirondack or the Finger Lakes region than he has with a resident of northern New Jersey, who, in his turn, feels a similar lack of rapport with a fellow Jerseyan from the southern part of the state, which is under the shadow of Philadelphia and its own particular community of interest.

Even if a particular problem can be adequately solved within the existing federal arrangement, an almost inevitable contest of power between the state and national government emerges and thus creates still another hurdle in the way of a more rational control of our society. Because of the image of two separate entities facing each other, an increase of one's power is assumed to decrease necessarily that of the other. Despite the evidence to the contrary, especially in the grant-in-aid programs, in which both governments have, in a sense, increased their powers, it is difficult to overcome the static conception of governmental power implicit in federalism.

It is true that in recent decades, the federal system has attempted, with a marked degree of flexibility, to override these difficulties by the formation of groupings, interstate compacts, and national-city programs. All these devices of "cooperative federalism," however, operate within the federal framework and are primarily considered as peripheral to, evasive of, or cutting across the fundamental national-state division. The basic problem posed by the shift of power and influence from the states to the national government remains whether the pressures that have forced these changes in the federal system can be placated or whether they will sweep away the system itself.

The strongest criticism of the federal system emphasizes that it cannot respond adequately to national needs because the supposed division between the national and the state governments masks the power of the states and the conservative interests with which they are allied. Herbert Wechsler believes that the whole federal apparatus is heavily weighted toward the interests of the states primarily because they play a prominent role in the composition of the "national" government, particularly in the choice of Congress and the presidency. Thus, he thinks that "the states are the strategic yardsticks for the measurement of interest and opinion, the special centers of political activity, the separate geographical determinants of national as well as local politics." With this built-in bias toward the states, when the national government, particularly Congress, does act, the body of such national action cannot be considered as in opposition to the states, but rather of such overwhelming necessity that it has broken through the state-oriented hurdles of the national political apparatus. As a result, "national action has thus always been regarded as exceptional in our polity, an intrusion to be justified by some necessity, the special rather than the ordinary case." [13] Thus, the American experience has justified the theoretical position of A. V. Dicey that "federalism tends to produce conservatism" and that it is "incompatible with schemes for wide social innovation." He wrote that, in essence, therefore, "federal government means weak government." [14]

From this characteristic of federalism stem the reactions of both conservatives and liberals. Franz Neumann, in a skeptical examination of the relationship between federalism and freedom, has approvingly quoted V. O. Key's statement that "a characteristic of the federal system seems to be that entrenched interests in the long run can better protect themselves in dealing with state legislatures than with Congress or with federal administrators." [15] William H. Riker, after a study of the principle of federalism and its operation in various countries, believes that the federal system in the United States has unquestionably worked in favor of privileged minorities in general and the southern whites in particular. He has thus stated that one's attitude toward federalism should be determined by one's view of these minorities. "The judgment to be passed on federalism in the United States," he has bluntly written, "is therefore a judgment on the values of segregation and racial oppression." [16]

Thus, the conservative elements that have opposed the shift in

[13] Herbert Wechsler, "The Political Safeguards of Federalism: The Role of the States in the Composition and Selection of the National Government," in MacMahon, *op. cit.*, pp. 98, 100.

[14] A.V. Dicey, *Introduction to the Study of the Law of the Constitution*, 9th ed., ed. E.C.S. Wade (London: Macmillan, 1950), pp. 173, 171, respectively.

[15] V.O. Key, Jr., as quoted in Franz L. Neumann, "Federalism and Freedom: A Critique," in MacMahon, *op. cit.*, p. 54.

[16] Riker, *op. cit.*, pp. 152–153.

the federal balance are naturally the strongest defenders of the concept of federalism itself. Similarly, the liberals maintain that the system has blocked or, at best, blunted the action of a national majority consensus and has hindered the fulfillment of a meaningful, coherent program of national reform. They even feel a degree of disenchantment with the grant-in-aid program because its force is diluted and its financial resources wasted as it moves through the various state mechanisms. The liberals pose the question, therefore, as to whether such a system, with its innate conservatism and its resultant weakness, can be adjustable enough to respond to the demands of a markedly changing society and decisive enough to carry through the necessary social and economic programs. With our knowledge of the operation of federalism and with the recognition of its flexible modifications during this generation, we can well ponder the answer.

The response is a difficult one because the dynamics of federalism do not operate in a vacuum, but rather in conjunction with other changes in the political structure. As we have seen, the reluctance of the country to face its role as a modern industrial society has derived to a large extent from the nature of legislative representation. As a result, the federal balance itself has been strongly affected by the inactivity of unrepresentative state legislatures. If this assumption is correct, it is clearly possible that the Supreme Court decisions on state legislative apportionment cases with their emphasis upon equality of the vote will decisively influence the federal balance and ease the strained relationship between state and national government. Thus, the federal system will be preserved and the states may receive a new charge of energy from their closer rapport with their populations.

Certainty of prediction in this field should be tempered. We cannot at the present determine whether the momentum of centralization can be stayed by a change in the composition of the state legislatures. Moreover, if there should be a true identity of interests between the state and national legislative majorities because both would reflect the country's popular majority, the degree of cooperation between them would so upset the federal balance that the survival of its structure would be a meaningless and irrelevant issue because it would already have been transmuted, in fact, into a centralized system.[17]

The shifts and changes within the federal structure have been among the most significant countervailing progressive forces that have balanced to some extent the backward characteristics of our politics. This play in the joints has eased the tensions that might have broken out under a more rigid and taut system. Thus, the dynamics of federalism well illustrates Hirschfield's organic compensation.

POLITICAL PARTIES

The nationalizing changes within the federal system and the future projection of this trend are significant because of their effect upon our political parties as well as in their own right. In the last decades, the trend of party development has moved in the same direction in which the country and the political system have tended. We are witnessing the birth pangs of a political party system somewhat different from the old, more national in scope, more ideological in content, more class-conscious in appeal, and more disciplined and responsible in practice. Since political parties develop in conformity with the nature of the political structure and with the character of the whole society, this responsiveness of American political parties is not remarkable. Thus, it should be expected that in a country marked strongly by geographical diversity and in a federal system in which the sovereign states play a prominent role, the party structure will be similarly diffused and based primarily upon the states. On the other hand, as the country becomes nationalized and as the federal balance, consequently, leans heavily toward the national government, a similar shift should be reflected in our parties.

Since the parties obviously cannot reflect changes in the political system until they have already occurred, their trend toward nationalization has been slower and more tentative than that of other political institutions. This necessary time lag is a paramount

[17] Thus, Martin Landau believes that the *Baker* v. *Carr* decision is of great significance in our political history because it closes the gap between an outmoded federal governmental structure and the increasing integration and centralization of American life. Landau, *op. cit,* pp. 241–248.

consideration when we are confronted with far-reaching proposals for party change. Drastic suggestions of united, well-disciplined, fully responsible, ideologically homogeneous parties may score heavily on grounds of logic and efficiency. One should, however, be cautiously skeptical of their efficacy because radical party reforms derive from fundamental historic changes and not from the deliberations of scholars.

The history of our political parties bears this out. A successful majority party coalition generally dominates an era's politics, and its sway ends only when one or more of its elements permanently desert it. Such major shifts in party clientele, however, do not occur for casual or transitory reasons but rather under the pressure of relentless historical forces, such as slavery and civil war in one instance and a worldwide economic depression in another. As a result, these dominant coalitions have been few and their reign has usually been long. Even fewer, however, have been the changes in the line-up of our major political parties. Throughout our history, there have been but two valid instances in which a majority party died or dissolved.

The modern trend of our parties' development toward national organization and class-oriented programs also reflects deep-seated historical causes. Since major political problems are increasingly becoming national ones, the parties are forced to think in national terms for organization and policy despite the resistance of their formal structure and the ingrained thought patterns of their members.

The major shift in the nature of our political parties began in the administration of Woodrow Wilson, who consciously attempted to secure a strong, disciplined, responsible national party committed to the enactment of a particular program. In this endeavor, he was strongly influenced by his study and interest in British politics and government—possibly too strongly influenced in the light of American political institutions and practices. The high peak of the application of his principles was reached in his first years of power when he guided the Democrats in Congress to pass a coherent legislative program.

Wilson's party reforms, however, proved short-lived. Despite his penetrating insight into the future of American politics, he seriously misjudged the immediate present—and this might also have been true for his view of international relations as well. The United States of his period, with its emphasis upon the states, was not ready to accept a nationalistic concept of politics. The American people would have to endure years of further nationalization of their social, economic, and cultural life as well as the traumatic shock of widespread economic dislocation before their political structure wuld be amenable to change. The concept of a strong national party would not emerge again until the administration of Franklin D. Roosevelt. Although he was a cannier and more politic leader than Wilson and undoubtedly learned from his errors, the main reason for the continuation of Roosevelt's party reforms in later years lay less in his character and ability than in the nature of his times. The New Deal, in initiating the dissolution of the old political system, began the fundamental change in our political parties. We have already seen how Roosevelt's social programs unintentionally hastened the obsolescence of the traditional urban machines and raised the greatest threat to their survival.

Roosevelt's specific party reforms emphasized, as did Wilson's, congressional passage of the president's legislative program. He initiated, for example, regular weekly meetings with his party's legislative leaders, thereby aiding the transformation of the party and the recognition of the chief executive as its leader. Roosevelt was similarly conscious of the relation of party to program when he unsuccessfully attempted to purge conservatives in the Democratic primaries of 1938 because they refused to support his policies. The setting of national party power over that of the states, combined with an emphasis upon ideological consistency as the prime test of party loyalty, placed too great a strain upon the sensibilities of Democratic members, officials, and legislators. Congress, in its turn, protected the interests of state party organizations from the specter of a national one, by preventing governmental employees from contributing to national campaigns. Even more significantly, the rest of Roosevelt's legislative program, the raison d'être of his views on party, came practically to a dead halt. The seeds, however, of national control and policy orientation had been firmly planted and would develop further in future years.

Later presidents would continue in the same direction of reforming the parties. This was most visible to the public in the expanding role of the president as party spokesman in midterm elections. Personal preference had little effect on this trend since the almost apolitical Dwight Eisenhower became as involved as the intensely political John F. Kennedy. Their activity negated the concept that the political party was a phantom-like national organization for three and two-thirds years and a real one only in the four months of presidential campaigning—if even then.

Party reform, however, was even more necessary for the party out of power, which had almost no continuity between elections because it lacked the authority, initiative, and influence of the presidency. The weakness of the defeated presidential candidate's titular leadership was recognized by all, especially by the man himself. The national committee was practically powerless as an effective national party instrument because its members sat solely as representatives of their state organizations and did not make up a truly independent body. The party's legislative leaders, as expected, tended to emphasize the congressional characteristics of localism and parochialism that were the basic attributes of the dominant state-controlled party system.

In late 1956 Paul Butler, the national chairman of the Democratic party, and various party leaders attempted to change this situation by establishing the Democratic Advisory Council, a group of prominent party members who were to study and discuss policy on a continuing basis. Because its purpose seemed at odds with the traditional concept of an American party, the council was a highly controversial body and it understandably had a short, feverish history in the face of strong opposition. The most sustained hostility came from the Democratic congressional elite, whose members refused to accept the seats offered them on the council. They believed that the council's very existence and its emphasis upon policy touched their vital interests and was alien to their fundamental political values. Since they were intimately linked with their state organizations, they hardly looked with favor upon an instrument for nationalizing the party structure. The council, moreover, could invade their own sphere of legislative influence, particularly since it would be more attuned than Congress to the nation's urban majority. In addition, they believed that a group could not present an effective party policy since such a policy was essentially the final product that emerged from the consensus hammered out in the various phases of the legislative process, rather than a neat, comprehensive program of specific items to which the party was committed. They discounted, for example, the party platform of the national nominating convention as a relatively insignificant concession to necessity that no one was expected to take seriously and believed that the debate over its composition should be as brief and as private as possible in order not to interfere with the truly serious political business of winning elections. To consider these debates with their dangerous divisive potential as the main core of party activity and to carry them on between conventions seemed ill-advised and unrealistic.

The combination of party nationalization and ideological emphasis laced together by disciplinary chords was seen in another Democratic party activity in these years, the debate over party loyalty and unity. To the world at large, it seemed a curious American phenomenon that persons could be members in good standing of a party, even be counted among its legislative leaders —and yet not support the party candidate for the presidency. Americans, however, with their recognition of the domination of state parties, saw little incongruity in this tolerance. They realized, moreover, how limited were the effective disciplinary resources the national party could command in this situation. The trend of political party development in the twentieth century, however, was steadily undermining the assumptions that had rendered such anomalies reasonable. In the 1920's and early 1930's, the problem of party loyalty had first broken out among the Republicans, when many leading members of the party's dissident midwestern progressive wing either abstained from supporting Republican presidential candidates or actively endorsed their opponents.[18] This rebelliousness against eastern business control of their party partly reflected the increasingly nationwide scope of significant political action. Thus, the midwesterners were realizing that a national voice was necessary for the protection of

[18] Clarence A. Berdahl, "Some Notes on Party Membership in Congress," *American Political Science Review*, XXXVI (April and June, 1949), pp. 319–321, 492–508; Ralph K. Huitt, "The Morse Committee Assignment Controversy: A Study in Senate Norms," *American Political Science Review* LI, 2 (June, 1957), 319–325.

their interests that had been generally neglected by their party spokesmen. When the old political system cracked in the 1930's, the nationalization of politics accelerated and the importance of national party policy increased. As a result, the problem of party unity reached new proportions—but within the dominant Democratic party.

By the late 1930's and early 1940's, as we have seen earlier, fissures had broken out within Roosevelt's successful alliance. As the southern Democrats began to be concerned about their lessened influence in party conventions because of the removal of the two-thirds rule, they developed doubts about the future projection of the liberal political trend they had originally encouraged. Increasingly, a sizable bloc of southern congressmen found themselves in opposition to the policies endorsed by the party majority outside the South. This faction, which included some of the most powerful and influential legislators, was the essential element in the formation of an informal conservative majority that checked, emasculated, or honed down progressive measures. Roosevelt understandably chose some of its most prominent members as the targets for his party purge in 1938. In 1940, this dissident sentiment was shown in the grudging support of the Democratic convention for Roosevelt's vice-presidential candidate, Henry Wallace. In 1944, in another vice-presidential race, the southern-backed candidacy of James F. Byrnes effectively blocked Wallace and allowed Harry Truman to emerge victorious. The selection of Truman was symbolically significant for Democratic politics because as a border state senator with a southern background and a faultlessly liberal voting record, he seemed to typify, as Samuel Lubell has emphasized, the party's moderate groups and "professional" politicians.[19] In succeeding years, these men would continue their attempt to achieve a consensus of the membership and to avoid an open clash between its southern and northern urban factions.

The intensity of the contending pressures became evident in 1948, when the convention, which nominated Truman for the presidency, became embroiled in a controversy over the platform on the subject of civil rights. A sharp division broke out between

[19] Samuel Lubell, *The Future of American Politics*, 2d ed. (Garden City, N.Y.: Anchor Books, 1956), ch. 2.

the liberal forces, which desired a strong civil rights plank with specific provisions, and the southerners, who did not want any mention of the subject whatsoever. The conflict was settled in the resolutions committee by the compromise of a mild civil rights plank phrased in general terms. On the floor of the convention, however, the liberals overthrew the counsels of the moderates and party professionals and refused to comply with the compromise plank. Led by Hubert Humphrey, then at the threshold of his senatorial career, they presented the strong plank once more. The vote on this proposal was as instructive as it was dramatic. The defeat of the liberal proposal was generally expected since the moderate plank was supported not only by the middle-of-the-road mediating groups in the party but also by practically the whole southern contingent as well. The liberals, however, despite the impressive alignment of forces against them, were successful by a narrow margin because of the vote of the large state delegations. Many of the leaders of these groups, although probably favoring compromise to avoid antagonizing the South, nevertheless felt that they could not explain a vote against a strong civil rights plank to their followers in the large cities. This vote reflected the new power balance in the party and impressed the South with the loss of its dominant position and with the realization that even with the help of its moderate allies and the sympathetic understanding of a number of machine leaders, the ultimate power in the party lay with the workers and the ethnic minorities of the large cities. It was appropriately symbolic that at the moment the vote was announced, some of the southern delegates left the convention in anger to become the nucleus of a States' Rights party, which ran Governor Strom Thurmond of South Carolina for the presidency. Although a majority of the southern states remained in Mr. Truman's electoral column, the South could no longer be considered a solidly Democratic region in presidential elections. This change in southern voting behavior forced the question of party loyalty upon all subsequent conventions.

The 1948 bolt did not prove a unique phenomenon since there would be similar defections in future elections. Although specifically touched off by the civil rights issue, they occurred within the framework of a general reaction against the liberal nationalizing tendencies of the New Deal and its offshoots. These defections, moreover, raised fundamental questions about the future of our political parties because they were expressed not by a separate candidacy but rather by support for Republican presidential candidates. The northern liberals, on their part, retaliated by demanding an advance pledge of support for the national ticket from the southern delegates. Their insistence not only irritated the southerners but displeased the moderates as well, because it both split the Democrats on the basis of doctrine and called into question the sovereignty of the state parties. In 1964, however, the culmination of the legislative battle over civil rights and the increasing identification of the Democratic party with social reform sharpened the ideological cleavage and encouraged a stricter sense of party discipline. The Republicans hastened this process by offering the conservative states' righters a meaningful alternative by nominating Barry Goldwater, a candidate from their right wing who had voted against the Civil Rights Act of 1964. By this time, even the moderates recognized the liberal contention that those who officially deserted the party should not be welcomed at future conventions or allowed to maintain their congressional positions as Democrats. The convention, moreover, in its commitment to civil rights, was even willing to subordinate state party control to the point of promising to refuse the seating of future delegates from states where party members were barred from the nominating process because of race. The candidates chosen by this convention symbolically indicated how far the party had changed in the space of a few years. Its presidential nominee—the man most responsible for the platform—was Lyndon Johnson, a southerner who personified throughout the 1950's the moderate Democrats who attempted to achieve a broad party consensus and to avoid sharp lines of difference. The vice-presidential candidate was Hubert Humphrey, the man who in presenting the strong civil rights plank at the 1948 convention triggered the series of events which eventually forced the party to assume a character seemingly at odds with its own traditions as well as the structure and content of our party system.

The South justifiably figures prominently in an account of the nationalization of our political parties. The South is the section of the country in which localistic sentiments have been strongest and most persistent, and in which the nationalizing forces in American life have been felt later and weaker than in the rest of the country. It has thus had, as we have seen, the greatest stake in the maintenance of states' rights and in the survival of the federal system itself. In addition, the substance and traditions of southern life have conflicted most sharply with that of its main partner in the Democratic party, the large cities. Thus, the ultimate test of the preservation of a loosely organized national party system is whether the South can retain its particular position in the party. The political shifts in the South, although fascinating in themselves, are primarily significant, therefore, because of their reflection on a magnified scale of the transformation of our party politics.

The South stands out especially as the showpiece of American political change when we examine its electoral statistics. Democratic strength has been eroding so steadily that the concept of a solidly Democratic South, one of the fundamental fixtures of our political history since the Civil War, has not been valid in presidential elections for half a generation.[20] In congressional and state contests, it can no longer be considered an absolute rule. Even if one should not take into account the extraordinary showing of the Republican party in the South in 1964, there can be no denial of the steady growth of Republican membership and popular following since the late 1940's. This trend has been a persistent one and will continue because it is solidly built upon a strong base, the expanding urban and suburban middle and upper classes, composed in large number of professional men and their families attached to burgeoning southern industry. Many of them are transplanted northerners who, by maintaining their Republican allegiance, have given the party a new respectability and have thus encouraged their southern-born peers to join them in accordance with their ideological leanings. The Democratic party, with the sloughing off of these conservative elements, has thus become more readily identified as the party of the small farmers and the urban workers. The Negroes, whose political significance increases as they become freed from the

[20] See V.O. Key, Jr., *Southern Politics in State and Nation* (New York: Knopf, 1950) and Alexander Heard, *A Two-Party South?* (Chapel Hill: University of North Carolina Press, 1952).

restraints upon their vote, primarily support the Democratic party because of its position on economic matters despite its role of maintaining white supremacy. This basic tendency will undoubtedly prevail even though, in the midsixties, temporary counterpressures developed that emphasized independent political action by Negroes.

This striking change in the southern vote fits into the pattern of our political transformation and has been matched, on a lesser scale, in other sections. The two parties did not, in fact, compete throughout most of the country because the localistic emphasis of the old political system fostered one-party control. In most of the New England and midwestern states, political domination by the Republicans was almost as tight as that of the Democrats in the South.[21] Many states had a recognized split in political control with the Democrats dominating the largest city and the Republicans, the rest of the state.

The leading authorities on American political parties generally agree that this former area control by political parties has been largely terminated by the development of a flourishing competitive two-party system throughout the country. Thus, the remarkable rise of a southern Republican party is matched by a Democratic resurgence in the traditionally Republican areas of northern New England and in the heart of the corn country in the Midwest. States which have never—or "hardly ever"—deserted the Republican column since the Civil War have in recent years shown Democratic majorities in congressional, gubernatorial, and presidential elections.[22]

Our parties are, therefore, becoming truly national ones divided upon national issues, thus reflecting the nationalization of our society and its political structure. This has not been a one-way process since the parties, in turn, have facilitated this na-

[21] See, for example, V.O. Key, Jr., *American State Politics: An Introduction* (New York: Knopf, 1956), pp. 18–28, and Austin Ranney and Willmoore Kendall, *Democracy and the American Party System* (New York: Harcourt, Brace and World, 1956), ch. 7, esp. pp. 161–164.

[22] Paul T. David, "The Changing Political Parties," in Marian D. Irish, ed., *Continuing Crisis in American Politics* (Englewood Cliffs, N.J.: Prentice-Hall, 1963), pp. 48–57, and E.E. Schattschneider, *The Semisovereign People: A Realistic View of Democracy in America* (New York: Holt, Rinehart, and Winston, 1960), pp. 89–96.

tionalization and have become more effective instruments through which the country has adjusted to new social and economic conditions. Just as the state-centered parties were the most appropriate units for a political system that sought to maintain the status quo in conformity with conservative interests, the newly emergent national parties will be equally suitable for a liberal political system whose prime quality is flexibility to change.

The Executive

Since the constitutional structure's separation of powers invites conflict between the legislature and the executive, it is not surprising that our governors and presidents have become the most direct and significant of all the progressive countervailing forces. The clashes between these two branches in recent decades have been, in fact, contests between the forces committed to the old political system and those associated with the new. The resolution of these conflicts in the shift of power and influence from the legislature to the executive parallels similar changes within the federal system and the political parties.

This trend to the executive stands out with particular sharpness at the state level since the legislative decline there is even more pronounced than at the national plane. Indeed, it is difficult for us to appreciate that under the first state constitutions, the governor's position was definitely subordinate to the legislature's. Moreover, the selection of the governor by the legislature was hardly designed to guarantee a strong personality in the executive mansion who would utilize even his restricted powers to the fullest. Allan Richards has described the governmental structure in the seven most typical state governments:

The people had such faith in the legislature that they allowed it to choose the other state officials, including the governor, who was limited to a one-year term and was ineligible for reelection. In only one of these seven states could he veto legislative acts. His appointing and pardoning powers were limited by an executive council also selected by the legislature. . . .[23]

[23] Allan R. Richards, "The Tradition of Government in the States," *The Forty-eight States: Their Tasks as Policy Makers and Administrators* (New York: The American Assembly, Columbia University, 1955), p. 41.

This faith in the legislature primarily stemmed from the territorial concept of republican liberty that was prevalent in the Revolutionary period, particularly among the small farmers. One can thus realize why, in an age of crude transportation facilities, the further away the location of political authority, the greater would be the popular mistrust since those in power would be less intimately and directly aware of conditions in a particular locality and their deliberations would take place further removed from the immediate surveillance of the citizens. Thus, there was a rising progression of civic mistrust beginning with the local government and reaching its peak with the national. By a similar standard, who in government was more worthy of trust than the representative of the locality? What more effective protection could there be for the people's interests than a body composed of these representatives?

The executive in the capitol, on the other hand, was a comparatively distant figure, less attuned to the interests of the people than *their* legislators. Just as the concept of a large republic was an elusive one to grasp at first because there had been no comparable enterprise in history so did the role and character of a republican executive seem difficult to comprehend. Jefferson, reflecting the democrat's instinctive suspicion of executive authority, feared that the American presidency, with its unlimited tenure, would become an elective kingship.[24]

The historical experience of the American colonies before their independence buttressed these predispositions. The lower houses of the legislatures had achieved a favorable reputation in the popular mind by their criticism of the arbitrary and unjust aspects of the rule of the royal governors. This attitude toward the executive and the legislature would remain even after British rule had ended.

The reversal of this view, particularly the fall in the legislature's prestige, occurred primarily in two phases of American history. By the first quarter of the nineteenth century, the state legislatures had forfeited a great part of their reputation by their

[24] See, for example, Jefferson's letter to James Madison, December 20, 1787, in Alpheus Thomas Mason, ed., *Free Government in the Making: Readings in American Political Thought*, 2d ed. (New York: Oxford University Press, 1956), pp. 248–250.

penchant for corruption. Simultaneously, the governor extracted executive powers from the control of the legislature. He also secured his election directly from the people—and for a lengthened term. The strengthening of the governorship was heightened in the period of Jacksonian democracy when the democratic transformation of the presidency reverberated throughout the state capitols of the country.[25] Suspicion of executive power dissolved with the realization that a popularly elected chief executive could be a more appropriate spokesman for the people than a legislature in which special interests could hold sway.

Although the second great change in the relative status of the executive and the legislature has been taking place in the present, its pattern is similar to that of the Jacksonian period. Once again, a majority of the people, many of them recently freed from their constitutional and political shackles by a strong democratic trend, identified themselves with the popularly elected executive rather than the minority-oriented legislature. The governor, chosen by a majority of an increasingly urbanized electorate, stood out in sharp contrast to the malapportioned legislature, under the virtually permanent control of the rural minority. This distinction was starkest when Democratic governors in northern states often found themselves saddled with Republican legislatures. It was also apparent, however, even when the governor was a Republican because he realized that his success at the polls would be determined in the metropolitan areas rather than in the rural sections and small towns that were the bases of strength for his party's delegation in the legislature. Since the governor would thus be sensitive to the problems of a modern society, the people looked to him and tended to ignore their legislators. Prestige and influence predictably shifted. Once more, the health of our politics was sustained by the flexibility of organic compensation.

The Presidency

The presidency is the most important of the countervailing forces that have allowed our political system to check its regressive characteristics and to adjust to the pressures of social and economic change. The increased power of the presidency is the

[25] Richards, *op. cit.*, pp. 42–46.

result of a cumulative drive derived from all the shifts previously outlined—the movement from states' rights to nationalism, from state parties to national ones, and from the legislature to the executive. Therefore, the institution that has risen highest in this century is the one to which all these trends have gravitated, the chief executive of a strong national government in command of a national party, the president of the United States. "The strong Presidency," Clinton Rossiter has written, "is the product of events that cannot be undone and of forces that continue to roll." [26]

Since the presidency is, in such great measure, the product of the basic currents of our twentieth-century history, it has become indelibly marked with our modern urban character. Because of this identity, the country's population look upon the president as its spokesman, the symbol of democracy, and the protector of its liberties. Thus, primarily through the democratizing experiences of the Jacksonian and New Deal eras, we have found ourselves in a position fundamentally opposite to the original distrust of executive authority, national power, and, above all, their combination in the presidency. Jefferson, our leading democratic philosopher, appropriately felt this distrust even when in the office himself. Two of the devices by which he limited its authority and power were the examples he set for future presidents by not addressing Congress in person and by not running for a third term. (Technically, the latter precedent can be attributed to Washington but his declining to run seems to have been primarily for personal reasons rather than on grounds of principle.) It is reflective of the changed nature of the modern presidency that two of this century's Democratic chief executives broke with these precedents of their party's founder: Wilson, by addressing Congress in person, and Franklin Roosevelt, by seeking and securing a third and then a fourth term.

The shaping of the modern presidency has not been a uniquely American phenomenon, but has rather followed a general pattern of twentieth-century Western political development in the increase of executive authority, particularly the concentration of power in the hands of one leader. In the previous

[26] Clinton Rossiter, *The American Presidency*, 2d ed. (New York: New American Library, 1960), p. 247.

century, democracy was primarily expressed in the operation of the legislature—as the common term "parliamentary democracy" indicated; in the twentieth, however, it has increasingly focused upon the executive.

This shift of emphasis has been largely an inevitable result of the complexity of the society which modern government has to regulate. Formerly, a conscientious and able representative could be reasonably conversant with the bulk of the subject matter on the legislative agenda and cast a truly deliberative vote. Parliamentary debates could thus be meaningful since they were concerned with comprehensible problems whose solution could be secured through the consensus of the legislative process. In modern times, however, the beacon of parliamentarianism has dimmed as it has been almost engulfed by a flood of technical and intricate proposed legislation. A mastery of the laws necessary to govern a complex society has gone beyond the limit of the single legislator, no matter how conscientious or able. In the British House of Commons (1928–29), it was claimed that sections of one bill being debated were understood by only three members, one of whom was the minister presenting it.[27] In addition to the sheer technical difficulty of modern legislation, its subject matter, with a predominant emphasis upon the demands of apparently irreconcilable economic classes, has become increasingly intractable to parliamentary compromise. Thus, in country after country, the prestige of legislatures dipped sharply and it became increasingly customary to dismiss these former arenas of great political debates as "talking shops," full of petty, posturing politicians, involved in their insignificant business while the real stuff of government was conducted elsewhere—at the party headquarters, around the cabinet table, and in the offices of the bureaucracy.[28]

In the American system of government, with our separation of powers, this trend was translated into increased influence for the president over Congress; in the British system, it meant an accel-

[27] W. Ivor Jennings, *Parliament* (Cambridge, England: Cambridge University Press, 1939), p. 277.

[28] For a modern analysis of the problems of legislatures, see Karl Dietrich Bracher, "Problems of Parliamentary Democracy in Europe," *Daedalus*, XCIII (Winter, 1964), 179–198.

eration of the shift from parliamentary government to cabinet government, and within the cabinet, an increasing concentration of power to the prime minister; in the less stable democracies, it was reflected in a tendency for parliamentary responsibility to be eroded by a constant reference to decree legislation, a virtual blank check given by the parliament to the cabinet; finally, in those countries where the democratic tradition was weak and its institutions relatively new, this trend to executive authority became an outright rejection of democracy itself and an acquiescence to glossy totalitarian systems which seemed to possess a vitality and realism lacking in the jaded parliamentary systems. Thus, it is comprehensible why some observers in the 1930's could easily entertain serious doubts about the relevancy of liberal-democracy in a highly technical age, so different from the simpler era in which it had been spawned. The recourse to dictatorship seemed but the inevitable projection of the trend toward executive power, a veritable "wave of the future." [29] In this testing of the essence of democracy, the institution of the democratic American presidency, with its fusion of power and responsibility, performed a role even greater than that of its Jacksonian predecessor, not only because the times were more complex and hazardous, but also because it served as an example to the whole democratic world.

In recognizing the general pattern of legislative decline under the pressures of a modern industrial, urban civilization, we can perceive the remarkable shortsightedness of rural, small-town America at the turn of the century in attempting to preserve the legislatures as defense bastions of its way of life against the city. These modern forces would inevitably have weakened the legislature under any circumstances. By guaranteeing, however, that the legislatures, because of their composition, could not reflect the new currents in our national society and could not adequately respond to its needs, the conservatives were hindering

[29] See Arthur Schlesinger, Jr., *The Politics of Upheaval* (Boston: Houghton Mifflin, 1960), p. 646; Carl L. Becker, *New Liberties for Old* (New Haven: Yale University Press, 1941), p. 121; and Harold Laski, *Parliamentary Government in England: A Commentary* (New York: Viking, 1938), ch. 1. "The wave of the future" is taken from the title of Anne Morrow Lindbergh's *The Wave of the Future: A Confession of Faith* (New York: Harcourt, Brace and World, 1940).

Congress and the state legislatures from achieving the performance of which they might have been capable and were thus
hastening the decline of the very political institutions upon which
they had irrevocably committed themselves. They not only put
their money on a horse destined to lose in the long run, but so
weighted it with the character of a receding era and the interests
of regressive minorities, that it lost all chances of making a credit-
able showing against a spirited and aggressive executive, spurred
by the dynamic forces that were transforming America.

THEODORE ROOSEVELT

The twentieth century had hardly begun before conservatives
were warned through the dynamic example of Theodore Roosevelt about the potential power of the presidency and its eventual
rapport with the disadvantaged groups in American society.
Thus, at almost the moment the system began to operate, the
institution that would eventually upset its equilibrium and become the leading instrument of its dissolution was already revealing intimations of this role.

With his innate gift of capturing the imagination of the
people, Roosevelt moved closer to the center of the political stage
than any executive since Lincoln. He not only acted vigorously in
his office, but articulated, as well, the classic defense of the strong
presidency. Indeed, whenever we distinguish between strong,
active presidents and weak, inert ones, we are basically following
Roosevelt's analysis.[30] The operation of the modern presidency,
as we shall see, leans heavily upon his model.

Since the presidency would become the symbol of the urban
dynamism that was transforming American society, it was appropriate that the first strong holder of the office in this century
might qualify as our first urban president.[31] More significantly,
Roosevelt clearly identified the presidency with social justice, as
Louis Koenig has pointed out, by throwing his weight on the side

[30] For Theodore Roosevelt's conception of the strong presidency, see
John P. Roche and Leonard W. Levy, eds., *The Presidency* (New York:
Harcourt, Brace and World, 1964), pp. 20–22. For the ironic rendition of
Roosevelt's views by his successor, William Howard Taft, as well as Taft's
justification for a more limited presidency, see also pp. 22–28.

[31] Rexford Guy Tugwell, *The Enlargement of the Presidency* (Garden
City, N.Y.: Doubleday, 1960), p. 297.

of social reform and criticizing the practices of the dominant power group. He thus indicated the path the later great presidents would follow. With uncanny prescience, he even touched on the problem of the Negro at a time of our deepest insensitivity to his civil rights. His entertaining of Booker T. Washington at the White House could be termed a gesture, but such gestures were notoriously rare in public life then—and even a generation later.[32] One can, by accenting Roosevelt's considerable weaknesses and inconsistencies, present the portrait of a man who actually accomplished comparatively little despite his bluster and extravagant language. He may very well have often reversed his own advice of "Speak softly and carry a big stick." Such criticism, however, does not do adequate justice to his major contributions in determining the development of the dominant political institution of our time.

In assessing Roosevelt's role, we should remember that his period in office was not propitious for the actions of a consistently strong executive since political power was structured primarily through Congress and the states. He also received rather dubious support from his own party, which was little inclined to show toleration for a full-scale program of social reform. Thus, as was true with Wilson's conception of political parties, the fulfillment of a vision was checked by the realities of the time.

Roosevelt's presidential performance, therefore, although unquestionably brilliant, was essentially a solo tour de force with little continuity of tradition or institutionalization of office. He later realized this in his disappointment with his chosen successor, William Howard Taft, who was as cogent and consistent a believer in a limited presidency as Roosevelt was of a dynamic and expanding one.

WILSON

Woodrow Wilson, on the other hand, did share Roosevelt's view of the presidency even though T.R., out of personal pique and partisan acid, refused to recognize this. The office was so transmuted in Wilson's term that this period can profitably be considered the essential transition between the inchoate vision of

[32] Louis W. Koenig, *The Chief Executive* (New York: Harcourt, Brace and World, 1964), pp. 298–300, 320.

the national executive perceived by the first Roosevelt in the White House and the fulfillment of this vision under the second.

The basis of Wilson's attitude toward the presidency was more cerebral than Theodore Roosevelt's, a product of his long analytical preoccupation with American politics. Historians acknowledge that as a political scientist and as a theorist of the presidency, Wilson stands above all men elected to the office. His concern for the American political structure was filtered through his deep regard for the British system of government. The Wilsonian presidency, with its emphasis upon personal leadership and party, bore a striking resemblance to the British prime ministership. His act of addressing Congress in person, for example, hewed much closer to British practice than American tradition. By fusing the strong presidency with determined party leadership, Wilson made the decisive step in shaping the modern American chief executive.[33]

Wilson's contribution to our politics has been somewhat clouded by the failures of his last two and a half years in office: the rejection of his plea for a Democratic Congress in the 1918 election, the refusal of the Senate to ratify the Treaty of Versailles and to allow us to enter the League of Nations, and his paralyzing illness and the resultant vacuum of leadership. What deserves emphasis are his first years of power, when theory and practice blended together in the achievement of an imposing legislative record and firm executive control. "Many historians," Rossiter has written, "think that the American Presidency, and with it our whole system of government, reached its highest peak of democracy, efficiency, and morality in the first four years of Woodrow Wilson." [34] Wilson, in office, thus fulfilled his early expansive concept of the presidency: "The President is at liberty, both in law and conscience, to be as big a man as he can." [35]

The coming of World War I added a new dimension to the

[33] For the high estimate of Wilson, see A.J. Wann, "The Development of Woodrow Wilson's Theory of the Presidency: Continuity and Change," p. 47, and August Heckscher, Woodrow Wilson: An Appraisal and Recapitulation," p. 245, in Earl Latham, ed., *The Philosophy and Policies of Woodrow Wilson* (Chicago: University of Chicago Press, 1958).

[34] Rossiter, *op. cit.*, p. 99.

[35] Woodrow Wilson, *Constitutional Government in the United States* (New York: Columbia University Press, 1908), p. 70.

scope of presidential leadership that went beyond even Wilson's expectations. It first increased the power and authority of the president by virtue of his being a leader during war. This development was not unusual since the greatest accretions of presidential power in our history have usually occurred in time of war, and thus some of our strongest presidents have been war presidents. The scope of the presidency increases in time of war because of the presidency's control over the military apparatus and its symbolism of national unity and patriotism. Although this pattern can be discerned in other countries, it is of special significance in the United States, where the political leader is also the formal chief of state as well as the titular commander-in-chief. Such a concentration of power and authority will usually have a marked effect upon the established governmental equilibrium. Moreover, the pressures of war that strengthen the executive usually work against the prestige and influence of a legislature because its debates are impaired and its sources of information are restricted.

In addition to this normal extension of presidential power during war, the involvement of the United States in world affairs inevitably rendered its leader a world figure, whose power and influence could hardly be equaled. Again, this change, with the other basic Wilsonian reforms, seemed ephemeral in the light of our policy of isolationism between the wars, when the United States, in apparently denying that its power was of international significance, cut its chief executive down to parochial size. As with the other legacies of the Wilsonian presidency, this one would not be fulfilled until the administration of Franklin Roosevelt.

Thus, Franklin D. Roosevelt's term of office underlined the limitations of Wilson's presidency, as Wilson's had Theodore Roosevelt's. Wilson's inability to maintain the momentum of his first four years in office was only secondarily influenced by his own personal limitations, the shift of public opinion, and sheer bad fortune. More significantly, a strong presidency required a willingness to challenge the basic assumptions of the existing political system, and a commitment to a thoroughgoing and consistent program of reform that could weld together the various disadvantaged groups into a new political coalition. This Wilson could not achieve because his party—indeed, he himself—was too basically conservative and too tied to the existing system to be a truly reforming force. Although the Democratic party, with its small-town, rural, southern base, was a more effective instrument for attacking the excesses of big business than was Roosevelt's Republican party, it was, nevertheless, of limited utility as a rallying point for the country's urban population with its strong southern and eastern European character; and it was a complete nullity as a hope for the southern Negroes living under the rule of white supremacy.

FRANKLIN ROOSEVELT

Roosevelt, however, was able to form the necessary coalition. When the old political system dissolved under the impetus of the depression, the ethnic minorities in the cities and the Negroes were able to join with the white southerners in the majority popular support for a program of economic recovery. The New Deal, the program of the new alliance, was of major historical importance in transforming the power structure and in expanding the government's economic and social responsibilities. The New Deal's impact upon the organization of government, however, was as significant as upon its role. In no segment of government was its effect stronger than on the presidency. National events forced the spotlight upon a dynamic president. Possessing a dominant, charismatic personality, as well as a deep conviction about the necessity of a strong executive, Roosevelt faced a country ravaged by national distress and presented to its people an ambitious economic program with a veritable cornucopia of new governmental projects and plans. The magnitude of the economic emergency and the energetic response of the New Deal drastically increased presidential powers and Roosevelt "burst the bonds of the Presidency as none of his predecessors had been able to do." [36] This change in the office differed from most previous ones because the strong presidency gained widespread acceptance.

Thus, if war had not broken out and if Roosevelt had retired after his second term, his period of office would still have ranked with the highest in our history and his impact upon the presi-

[36] Tugwell, *op. cit.*, p. 410.

dency would have been the greatest in this century. With the coming of World War II, however, the country and its president had their second "rendezvous with destiny." The dimensions of the office, already stretched—and stretched, some felt, beyond constitutional limits—by years of exciting and significant domestic reform, expanded even further. The natural gravitation of power and authority to the executive which, as we have noted, usually occurs in time of war was here exaggerated by the mammoth proportions of the historic conflict, particularly its global scope, the hitherto unbelievable drain of financial and material resources, the millions of persons involved in its conduct, and its shattering impact upon political institutions and control on at least three continents. Its ideological nature, moreover, transformed the head of the most powerful democratic nation into the leader of the free world. Unlike our previous withdrawal after Wilson's international involvement, the leadership thrust upon the country and its presidency could not be relinquished.

THE ATTACK ON THE PRESIDENCY

A combination, therefore, of historical forces, domestic and foreign, strengthened and expanded the presidency. Roosevelt's administration was a climactic one because it left the office permanently and irreversibly transformed. We noted earlier, however, that this basic change was only imperfectly apprehended at the time since many so instinctively associated it with Roosevelt himself that they felt it could not survive his death. Thus, in the late 1940's and 1950's, a second attempted reaction (see pp. 72–76) to the main reforms of the New Deal leveled much of its attack against the main instrument of its fulfillment, the strong, modern presidency.

One of these attempts was successful, the passage of the Twenty-second Amendment in 1951, which limited the presidential tenure to two terms. Conservatives attained this goal because Congress, under temporary Republican control, presented the change to the rural-dominated state legislatures. Their endeavor seemed to fly in the face of history since only a short time earlier, the American people, threatened by international crisis and impending war, had elected a president for a third term, as well as a succeeding fourth. There could be, of course, no guaran-

tee that future emergencies would accommodatingly fall some-
where in the middle of the first term rather than disconcertingly
near the end of the second. The advocates of the amendment,
however, maintained that it was justified by history itself with the
record of Roosevelt's alleged autocratic tendencies. This emphasis
upon F.D.R., however, fed the suspicion that the amendment was
less the product of thought and reflection than of animosity toward a man whom his enemies could not defeat while he was
alive. "It is to be suspected," says Tugwell, "that most of those
who voted for it knew it to be unwise, and certainly most were
soon willing to admit regret." [37]

The linking of Roosevelt with dictatorship revealed an animosity as much against the strong presidency he symbolized as
against the man himself. The primary criticism against the
amendment is not, however, concerned with the timing of a possible emergency, but rather with the effect upon the normal
operation of the office. A chief executive, particularly in the last
two years of his second term, will lose much of the authority and
power of his position by virtue of the certain knowledge of its
termination. When the prohibition of a third term was a tradition
rather than a constitutional provision, the possibility that a president might run gave him an impressive whiphand over a recalci-
trant Congress. Rossiter is, therefore, correct in considering the
amendment an attack upon the modern development of the presidency:

The real logic of the Twenty-second Amendment is . . . that it helps
to shift the balance of power in our government away from the executive and back toward the legislature, thus reversing a trend that had
appeared irreversible by any ordinary exertion of the will of Congress. . . .
. . . . .
And I submit that it was not the possibility of dictatorship but the
reality of the strong Presidency, not the shadow of a third-term President but the substance of any President, that gave force to the successful drive for the Twenty-second Amendment.[38]

A still more direct and drastic limitation of the office was the
Bricker amendment proposed in the early fifties, which could
easily rank as one of the most radical constitutional changes ever

[37] *Ibid.*, p. 444.   [38] Rossiter, *op. cit.*, p. 226.

considered by Congress. A throwback to the Articles of Confederation, it virtually allowed the states to have a veto upon any treaties or executive agreements that would in any way affect them. If successful, it would probably have made the conduct of foreign affairs extraordinarily difficult in an age that places a high premium upon quick decision-making.[39] Its serious consideration by Congress—a milder version of it came within one vote of the necessary two-thirds approval of the Senate—becomes comprehensible only as a reflection of conservative distrust of the modern presidency, compounded with hostility to Roosevelt's foreign policy.

TRUMAN AND EISENHOWER

The attack on the presidency in this period basically failed, as did the general conservative reaction of which it was such a significant part. The permanency of the changes achieved under Roosevelt was not fully appreciated until they were continued by successors of a different stripe: Harry Truman, who did not seem to possess the remarkable abilities and heroic stature appropriate for the strengthened office, and Dwight Eisenhower, who seemed to have neither the appropriate temperament nor political philosophy.

The presidency, however, overrode these limitations. Truman proved to have powers of character and perception that had generally eluded contemporary observers of his earlier career who could see little more than a former haberdasher and a run-of-the-mill product of an unsavory political machine. Moreover, without any intellectual pretensions, he was extremely well-read in American history and had developed a strong interest in the study of the presidential office. Thus, in this period of stress, the modern presidency was in the safe hands of one eager to protect it from shortsighted men who lacked his historical perspective and depth.

An even more challenging test to the presidency came when it was secured by the Republican party in the Eisenhower era. The Republicans in power, however, proved as little able to curtail the

[39] While the Bricker amendment was being considered, a penetrating analysis of its implications was written by Henry Steele Commager in "The Perilous Folly of Senator Bricker," *The Reporter*, IX, 6 (October 13, 1953), 12–17.

presidency as they were the role of government itself. Eisenhower, it is true, did enter office determined to reinforce the traditional separation of powers between the executive and the legislature, which he felt had become blurred by an overly energetic presidency. However, the responsibility of office, the basic facts of political life, and the realization that history could not be undone forced him to approach closer with each succeeding year to the model of the strong presidency. For example, Eisenhower began his term opposed to the practice, which had become institutionalized under Truman, of the president's handing Congress its basic legislative agenda for the year. Yet within a short time, the members of his administration came to the conclusion that the presentation of such a detailed program was the only feasible means by which the executive branch could deal with the legislative.[40]

THE ELECTORAL COLLEGE

The parallel development of the new presidency and the new political system has not been a fortuitous one since they were both products of the same historical pressures. Similarly, the modern presidency has been justifiably identified with the nation's urban population, those most directly involved with these pressures.

As is the case with Congress' relation to the rural areas, the chief reason for the identification of the presidency with the cities is found in the manner of its election. Since the Electoral College allots each state electoral votes according to the number of its congressmen and senators, it does accord an extra weight to the sparsely populated states because they are given a minimum of three votes. Thus, they do have a theoretical comparative advantage over the other states.[41] In practice, however, the Electoral College operates to the advantage of the heavily populated states since the candidate who receives a popular plurality in a state

[40] Richard E. Neustadt, "Presidency and Legislation: Planning the President's Program," *American Political Science Review*, XLIX, 4 (December, 1955), 980–1021.

[41] Senator Paul Douglas, speech in Senate, March 26, 1956, *Congressional Record*, Vol. 102, pt. 4 (Washington, D.C.: U.S. Government Printing Office, 1956), pp. 5562–5563.

receives the total of its electoral votes. The stakes in the presidential election, therefore, lie in the most populous states, such as California, New York, Pennsylvania, and Illinois, since victories there will largely determine the election result.

As can be surmised from the very number of their people, these states tend to be heavily urban—even though there is, of course, no perfect correlation between size of population and urbanism. Lewis Froman, Jr. has pointed out that the eleven most populous states in 1960, whose electoral vote by itself could give a presidential candidate a majority of one, had a mean 77.7 per cent of their population classified as urban. On the other hand, all of the other states had a comparable mean of only 57.3 per cent. Furthermore, these eleven most populous states have a more competitive two-party system than the other states (73 per cent of them are classified as of the two-party variety, whereas only 49 per cent of the others so qualify).[42]

Thus, within the populous states, the fate of their presidential contests since 1932 has usually been decided in the cities, and often in the one largest city of the state. The presidential campaign, therefore, not only centers upon these states, but the brunt of its appeal is aimed at the population of their metropolitan areas. The president is, thus, sensitive to the interests and demands of the citizens of New York, Chicago, Los Angeles, and other large cities.

The modern character of the presidency and its commitment to urban interests often form an underlying theme in reforms proposed for the Electoral College. Most of these proposals, particularly the least likely possibility of direct majority election, can plausibly be defended on the grounds of securing the most direct and true reflection of the country's character. This defense, however, loses much of its validity when examined within the context of the entire political structure. Power in choosing the president is now, as we have seen, an urban countervailing force to the rural-dominated Congress. The groups that are politically rebuffed by the static nature of the legislature receive some compensation from their added power in choosing the executive. A rough and ready, practical balance of power, therefore, becomes apparent,

[42] Lewis A. Froman, Jr., *People and Politics: An Analysis of the American Political System* (Englewood Cliffs, N.J.: Prentice-Hall, 1962), p. 88.

even though this is not quite what the Founding Fathers had in mind when they thought that they were applying it in the formulation of the apparatus of government. Consequently, any change in this urban advantage in the presidency without a corresponding change in the rural bias of Congress would have thrown the whole political balance heavily on the side of the rural areas.

This antiurban theme emerged in full force in the Mundt-Coudert version of reform that would have retained the electoral system but would have had one elector chosen by each congressional district.[43] This method would have allegedly eliminated the friction resulting from the difference in political attitudes between the Congress and the president by having them both derive their authority from the same constituencies. This objective was to be attained, however, by rendering the presidency as rurally oriented as the then malapportioned House of Representatives. Thus, the metropolitan areas would have rather cynically been deprived of any governmental organ in which their interests would be accorded adequate representation.

These urban criticisms of a change in the mode of electing the president will be significantly weakened if the Supreme Court's reapportionment decisions, particularly *Wesberry* v. *Sanders,* change the composition of the House of Representatives to correspond to the country's metropolitan orientation.

Yet, even such a change in the character of Congress might not eliminate misgivings about the effects of these proposals. For example, the most likely form of electoral reform, the proposed Lodge-Gossett amendment, would retain the electoral votes of the states but divide them in proportion to the party vote; that is, a party that received 60 per cent of the state's popular vote would receive a commensurate 60 per cent of its electoral vote. The retention of the electoral votes would preserve the advantage of the states with a very small population, while its division would remove the benefits to the very large ones. We noted earlier the correlation between a state's population, its urban character, and its party competitiveness. Thus, the margin of a party's victory would be higher relatively, and even absolutely in many instances, in a

---

[43] The definitive attack upon electoral reform proposals was made by Senator Douglas in his Senate speech of March 26, 1956, *op. cit.,* pp. 5535–5574, esp. pp. 5553–5574.

small one-party state than in a large one in which the two parties usually battled on somewhat even terms. As a result, the election campaign might well concentrate upon the one-party states with their static economy and population mold. This would be an especially unfortunate development at the present time when one of the healthiest currents in our political life is the release of many states from semipermanent one-party domination. This trend might be arrested and even reversed if electoral advantages could still accrue to one-partyism.

THE FUTURE OF THE PRESIDENCY

Less likely than a change in the nature of the president's constituency through enactment of such a reform is a diminution of the office itself since both the character and the strength of the presidency are in great degree the product of irreversible historical forces that have changed the face and substance of American society. Indeed, so impressed are we with the problems facing a president that a modern political scientist, Herman Finer, feels that the nature and dimensions of the office have gone beyond the limits and capacity of one human being:

The quality of the government of the American nation is staked almost entirely on a gamble—the gamble of the sufficiency of one man's personal qualities of mind and character and physique, pitted against the appalling tasks that history has thrust on the office of the President of the United States. It is an intolerable hazard by every criterion, decision-efficiency or democratic responsibility.[44]

He suggests some form of sharing this awesome authority that would be closer to the collective responsibility of the British cabinet.[45] Despite the rigor of Finer's analysis of the presidential predicament and the reasonableness of his solution, he failed to acknowledge the difficulty of diffusing presidential power and responsibility when their concentration had been formed by basic historical trends.

Although one can recognize the almost inexorable character of the historical forces which have shaped the modern presidency,

[44] Herman Finer, *The Presidency: Crisis and Regeneration, An Essay in Possibilities* (Chicago: University of Chicago Press, 1960), p. vi.
[45] *Ibid.*, esp. ch. V–VII.

one can also have misgivings about such a concentration of power. One can regret that this trend was accelerated and intensified by the commitment to an older society by part of the political structure. As a result, the drastic countervailing force of a powerful national executive became necessary in order that the country's population might secure a realistic awareness of its problems and some degree of relief.

Apprehension is increased, moreover, by the rather casual way in which men are recruited for such a responsible office. Individuals have been considered for the presidency and have even run for it with only limited political experience—and some with none at all. Thus, our system stands out in contrast to others in which men can achieve positions of high leadership only after having had much training in the lower rungs of the governmental apparatus. In Great Britain, for example, a person appointed prime minister has generally been in the public eye for many years and has held a number of ministerial posts.[46]

Admittedly, experience should not be considered the sole, or even the overriding, criterion for the highest public office. More than one mediocrity has bobbed to the surface in the flow of British politics. At times, the ascent up the party's hierarchical ladder can drain out the very qualities of character and ability that are the most essential for the executive task. Moreover, one must fully realize that the unique nature of the office renders suitable training for it a somewhat fanciful conception. Some of our presidents with the most varied backgrounds in public life, such as Buchanan, have proven failures. Even Madison was a unsuccessful president despite the fact that he had been an influential legislator, secretary of state, and "father of the Constitution," no less. Similarly, some presidents with a rather meager prior public record have proven extremely effective; the classic case, of course, was that of Lincoln. Even Wendell Willkie, a thoroughly fresh personality on the political scene, who did not win the election, possessed remarkable talents and generated new ideas. One can easily acknowledge, therefore, that political expe-

---

[46] See Finer's contrast between the chanciness of the American system of choosing chief executives and the virtual guarantee of experience of the British system. *Ibid.*, ch. VI.

rience per se is no more a guarantee of a great president than judicial experience is assurance of a great Supreme Court justice because the peculiar demands of each office really transcend any other type of experience.

With all due recognition to these reservations, however, there is still no more valid test for judging a man's capabilities for our highest office than from his past record. The longer and more varied his previous career, the more evidence we have for our judgments about his intellectual powers, his political and administrative talents, and the general tenor of his convictions. The choice of a president with little experience may prove a very successful gamble. "But success in a lottery is no argument for lotteries," wrote Bagehot, in refusing to admit the wisdom of our method of naming presidents, despite Lincoln's victory in 1860.[47]

Our unsystematic and sporting attitude toward presidential nominations is also exhibited by our easy acceptance of the virtual ending of the political careers of many of our defeated presidential candidates. Our prodigal use of political talent clearly differs from British practice. By their cabinet system, when a party is defeated in a parliamentary election, its leader is not dismissed automatically. The very fact that a man has worked his way up to the top of his party is accepted as evidence that he still has a great deal to offer in public affairs. He remains in the center of political life, the leader of the opposition in Parliament, always ready to command the party in the next election contest.

In our system, however, we feel no such necessity for hoarding our political leadership. Thus, a man may secure the presidential nomination and be considered by almost half the country as the most fitting individual to lead it; but with his defeat, unless already in another office, he will be relegated to private life. After losing their chance to head the nation, Stevenson in 1952 and 1956 and Nixon in 1960 were forced to take the alternative of practicing private law. The turn of fate to either greatness or near obscurity can be as sudden as the contrast between the two alternatives is sharp. The wasteful obsolescence of our political leadership, therefore, aptly complements its casual recruiting.

The very forces, therefore, of mechanization, cultural unity,

[47] Walter Bagehot, *The English Constitution*, "The World's Classics" (London: Oxford University Press, 1949), p. 28.

and democracy that have been instrumental in shaping the nature of the presidency and in increasing its powers and responsibilities to overwhelming heights have possibly by their combination limited our effectiveness in discovering, training, and utilizing the most capable men in political life for this post. Our lack of concern derives partially from a rather optimistic reading of American history, particularly in respect to the presidency. Indeed, even this work's emphasis upon how the basic characteristics of our recent history and the nature of the modern office have rendered unlikely individuals competent or outstanding presidents might lead to the mistaken fatalistic view that "the office makes the man." There can be no guarantee, however, despite the implications of some political commentators and scholars, that divine forces watch protectingly in the wings of our political conventions and, with an unseen hand, guide the deliberations of the delegates through what appears to be blind chance and petty maneuvering to the predestined choice of "the best man" as our potential national leader. The individual with the best organized convention team and the most advanced walkie-talkie system may not be the best for the country. The imposing authority of Napoleon to the contrary, God is not on the side of the biggest battalions, politically no more than militarily.

It was once common practice at the conventions for windy orators to exclaim that the peoples of the world were watching their proceedings with rapt attention and that their deliberations would be recognized as of historic importance on every continent. It was all good sport, taken seriously by no one, least of all the speakers themselves. The sport, fortunately or not, is over. The world *is* watching, not completely without misgivings, the proceedings of our conventions because the lives of hundreds of millions may be directly affected. With the fate of the world hinging so largely upon the quality of our political leadership, however, there should surely be no reservations about our seeking the very best of which we are capable. When one British periodical was assessing the claims of the leading presidential contenders in 1960, it acknowledged that they were all competent men. "But the United States," it added, "does not need a competent President. She needs a great one—and so does the world." [48]

[48] *Manchester Guardian Weekly*, LXXXII, 10 (March 10, 1960), 1.

Chapter VI

The Supreme Court and Judicial Review

In our analysis of the dynamics of American politics, we have seen how the legislature has become increasingly conservative and how the executive, partially as a reaction to this role of the legislature, has become increasingly liberal. Within the general tension between these two branches that represent the basic conflict between stability and change which every society continuously endures, our court system, particularly the Supreme Court, plays an extraordinary and highly significant role. Its main function is nothing less than the resolution of this conflict. "Law must be stable," wrote Roscoe Pound, "and yet it cannot stand still. Hence all thinking about law has struggled to reconcile the conflicting demands of the need of stability and the need of change." [1] Despite its recognition by legal scholars and political scientists, this role has seldom been explicitly acknowledged by the public, even though the Court has generally been accorded great respect and has acquired a prestige and influence unequaled by the chief judicial bodies of other countries. This respect has been given the Court not for its true role, but rather for a purported, quasi-mystical one, quite alien to the secular, pragmatic character of our political institutions.

This confusion as to the Court's function derives from the fact that it resolves the conflict between stability and change by interpreting the Constitution. In this interpretation, it eventually reflects the basic influences of the time by generally upholding the

[1] Roscoe Pound, *Interpretations of Legal History* (New York: Macmillan, 1923), p. 1.

[182]

interests of the country's leading social and economic forces and the demands of its dominant political majority. In the process, it reflects as well the prevailing intellectual theories of each particular period. Thus, the Court meets what Holmes called "the felt necessities of the time" by responding to change and acquiescing to the stable and insistent needs of the people.[2]

The Court responds to these pressures in a fundamentally different manner from the other branches of government. The President and Congress can explicitly state that they are acting because of the demands of the moment and that they are reflecting the popular will. This the Court cannot do. It must rather justify change not in terms of contemporary necessities, but in the words of a constitution drafted in 1787. This is possible because the Constitution's lucidity and simplicity of expression does not conflict with a useful broadness and ambiguity of meaning. The Court thus has the opportunity of shaping this remarkably malleable material according to the prevailing political, social, economic, and intellectual views.

The Court's function, therefore, is not only to adjust to change, but to sanction it in terms of the Constitution, thereby preserving the existing institutional machinery. This function fosters the myth that the Court pursues no political or policy-making function, but merely examines the words of the Constitution to determine whether a particular law is valid. The classic statement of this myth was presented with unmistakable simplicity by Justice Owen Roberts in the majority opinion in *United States* v. *Butler:*

There should be no misunderstanding as to the function of this court in such a case. It is sometimes said that the court assumes a power to overrule or control the action of the people's representatives. This is a misconception. The Constitution is the supreme law of the land ordained and established by the people. All legislation must conform to the principles it lays down. When an act of Congress is appropriately challenged in the courts as not conforming to the constitutional mandate the judicial branch of the government has only one duty,—to lay the article of the Constitution which is invoked beside the statute which is challenged and to decide whether the latter squares with the

[2] Oliver Wendell Holmes, Jr., *The Common Law* (Boston: Little, Brown, 1881), p. 1.

former. All the court does, or can do, is to announce its considered judgment upon the question. The only power it has, *if such it may be called*, is the power of judgment. This court neither approves nor condemns any legislative policy. Its delicate and difficult office is to ascertain and declare whether the legislation is in accordance with, or in contravention of, the provisions of the Constitution; and having done that, its duty ends.[3]

Roberts' statement, written in 1936 when the Court was deeply immersed in controversy, was challenged in a blistering dissent by one of his colleagues, Justice Harlan Fiske Stone, who said that the Court was giving "a tortured construction of the Constitution" as it sat "in judgment on the wisdom of legislative action." Stone warned that "the only check" upon the judiciary's "exercise of power" was its "own sense of self-restraint." [4]

Stone's words only provoked another justice the next year, George Sutherland, to reinforce Roberts' view on the Court's function:

The suggestion that the only check upon the exercise of the judicial power, when properly invoked, to declare a constitutional right superior to an unconstitutional statute is the judge's own faculty of self-restraint, is both ill-considered and mischievous. Self-restraint belongs in the domain of will and not of judgment. The check upon the judge is that imposed by his oath of office, by the Constitution and by his own conscientious and informed convictions; and since he has the duty to make up his own mind and adjudge accordingly, it is hard to see how there could be any other restraint. . . .

. . . . .

It is urged that the question involved [the constitutionality of state minimum wage laws] should now receive fresh consideration, among other reasons, because of "the economic conditions which have supervened"; but the meaning of the Constitution does not change with the ebb and flow of economic events. We frequently are told in more general words that the Constitution must be construed in the light of the present. If by that it is meant that the Constitution is made up of living words that apply to every new condition which they include, the statement is quite true. But to say, if that be intended, that the words of the Constitution mean today what they did not mean when written—that is, that they do not apply to a situation now to which

[3] *United States* v. *Butler*, 297 U.S. 1, 62–63 (1937), author's italics.
[4] *Ibid.*, 79, 87, dissenting opinion.

they would have applied then—is to rob that instrument of the essential element which continues it in force as the people have made it until they, and not their official agents, have made it otherwise. . . .

. . . . .

The judicial function is that of interpretation; it does not include the power of amendment under the guise of interpretation. To miss the point of difference between the two is to miss all that the phrase "supreme law of the land" stands for and to convert what was intended as inescapable and enduring mandates into mere moral reflections.[5]

According to this myth, sharply etched by the absolute language of Roberts and Sutherland, the Constitution under which we live today is the same document, save for formal additions, that was drafted and approved in the late eighteenth century. Therefore, no matter how profound the manifestations of social and economic change and no matter how much at odds with anything the Founding Fathers could ever have imagined, the Court's role is to declare, "Ah yes, this is, of course, justified under the words of the Constitution. Rest assured! We are still operating under its wise, benevolent, and prescient wisdom."

The judicial myth has always had its doubters and skeptics. Many found it difficult to share the Court's apparently ingenuous view that it was but the humble and powerless servant of a glorious and wise Constitution. It smacked too much of Gilbert and Sullivan's Lord Chancellor's statement after his effusive praise of the law: "And I, my lords, embody the law." Justice Holmes, who consistently deflated his colleagues' bland presumptuousness throughout his career on the Court, once quoted an early eighteenth-century bishop upon the power of those who "merely" interpret: "Whoever hath an absolute authority to interpret any written or spoken laws, it is he who is truly the lawgiver, to all intents and purposes, and not the person who first wrote or spoke them." [6]

[5] *West Coast Hotel Co.* v. *Parrish*, 300 U.S. 379, 402–404 (1937). Here, however, Sutherland was speaking for a conservative minority rather than a majority.

[6] Holmes' quotation from Bishop Hoadly is found in James B. Thayer, "The Origin and Scope of the American Doctrine of Constitutional Law," *Harvard Law Review*, VII (1893), 129.

The myth becomes vulnerable when the Court divides, thus presenting diametrically opposite opinions as to what the Constitution really states. These divisions, at times, embitter the personal relationship between the justices precisely because they are assumed only to be reading the words of the Constitution and not presenting their own political views. In the more genial ambiance of Congress, legislators debate about which policy is the wiser or the more expedient, usually recognizing that reasonable men can differ and fallible men can be wrong. When the justices divide, however, they are not supposed to differ upon what is wise or expedient, but rather upon what the words of the Constitution mean. Thus, the justice finds himself closeted in the same room with colleagues who cannot comprehend what such simple words like *liberty* or *equality* mean, words which any reasonable man— let alone a member of the Supreme Court—should be able to understand. In this environment, discussion is often ineffective because these words are really the keys to an individual's basic political, social, and economic philosophy. The judicial atmosphere can thus become charged and tempers triggered to the point of explosion. "Perhaps no discussions in the world," Arthur Schlesinger, Jr., has written, "proceed at higher intellectual tension." Indeed, Justice Robert Jackson once even raised doubts about the rationality of the majority of his colleagues when he wrote in a searing dissent: "Today's judgment will be more interesting to students of psychology and of the judicial processes than to students of constitutional law." [7]

If the judicial myth is jarred when the Court is divided, it is even more shaken when it reverses itself, especially within a short span of time. Such a shift naturally raises fundamental questions about the nature of judicial review. If the Constitution means one thing in one generation or one decade and the opposite the next, can it be considered as having *a* meaning which the Supreme Court can discover? At such times, it strains credulity to insist that the Court is not involved in determining policy and that its role is solely a passive, apolitical, interpretative one. The criticism is then voiced that the highest branch of the judiciary is a legisla-

[7] Arthur M. Schlesinger, Jr., "The Supreme Court: 1947," *Fortune*, XXXV (January, 1947), 73; *Zorach* v. *Clauson*, 343 U.S. 306, 325 (1952), dissenting opinion.

ture as well as a court—and a super-legislature, at that, because it enters the legislative contest only after the Congress and the president have already played their hands.

The image of nine appointed men (or, more exactly, five of the nine) decisively influencing the basic policy decisions of the nation theoretically ought to be an unsettling one for a democracy. How can such a body, not responsible to any other branch of government and apparently immune from the currents of public opinion, operate in this way in a country so consciously democratic?

The anomalous position of the Court and its supporting myth in our political system is primarily comprehensible in terms of the judicial function of achieving a harmony between the forces of stability and change. Despite obvious facts to the contrary, the myth that the Court does not make policy has endured because it fulfills a basic need of our national political psyche. We desire the reassurance of permanence and continuity afforded by a stable political structure, but, at the same time, we want the advantage of its ready adjustment to social and economic change, in order to satisfy our wants.

The Court, in attempting to reconcile opposite tendencies, is faced with an inordinately difficult and often thankless task because it cannot completely resolve the tension of these conflicting forces. At times, the Court has been criticized for being too radical, for taking too advanced a political position, or for acquiescing too readily to the transitory popular will. Thus, it is attacked for breaking too sharply with the past and for undermining the stability of the institutional structure by destroying a sense of continuity. The Warren Court, with its decisions on civil rights, civil liberties, apportionment, and school prayers, has been subjected to this line of criticism. The sense of breaking with the past may have been felt even more sharply during the Roosevelt administration when the Court took a markedly liberal turn after the Court-packing controversy. At that time, Justice Roberts, the last of the conservative majority of the "nine old men," shook his head sadly at the reversals of past precedents. When the Court declared in 1944 in the case of *Smith* v. *Allwright* that, contrary to a previous decision, the white primary was unconstitutional, in a lone dissent, Roberts expressed the fear that Supreme Court decisions would be placed in the same category "as a restricted railroad ticket, good for this day and train only." "I have no assurance," he wrote, "in view of current decisions, that the opinion announced today may not shortly be repudiated and overruled by justices who deem they have new light on the subject." [8]

The Court, however, has more often been attacked from the opposite side, for being too conservative in preventing the popular majority will from being carried out and in laggardly adjusting to current social and economic needs. The Court is then pictured as being so enveloped in the dry abstractions of constitutional language that it has lost touch with the real world. Felix Frankfurter, well before his own appointment to the Supreme Court, once wrote a withering blast against an opinion of Chief Justice Taft in a labor case: "For all the regard that the Chief Justice of the United States pays to the facts of industrial life, he might as well have written this opinion as Chief Justice of the Fiji Islands." [9]

In placing side by side both sets of the Court's critics, we can observe that, in balancing change and stability, it can easily be accused of listing too much to one side or the other. What stands out, however, is that the Court has, in the long run, adjusted to the country's basic changes in a manner that has preserved our feeling of adherence to the Constitution. This has usually meant that the views of the majority have eventually been rationalized in terms of our fundamental law. Robert Dahl rightly believes that the bestowal of this "legitimacy" is, in essence, the Court's main function. [10]

There is little mystery behind this rapport between the Supreme Court and the majority of the people. The justices are, after all, appointed by presidents who do represent this majority. It is, thus, reasonable to assume that truly stable political majorities will be reflected by similar majorities on the Court, that a

[8] *Smith* v. *Allwright*, 321 U.S. 649, 669 (1944), dissenting opinion.

[9] Felix Frankfurter, "The Same Mr. Taft," *New Republic*, XXVII (1921), 230–231; quoted by Max Lerner, ed., *The Mind and Faith of Justice Holmes: His Speeches, Essays, Letters and Judicial Opinions* (Garden City, N.H.: Halcyon House, 1943, 1948), p. 157.

[10] Robert A. Dahl, "Decision-making in a Democracy: The Role of the Supreme Court as a National Policy-maker," *Journal of Public Law*, VI (1957), 294.

prolonged liberal or conservative trend will eventually result in a liberal or conservative Court. Mr. Dooley, Finley Peter Dunne's fictional saloon-keeper about the turn of the century, said with his customary sagacity that "the Supreme Court follows the election returns." [11] This does not mean, of course, that the justices change their minds according to the result of an election or that they consciously consider themselves representatives of the majority will. It does mean rather that presidents tend to name justices whose basic political philosophy and general line of constitutional interpretation, as far as can be gathered from their previous record and background, is similar to their own.

This majoritarian influence upon the Court by presidential appointment cannot be direct or infallible. Liberal presidents have been known to appoint conservative justices, and conservative presidents have acted in a similar contrary fashion. In addition, the opinions of some justices have not been what was generally expected at the time of their appointment. Thus, the president, in making his judicial choice, is in a position as potentially ironic as it may be decisive. Once appointed and confirmed, the justice cannot be removed because the president disagrees with the pattern of his opinions. Indeed, he may well remain on the bench long after the chief executive has left office. "The good that Presidents do is often interred with their administration," wrote *The Nation*. "It is their choice of Supreme Court justices that lives after them." [12]

The possible unpredictability of a justice's record on the Court is not the only element of chance with which a president must contend. Although Dahl has calculated that, throughout our history, an average of two Supreme Court appointments have been made each presidential term, there is no guarantee as to how many justices a president will actually have the opportunity to appoint since this is decided by the vagaries of retirement or

---

[11] Finley Peter Dunne, *Mr. Dooley at His Best,* ed. Elmer Ellis (New York: Scribner's, 1938), p. 77. The present author has taken the liberty, in deference to an age less familiar with and less tolerant of dialect humor, to present Mr. Dooley's words in recognizable English.

[12] Editorial, *The Nation,* January 14, 1939, p. 52, quoted in Marian D. Irish and James W. Prothro, *The Politics of American Democracy,* 3d ed. (Englewood Cliffs, N.J.: Prentice-Hall, 1965), p. 479.

death.[13] Thus, popular majorities can conceivably wait for a considerable period of time before their outlook can be reflected on the Court.

The Court is usually cognizant of the popular majority's opinion even in those instances where it does not follow it. When it finds itself in disagreement with both the president and Congress, it will generally move warily to deflect from a direct confrontation or to avoid contact altogether. It thus recognizes that its influence, great and even decisive, is seldom exerted effectively when in direct opposition to the political arms of government.[14] It is outmatched because it lacks their power and the authority they derive from popular sovereignty. Its members thereby heed the advice of the British jurist, Francis Bacon: "Let them [judges] be lions, but yet lions under the throne." [15]

The justices have usually been aware of the necessity of adaptability. "The Court must sail by the wind," wrote Charles Curtis, Jr., "as well as by the stars." [16] Over the years it has developed a goodly number of justifications for judicial self-restraint, for not passing judgment. It thus has at hand a whole armory of tactical devices for trimming its sails and avoiding the overwhelming waves of popular disapproval. At times, they will be used to gain a breathing spell for a quieter period. The Court, for example, has the power, through the writ of certiorari, of determining the great majority of cases it is going to hear. It can thus, when judgment might prove uncomfortable, refuse to have cases come before it, and, moreover, state no reason for its refusal.[17] Finley Peter Dunne's Mr. Dooley had little sympathy

[13] Dahl, *A Preface to Democratic Theory* (Chicago: University of Chicago Press, 1956), p. 110.

[14] Dahl, "Decision-making in a Democracy," pp. 279–295.

[15] Cited in Charles P. Curtis, Jr., *Lions under the Throne* (Boston: Houghton Mifflin, 1947), p. 165.

[16] *Ibid.*, p. 324.

[17] For an illuminating study of the Court's self-serving use of judicial self-restraint, see John P. Roche, "Judicial Self-restraint," *American Political Science Review*, XLIX (September, 1955), 762–772. One of Roche's sharpest attacks is upon the Court's use (or misuse) of the writ of certiorari. In a footnote on p. 766, he cites a series of articles, coauthored by Professor Fowler Harper, running in the *University of Pennsylvania Law Review* from December, 1950, to February, 1954, and entitled "What the Supreme Court

with the dilatory attitude of the Court toward pressing problems: "If you are looking for a game of quick decisions and base hits, you have got to have another umpire. It never gives a decision till the crowd has dispersed and the players have packed their bats in the bags and started for home." [18]

The Court has also avoided judgment in a number of cases by labeling them "political" and claiming that their nature rendered them suitable for settlement only by the political arms of government. The Court, for example, sidestepped apportionment cases for years on the plausible grounds that there were fewer subjects more steeped in politics than the composition of a legislature.[19] More than one analyst of these "political" cases has come to the conclusion that they actually had no common objective character except their avoidance by the Court.[20]

Even if the Court should hear a case involving a major principle of contention, there is no certainty that it will declare itself on that issue. Often, when the country has wondered how the Court would act in a highly charged or particularly delicate situation, it has confounded predictions by deciding the case on the basis of some minor legal point or procedural technicality.[21] It has then stated that it is only a court of law that decides individual cases and that it always avoids, if possible, judging upon broader, substantive issues. "This Court reaches constitutional issues last, not first," Justice Frankfurter once tartly instructed a lawyer arguing before it.[22] This position would receive a great deal more respect if one were not aware of the many times

Did Not Do in the 1949 Term" to "What the Supreme Court Did Not Do during the 1952 Term."

[18] Dunne, op. cit., p. 73.

[19] See Frankfurter's argument in Colegrove v. Green, 328 U.S. 549, 553–554 (1946).

[20] Jack W. Peltason, Federal Courts in the Political Process (New York: Random House, 1955), p. 10; Roche, op. cit., p. 768.

[21] Two such cases were Hirabayashi v. United States, 320 U.S. 93 (1943), in which the Court dodged the question of the wartime evacuation of Americans of Japanese descent from the West Coast, and Peters v. Hobby, 340 U.S. 341 (1955), in which it similarly avoided the issue of the constitutionality of the use of secret witnesses in loyalty hearings. See Roche, op. cit., pp. 768–769, 772.

[22] Quoted in C. Herman Pritchett, Congress versus the Supreme Court— 1957–1960 (Minneapolis: University of Minnesota Press, 1961), p. 99.

that the Court could have decided cases on limited grounds but gratuitously declared itself on major policy questions.

The conception of a Supreme Court reflecting the majority view, or at least bending with it, is at odds with the more common image of a stubborn conservative Court blocking the flow of progress demanded by an insistent popular majority. Modern reexaminations of the Court's history, however, have convincingly shown that there have actually been very few periods when it has openly challenged a stable political majority.[23] Those majorities that have been checked by the judiciary have proven upon inspection to lack the requisite strength and character. Its record, Dahl states, justifies the expectation "that the Court is least likely to be successful in blocking a determined and persistent lawmaking majority on a major policy and most likely to succeed against a 'weak' majority; e.g., a dead one, a transient one, a fragile one, or one weakly united upon a policy of subordinate importance." [24] A determined stable political majority will, therefore, in the long run be able to carry out its will. As Alpheus Thomas Mason has written: "In a free society all governing institutions must ultimately respond to the dominant political forces of the country as revealed at the ballot box." [25]

In discussing the Court's eventual adjustment to the popular will, it is difficult to avoid the phrase "in the long run." Edward S. Corwin declared: "In the long run the majority is entitled to have its way, and *the run must not be too long either.*" [26] It can, however, mean a considerable length of time which may try the patience of many persons. John Maynard Keynes, in his exasperation at its use in economics, made the classic rebuttal: "In the long run, we will all be dead." There is no question that the phrase can easily be used insensitively to excuse or rationalize

[23] Robert G. McCloskey categorically states: "At no time in its history has the Court been able to maintain a position squarely opposed to a strong popular majority." See his *The American Supreme Court, 1789–1960* (Chicago: University of Chicago Press, 1960), pp. 23, 196.

[24] Dahl, "Decision-making in a Democracy," p. 286.

[25] Alpheus Thomas Mason, *The Supreme Court: Palladium of Freedom* (Ann Arbor: University of Michigan Press, 1962), p. 148.

[26] Edward S. Corwin, *Court over Constitution: A Study of Judicial Review as an Instrument of Popular Government* (Princeton: Princeton University Press, 1938), p. 127.

present injustices. For example, in 1918 the Court, in the case of *Hammer* v. *Dagenhart*, declared unconstitutional the federal law prohibiting the use of child labor in the production of goods involved in interstate commerce. When the Court changed its position in 1941 and held, in *United States* v. *Darby*, that such a prohibition was constitutional, a bitter question was raised as to "how the Court could make up for the 'stunted minds and broken lives' of children whom it had surrendered to exploitation in the years since 1918." [27]

Despite its limitations, "the long run" is a necessary perspective for the historian, and we must thus recognize that the Court's eventual response to popular needs and demands is the dominant motif of its history. Its temporary resistance—stubborn, frustrating, stupid, and even cruel—is part of the price we pay for the Court's adherence to the previously mentioned principles of consistency and continuity. The knowledge that the Court will bend grants it the tolerance to accomplish this in its own manner and in its own time.

The Court and the Country

The Court primarily adjusts not because of any political pressures, however subtle or indirect, but rather because the justices do not live in an isolated world. Thus, the changes reflected by majority opinion are felt by them as much as by their fellow countrymen, and the most perceptive justices have acknowledged this. "Judges are men, not disembodied spirits," Justice Frankfurter pithily commented.[28] Similarly, Justice Cardozo had in an earlier period eloquently stated the relationship of judges to the rest of society: "The great tides and currents which engulf the rest of men, do not turn aside in their course, and pass the judges idly by." [29]

The receptivity of the justices to the characteristics of their so-

[27] *Hammer* v. *Dagenhart*, 247 U.S. 251 (1918); *United States* v. *Darby*, 312 U.S. 100 (1941); Lerner, *op. cit.*, p. 168.

[28] Quoted in Henry J. Abraham, *The Judicial Process: An Introductory Analysis of the Courts of the United States, England and France* (New York: Oxford University Press, 1962), p. 283.

[29] Quoted in *ibid.*, pp. 287–288.

ciety is seen most clearly when the Supreme Court of one generation overrules that of another. The members of the Court are not consciously attempting to overrule past interpretations of the Constitution in the light of new political, social, economic, and cultural forces. Rather, they read the Constitution differently because they are products of a different era, "children of their times." [30] Thus, when the Court in the late nineteenth century declared that state regulatory and social legislation violated the Fourteenth Amendment's guarantee of liberty, it was not consciously reading Herbert Spencer's extreme laissez-faire philosophy into the Constitution. It was, however, reflecting the fact that his views were the prevailing intellectual theory of the time. The justices were, thus, so "drenched" in Spencer's philosophy that they failed to realize their own commitment to it.[31] As Keynes pungently noted:

The ideas of economists and political philosophers, both when they are right and when they are wrong, are more powerful than is commonly understood. Indeed the world is ruled by little else. Practical men, who believe themselves to be quite exempt from any intellectual influences, are usually the slaves of some defunct economist.[32]

When the Supreme Court of the later New Deal upheld legislation similar to what it had previously invalidated, a similar process was at play. In interpreting the word *liberty*, the justices were unconsciously reflecting the changed political, economic, social, and intellectual climate of the country. America's attitude toward free enterprise and its concept of property had changed through the experience of the depression and decades of industrialism. When the justices accepted an expanded role for government in the economy as constitutional, they were not purposely reading Keynes' *General Theory of Employment, Interest and Money* into the Constitution, but rather were living in a society in which the basic principles of economics were being uprooted by his theory. If a work could possibly be the most influential of the generation, it must be assumed that it left its mark upon the Court as well.

[30] McCloskey, *op. cit.*, p. 182.   [31] Curtis, *op. cit.*, p. 332.
[32] John Maynard Keynes, *The General Theory of Employment, Interest and Money* (New York: Harcourt, Brace, 1936), p. 383.

We shall later examine a similar situation when the Court shifted its position on racial segregation, upholding its validity in the 1890's and declaring it unconstitutional in the 1950's. In each instance, its interpretation of the word *equal* in the Fourteenth Amendment was not a self-contained exercise in legal semantics, but rather a reflection of an age—even though the period's character, in turn, was reinforced by the Court's action.

Constitutional Adjustment

Many persons believe that the concept of the continuous re-examination and reinterpretation of the Constitution undermines the permanence of our basic values and the stability of our institutions. To them, a constitution that is constantly having new meaning read into it is really no constitution at all. They want the Supreme Court to relieve the pressures of doubt and uncertainty upon all government officials by giving *the* permanent, authoritative interpretation of the Constitution and thus settling all issues once and for all.

It is possible to understand, therefore, why in the midthirties, a time when the Court's decisions were subjects of bitter political controversy, as eminent a constitutional scholar as Robert Cushman could present a plan which attempted to still all doubts about judicial interpretation.

This proposal is that we adopt clarifying amendments to the Constitution which will sharpen the meaning of its clauses, make clear the scope of its delegations of power, and the impact of its limitations. The Court in construing the commerce clause or the due process clause is engaged in making broad decisions of policy which do not properly belong to a judicial body. We could relieve it of that power by clarifying those clauses so that their meaning and application is no longer a matter of honest dispute. If we wish to make sure that the power of Congress under the commerce clause includes the regulation of laboring conditions under which goods are made for the interstate market, then let us say so with definiteness and precision. If we are tired of having the due process of law clause used by conservative judges to throttle needed social legislation, let us make clear what we wish the due process limitation to mean, or discard it altogether. I believe we should all be better satisfied if, without impairing the integrity or the traditions of our judicial system, we left to the Court the task of applying constitutional clauses which have reasonably definite meaning, instead of attacking it for giving what we feel is the wrong meaning to clauses so vague as to have no clear and concrete meaning of their own. Our whole judicial system would gain in efficiency, and in public confidence, under such a change. . . .[33]

Despite the reasonableness of its presentation, this proposal missed much of the fundamental character of the Constitution and the genius of the system of judicial review. Of course, it is possible to clarify the Constitution and to pinpoint its phrases so clearly that confusion would be virtually eliminated as to what is or is not constitutional. What a price, however, we would pay for such precision and clarity! We would be inextricably tying our basic system of government to the needs and demands of one particular era, to the assumptions and precepts of one particular philosophy. We would be making an almost irrevocable commitment that could be changed only by drastic upheaval in the country's social and political life—and all in the name of precision and clarity.

Although the men who wrote the Constitution were unquestionably a bold and imaginative group, they refrained from legislating clearly and precisely for posterity. They rather let future generations fill in the broad outlines they had established because they recognized that they could not foresee and provide for all details. It was in this spirit that Chief Justice John Marshall emphasized the necessity of a broad interpretation of the Constitution in the Court's opinion in *McCulloch* v. *Maryland*. He counseled his fellow justices that "we must never forget, that it is a *constitution* we are expounding," one he described later in the opinion as

intended to endure for ages to come, and, consequently, to be adapted to the various *crises* of human affairs. To have prescribed the means by which government should, in all future time, execute its powers, would have been to change, entirely, the character of the instrument, and give it the properties of a legal code. It would have been an unwise attempt to provide, by immutable rules, for exigencies which, if

[33] Robert E. Cushman, "The Role of a Supreme Court in a Democratic Nation," a lecture given at the University of Illinois on March 9, 1938. Reprinted in Benjamin Munn Ziegler, ed., *Desegregation and the Supreme Court* (Boston: Heath, 1958), pp. 33–34.

foreseen at all, must have been seen dimly, and which can be best provided for as they occur.[34]

A sharp distinction can be drawn between the temporary and the permanent aspects of the political attitudes of the Founding Fathers (or, in a sense, between their legislative and constituent roles). One of the most important provisions in the Constitution gave Congress the power to regulate interstate commerce. Thanks to John Marshall's broad interpretation in *Gibbons* v. *Ogden* of the provision's key words—*regulate, interstate,* and *commerce*—much vigorous and extensive governmental activity has stemmed from this simple phrase. In no sense, however, does this mean that the Founding Fathers or John Marshall ever expressed themselves in favor of any later specific applications of it.

Alexander Hamilton, for example, with his meager concern for the sensitivity of the states, was probably the individual at the Philadelphia Constitutional Convention with the most farsighted vision of the potential extension of national powers. Yet even this extreme nationalizer stated that agriculture was an example of a subject which could not conceivably fall under national regulation.[35] In excluding agriculture, Hamilton was speaking more in the character of a legislator than a constitutional drafter, a man whose vision of the future, despite its breadth, was still limited by his contemporary world, in which the farmer, working his plot of land, was the epitome of localism, the man in society furthest removed from the flow of interstate commerce.

In the twentieth century, agriculture largely lost its localistic character and became enmeshed in not only interstate, but international, commerce as well. The Court of the early New Deal period, as we shall see, was an exceptional one in our judicial history because of its adamant refusal to recognize the basic reality of American life. It thus virtually insisted that agriculture had been a local activity, was then a local activity, and would remain one ad infinitum. "It does not help to declare," wrote the Court in 1936, "that local [agricultural] conditions throughout the nation have created a situation of national concern; for this is but to say that whenever there is a widespread similarity of local conditions, Congress may ignore constitutional limitations upon its powers

[34] *McCulloch* v. *Maryland,* 4 Wheat. 316, 407, 415 (1819).
[35] Alexander Hamilton, *The Federalist,* Number 17.

and usurp those reserved to the states." Similarly, it declared the same year that "the local character of mining, of manufacturing, and of crop growing is a fact, and remains a fact, whatever may be done with the products." [36]

The Court made a sharp shift from this obdurate position and within a short time recognized the character of agriculture in a highly interrelated economy, barely imaginable a century and a half before. Indeed, the Court moved so far as to declare that the farmer's production came under national regulation even if none of it ever left the physical limits of his farm.[37] Thus, the Court adjusted the fixed but flexible words of the Constitution to a changing world.

The Judicial Balance

In placing this emphasis upon change, we should not overlook that the Court's balancing function requires it to adjust to change in such a manner as to preserve the concept of a permanent constitutional structure and a continuing political tradition.

One method by which the Court can achieve this is by adjusting to change more gradually and hesitantly than the rest of society. The conservatism exhibited in this time lag is an expected characteristic of the judiciary. The British legal scholar A. V. Dicey believed that judges were even more laggard than legislators in keeping abreast of prevailing intellectual currents. He wrote, "If a statute . . . is apt to reproduce the public opinion not so much of to-day as of yesterday, judge-made law occasionally represents the opinion of the day before yesterday." [38]

In accordance with this judicial conservatism, by the time the Court finally recognizes a theory, it is no longer held by the rest of society. The Court, nevertheless, defends it from the claims of newer theories, which have already been accepted by the other political institutions as well as by the universities and the journals of opinion. Thus, the Court can find its philosophical *obiter dicta*

[36] *United States* v. *Butler, op. cit.,* 74–75; *Carter* v. *Carter Coal Co.,* 298 U.S. 238, 304 (1936).

[37] See *Wickard* v. *Filburn,* 317 U.S. 111 (1942).

[38] A. V. Dicey, *Law and Public Opinion in England during the Nineteenth Century,* 2d. ed. (London: Macmillan, 1917), p. 369.

(statements in its opinion—often the most controversial and quotable—which are not necessary for the determination of the decision and are not legally binding) hailed as wisdom in one decade and hooted at in the next. The Court eventually does adjust even though these changes are acknowledged even more hesitantly than they are made.

This hesitance is not based upon perverse coyness, but rather upon the fundamental necessity that a rule of law should be applied with a rational predictability. The Court, as a result, usually shifts slowly and gradually from one position to another in order to maintain the thread of continuity, and it follows the rule of *stare decisis*, grounding its opinions upon past precedents and also creating a foundation for future decision. This process may be partially obscured by the emphasis given those instances when the Court has changed its mind by overruling a previous line of opinions or reversing a particular decision. These sharp breaks with the past, important and dramatic as they are, nevertheless, are the exceptions rather than the rule.

The Court's characteristic mode of operation is aided by the fact that issues come to its attention enveloped within the substance of particular cases. Although this dependence upon individual cases restricts the scope of its power, the advantages are patent since the Supreme Court can emphasize its role as a court rather than as a policy-making body. We have already seen how the Court can evade deciding basic issues by stating that the cases in question can be decided upon a minor point. It can justify this evasion by declaring that it is a court of law concerned with the settlement of cases per se rather than with their accompanying issues.

The greatest advantage to the Court becomes apparent when it executes one of its major shifts of constitutional principles in a gradual step-by-step approach. "An idea," McCloskey has written, "could be implied today, obliquely stated tomorrow, and flatly asserted the next day." [39] At the first stage of this process, the Court denies that it is beginning to change from a former line of binding precedents. Although Case B has been decided differently from Case A, the Court patiently explains in its opinion that, despite their similarity, the facts in one case differed

[39] McCloskey, *The American Supreme Court*, p. 36.

in some measure from those in the other. Thus, no change of principle occurred, since there were differences in two separate cases. This rationale becomes somewhat strained when the process goes one step further with a projection of the trend of change in Case C. The Court, nevertheless, stoutly insists that it is not deciding basic principles—which is not its function—but rather judging on the basis of facts.

By the time this process has fully evolved, the fiction that a change has not occurred is bankrupt. The old standard of the Court has been deserted, either unremembered or mentioned hurriedly in passing. It is at this stage that the Court will finally acknowledge its pattern of behavior by overruling the original decision and rejecting the former principle. At this point, the Court's action is in the nature of a coup de grâce since it can point for support to the unraveling of a whole skein of judicial opinions.

The Court's use of a step-by-step approach to change does not mean that it is necessarily conscious at the earlier stages as to what the ultimate conclusion of a particular line of decisions will be, and that it is thus attempting to soften the impact of a new principle by inserting it as gently as possible into the prevailing interpretation of the Constitution. The justices rather utilize this gradual method because this is the way they instinctively react.

The Court facilitates its mobility by a natural tendency to insert reservations even when it is committing itself to a particular position. These reservations may be imbedded in the text of its opinions or are closer to the surface in dissenting ones or in those majority views which are exceptions to the prevailing judicial tenor. They allow the Court, even at the point of furthest advance, to keep its rear lines open for a possible retreat.[40] If a change does occur, a workable set of precedents can be devised to support it.

The State and Free Enterprise

In the earlier analysis of American political history, we noted the radical transformation of society by the intense acceleration of industrialization after the Civil War. This powerful thrust of

[40] *Ibid., passim.*

American capitalism raised fundamental questions about the nature of individual freedom and its relationship to society. Thus, the country's population in the first postwar generation was groping for some effective accommodation of big business within the fabric of the national community. At the same time, it was also troubled by another aspect of the same problem of individual freedom and the responsibility of society, the position of the newly emancipated Negroes.

During this period, the Court pursued its usual principles of judicial adaptation to prevailing sentiments more consistently than at any other time. Its decisions faithfully reflected not only the country's ambiguity and uncertainty toward the problems of business regulation and the southern Negroes, but also a steady movement toward the eventual solution of freedom for business and the subordination of the Negroes.

This pattern of the Court's behavior is apparent in the field of business control, particularly when it grappled with the question as to whether the Fourteenth Amendment's injunction against a state's depriving "any person of life, liberty, or property without the due process of law" limited the state's power to regulate business. The importance of the issue cannot be underestimated because the Court was in effect weighing the decision as to whether to acquiesce to the momentum of industrialism or to check it in response to the interests and values of an older society. Max Lerner has validly described this era as "one of the fateful periods in our national life . . . [when the] Court stood poised between the agrarian revolt, which had been stirred by the growth of monopolistic capitalism, and the business interest whose new militancy concealed their uneasiness." [41] One can trace the hesitant step-by-step progress toward a judicial solution as the Court tread its ground carefully. First, it accepted state regulation of business activity apparently without any qualification; later, the Court continued its acceptance, but with some reservations; these reservations were later expanded and made more definite until finally state legislation was explicitly voided and the Fourteenth Amendment became a solid and virtually impenetrable check against state regulation.

Thus, in the Slaughterhouse Cases in 1873, the Court refused

[41] Cited in McCloskey, *Essays in Constitutional Law,* p. 135.

to decide against regulation because it maintained that the amendment had not changed the relationship between the state and national governments except on the question of Negro rights. In 1877, the Court similarly held aloof from invalidating state control of rates charged by grain elevators because it believed the state was justified in regulating a business in which the public had an interest.[42]

In less than two decades, however, the Court gradually shifted its position and protected business from state control. At what precise case the Court reached the turning point is a debatable question. To some, it was in 1887, when the opinion in *Mugler* v. *Kansas* limited the state police powers to a greater degree than formerly, even though the state prohibition measure at issue was accepted as constitutional. To others, the decisive year was 1888, when the Court, still upholding the states' power to fix rates—in this instance for railroads—narrowly defined and delimited the category of businesses which could be so regulated. Some might claim, however, that the decisive turning point occurred a little aside from the general pattern of these cases, when the Court explicitly stated in 1886 that the Fourteenth Amendment's guarantee to persons of "the equal protection of the laws" applied to corporations as well as individuals.[43]

There is, however, little question as to when this period of judicial transition and hesitation was terminated. In 1890, the Court carried out to the end the implications of the trend of its line of decisions toward a full-scale laissez-faire interpretation of the amendment. It declared that the reasonableness of railroad rates was a subject for final determination by the judiciary, not by a commission appointed by the legislature.[44] The Minnesota Rate decision," wrote Alpheus Thomas Mason and William Beaney, "thus completed a judicial revolution." They quoted approvingly the comments of a judge: "It is from that decision that I date the

[42] Slaughterhouse Cases, 16 Wall 36 (1873); *Munn* v. *Illinois*, 94 U.S. 113 (1877).

[43] *Mugler* v. *Kansas*, 123 U.S. 623 (1887); *Georgia Railroad and Banking Co.* v. *Smith*, 128 U.S. 174 (1888); *Santa Clara County* v. *Southern Pacific Railroad Co.*, 118 U.S. 394, 396 (1886).

[44] *Chicago, Milwaukee and St. Paul R.R. Co.* v. *Minnesota*, 134 U.S. 418 (1890).

flood." [45] The Supreme Court, therefore, ended its inner struggle and made its commitment to the encouragement of free enterprise.

The judicial period of doubt on the future of capitalistic development closed at about the same time that the country ended its own period of indecision with the establishment of a new conservative political system. The Court reflected and reinforced in the succeeding two decades the fastening of this system upon the country. Thus, in the year before the crucial election of 1896, when the forces of American politics were undergoing a fundamental realignment, the Court made two controversial decisions favorable to big business. One declared the federal income tax unconstitutional. The other seriously weakened the Sherman Antitrust Act by interpreting the congressional power of regulating interstate commerce so narrowly that a giant sugar trust eluded the scope of the law.[46] In 1905, the Court, in line with its new interpretation of the Fourteenth Amendment, not only declared unconstitutional a New York State law regulating hours of labor in the baking industry, but also characterized all laws of this nature as "mere meddlesome interferences with the rights of the individual." [47]

The Supreme Court of these decisive years came under scalding criticism not only from its contemporaries but from later legal commentators as well. Although this liberal criticism is valid, one should bear in mind, in evaluating the Court's record, that it was, as noted earlier, reflecting the dominant contemporary intellectual philosophy—indeed, if anything, lagging behind the rest of the country in accepting the extreme laissez-faire philosophy.[48] It also, in great degree, agreed with the leading economic and political interests of the time. Thus, when John Frank criticized

[45] Alpheus Thomas Mason and William M. Beaney, *American Constitutional Law: Introductory Essays and Selected Cases* (Englewood Cliffs, N.J.: Prentice-Hall, 1955), p. 387.

[46] *Pollock* v. *Farmer's Loan and Trust Company*, 158 U.S. 601 (1895); *United States* v. *E. C. Knight*, 156 U.S. 1 (1895).

[47] *Lochner* v. *New York*, 198 U.S. 45, 61 (1905).

[48] Walton H. Hamilton has emphasized how reluctantly and grudgingly it did acquiesce. See his "The Path of Due Process of Law," in Conyers Read, ed., *The Constitution Reconsidered* (New York: Columbia University Press, 1938), pp. 188–190.

the Court for its supine service to the "robber barons," he, nevertheless, asked: "Yet, can it be said that what the Court was then doing was less than what the country, or at least a large share of it, wanted?" [49]

There was, admittedly, opposition to the growing power of big business by large sections of the population, even by imposing majorities in a number of states. State Granger laws were enacted which regulated business, especially the railroads, and Congress passed similarly motivated legislation. The crosscurrents of American politics, however, prevented this feeling from being translated effectively into a stable majority coalition. The Court, therefore, can hardly be accused of running counter to a public opinion which could achieve political expression only fitfully and temporarily.

We have, thus, seen that the Supreme Court generally followed the traditional operating rules of judicial behavior in conforming to social, economic, and political changes in both the post-Civil War period when our politics was in a state of flux and indecision, and later during the crucial transition period when the new conservative political system was being successfully installed. Thus, the Court, after years of doubt, placed the full force of its authority behind the fundamental principles of the new system.

The succeeding period, when the system was in operation, proved one of the most challenging in the Court's history. The challenge was implicit in the character of the system and in the nature of the Court's function. The main purpose of the system, as we have seen, was resistance to the forces of social, economic, and political change. The Court was thus placed in an obvious dilemma. Although its function was undoubtedly to protect stable institutions, it was, at the same time, to adjust to change—yet change was not adequately reflected in the political process itself. The disadvantaged groups, by their pressure for political expression, did at times break through the conservative defenses and secure a measure of reform; they lacked, however, the unity, the resources, and the determination to achieve a significant transformation of the conservative mold.

The Court in this period, consequently, had a checkered

[49] John P. Frank, *Marble Palace: The Supreme Court in American Life* (New York: Knopf, 1958), p. 154.

record reflecting both the prevailing conservatism and the inter-
mittent liberalism. In some years, particularly from 1908 to 1917
when progressivism and Wilsonian liberalism were at their peak,
the judiciary seemed to proceed in the path indicated by the new
social, economic, and intellectual trends. By utilizing the reservations and exceptions to the general run of its conservative opinions, the Court was able to interpret Congress' power to regulate
interstate commerce, in a number of cases, broadly rather than
narrowly in sanctioning national regulation; similarly it modified
its rigid Spencerian interpretation of the Fourteenth Amendment
by declaring state laws regulating maximum hours of work as
constitutional.[50]

In both types of cases, the Court was adjusting to demands
impelled by the changing nature of American society. The broad
interpretation of the commerce power was a recognition of the
interdependent nature of the economy and the resultant artificial-
ity of state lines. The new interpretation of the Fourteenth
Amendment was another form of appreciation of economic realities over abstract theory. The Court, enlightened by the statistics
of the Brandeis brief, recognized that a modern industrial country
required some degree of state regulation to guarantee its workers
the minimum necessities of a civilized life.

These liberal turns, however, were the exception rather than
the rule since the Court, in general, hewed to the conservative
line. As Wilsonian liberalism dimmed, the Court refused to
accept national and state social legislation as constitutionally
legitimate. It returned, for example, to a strict interpretation of
the commerce power when it invalidated a national child labor
act. When the law's advocates attempted to elude this trap by
achieving the same end through the national taxing power, the
Court predictably rebuffed these efforts as well by a narrow
interpretation of the Constitution.[51] In the 1920's, it also exhibited a harsh attitude toward state regulatory laws, which it

---

[50] On the expansion of the commerce power, see *Swift* v. *United States,*
196 U.S. 375 (1905), and *Stafford* v. *Wallace,* 258 U.S. 495 (1922); on state
laws regulating hours of work, see *Muller* v. *Oregon,* 208 U.S. 412 (1908),
and *Bunting* v. *Oregon,* 243 U.S. 426 (1917).

[51] *Hammer* v. *Dagenhart, op. cit.; Bailey* v. *Drexel Furniture Company,*
259 U.S. 20 (1922).

consistently cut down on the grounds that they did not deal with activities affecting the public interest.[52] The Court probably achieved its greatest notoriety in liberal circles at this time when it invalidated a District of Columbia minimum-wage law to protect women and minors.[53] In justifying its position by utilizing the wage theory of classical economics, the Court was repeating the principles applied by its predecessors in the 1890's and the early twentieth century.

In this period, the Court's position could still be justified as conforming with the general thinking of the American people, particularly as reflected in the political hegemony of the business-oriented Republican party. McCloskey has been critical of those who blame the Court for an illiberality which, in fact, belonged to the people themselves: "The fact that there was not more . . . [regulatory] legislation, the fact that Americans during the 1920's tolerated so great a measure of social injustice—this is to be attributed to public apathy amounting to callousness, not to the Supreme Court." [54]

When this basic public attitude was changed by the force of the depression and the New Deal, the Court's inability to recognize the nature of fundamental economic and social change placed it in a vulnerable position. The Court had become so accustomed to accenting the value of stability in its function at the expense of adjusting to change that it instinctively clung to the old constitutional formulas. The justices had linked their views so closely with the conservative interests of the old dominant coalition that they were unable to recognize the true dimensions of its opposition. They thus provoked one of the major conflicts in American judicial history.

Civil Rights after the Civil War

The commitment of the Court to the establishment and maintenance of the conservative political system of the first third of the century was by no means restricted to its defense of big business. It was a support for the other segments of the system,

[52] For one such example, see *Ribnik* v. *McBride*, 277 U.S. 350 (1928).
[53] *Adkins* v. *Children's Hospital*, 261 U.S. 525 (1923).
[54] McCloskey, *op. cit.*, p. 152.

rural control over the cities and white southern domination of the Negroes. There were, however, comparatively few cases in which rural domination itself could be considered an issue. The position of the Court does become evident once we recognize that the prime motivation of the rural population in seeking this political power was to preserve the values of its way of life from being corrupted by the cosmopolitan culture of the cities. In this light, a number of Court decisions, such as the upholding of Congress' power to prevent the interstate commerce of lottery tickets, alcohol, and women for immoral purposes, can be seen as supporting rural values as much as those of the Progressive elements in the cities.[55] The Court was similarly reflecting the limits of this Puritanical morality, as Holmes suggested in a dissent, when it refused to sanction as constitutional the national power to check another evil, child labor.[56]

Indisputable, however, was the Supreme Court's support of the third element in the political system, the white domination of the southern Negro. Indeed, the step-by-step transformation of the Fourteenth Amendment into a defense of laissez-faire was to a degree paralleled by the Court's emasculation of the amendment as a defense of Negro civil rights, which had been its original purpose.

The Court began this process of interpretation in 1873 with its decision in the Slaughterhouse Cases, when it refused to accept the Fourteenth Amendment as a protection of business from state regulation. In justifying its position, the Court declared that the unquestionable purpose of the amendment's "equal protection of the laws" clause was solely to protect the rights of the Negroes.[57] At the same time, however, it narrowly interpreted the "privileges and immunities" clause to include only a small number of guarantees of United States citizens. During this period, the Negro's right to vote was in an ambiguous position because the Court emphasized that the states had retained the responsibility for the establishment of voting qualifications while at the same

[55] *Champion* v. *Ames* 188 U.S. 321 (1903); *Clark Distilling Co.* v. *Western Maryland Railway Co.* 242 U.S. 311 (1917); *Hoke* v. *United States* 227 U.S. 308 (1913).

[56] *Hammer* v. *Dagenhart, op. cit.,* 280.

[57] Slaughterhouse Cases, *op. cit.,* 71.

time it insisted that these qualifications could not violate the provisions of the Fourteenth and Fifteenth amendments.[58]

In the 1880's and early 1890's, the trend of Court decisions generally showed an increasingly less benevolent attitude toward the Negro, a shift which reflected national feeling on the race question. The ending of Reconstruction and the weakened position of the radical Republicans in Congress were strong indications of the future pattern of southern race relations and the indifference of the rest of the country. The Court, in its Civil Rights Cases decision in 1883, whittled away at the effectiveness of the Fourteenth Amendment by holding as unconstitutional, congressional legislation designed to implement the amendment's provisions by outlawing discrimination in public facilities and conveyances. The Court stated that the amendment's language was purely a check on discriminatory state action and in no way a grant for positive national legislation.[59]

The Court moved further in the same direction by checking the use of national powers to restrict state segregation laws. In 1890, it stated that a Mississippi statute requiring segregated facilities on railroads could not be declared unconstitutional because of its effect upon interstate commerce. This was an ominous decision for the southern Negro because, twelve years earlier, the Court had stated that a state law forbidding segregation was an infringement upon the commerce power.[60]

The ground was being set, therefore, for the Court to take the climactic turning point that would eliminate Fourteenth Amendment protection of Negro rights against state legislation. In 1896 it at last declared, in the historic decision of *Plessy* v. *Ferguson*, that state segregation laws could not be considered a violation of the amendment's "equal protection of the laws" clause as long as the facilities in question were "separate but equal." [61] Thus, the Court seemed to have come full circle from its Slaughterhouse decision in 1873 when it had stated that the avowed purpose of the clause was solely the protection of the Negro.

[58] *United States* v. *Reese*, 92 U.S. 214 (1876); *United States* v. *Cruikshank*, 92 U.S. 542 (1876); *Ex parte Yarbrough*, 110 U.S. 651 (1884).

[59] Civil Rights Cases, 109 U.S. 3 (1883).

[60] *Louisville, New Orleans, and Texas Railway* v. *Mississippi*, 133 U.S. 587 (1890); *Hall* v. *DeCuir*, 95 U.S. 485 (1878).

[61] *Plessy* v. *Ferguson*, 163 U.S. 537 (1896).

The Court maintained, however, that it was not breaking precedent because it still acknowledged that "the object of the amendment was undoubtedly to enforce the absolute equality of the two races before the law." [62] It presented, however, such a narrow, legalistic interpretation of *equality* that it was of little use as a protection of the Negro within the context of southern life:

A statute which implies merely a legal distinction between the white and colored races . . . has no tendency to destroy the legal equality of the two races. . . .

. . . . .

Laws permitting, and even requiring, their separation in places where they are liable to be brought into contact do not necessarily imply the inferiority of either race to the other. . . .[63]

It thus summarily rejected any invidious implications of superiority and inferiority that might be drawn from a legalized system of segregation. "If this be so," the Court noted, "it is not by reason of anything found in the act, but solely because the colored race chooses to put that construction upon it." [64] "The curves of callousness and stupidity intersect at their respective maxima," pungently wrote Charles Black, Jr., about this remarkable statement, described by two other legal authorities as "an utterance rarely equaled for irony." [65]

The Court's refusal to acknowledge the obvious purpose of the segregation law was hardly based upon ignorance about race relations in the South. Its opinion revealed a sympathetic rapport with the southern whites. Justice Henry Brown noted the distinction between the whites and the Negroes as one "which is founded in the color of the two races, and which must always exist so long as white men are distinguished from the other race by color." Thus the Fourteenth Amendment, which granted the acknowledged legal equality between the races, "in the nature of things . . . could not have been intended to abolish distinctions based upon color, or to enforce social, as distinguished from political equality, or a commingling of the two races upon terms un-

[62] *Ibid.*, 544.   [63] *Ibid.*, 543, 544.   [64] *Ibid.*, 551.
    [65] Charles Black, Jr., "The Lawfulness of the Segregation Decisions," *Yale Law Journal*, LXIX (January, 1960), 422n.; Mason and Beaney, *op. cit.*, p. 455.

satisfactory to either." Moreover, the Court implied that even if that were the object, it would be unattainable because "legislation is powerless to eradicate racial instincts or to abolish distinctions based upon physical differences, and the attempt to do so can only result in accentuating the difficulties of the present situation." "If one race be inferior to the other socially," the Court magisterially declared, "the Constitution of the United States cannot put them on the same plane." [66]

The only dissenting opinion came from Justice John Harlan, who had also been a minority of one in 1883 when the Court refused to accept as constitutional a federal civil rights law. Harlan, who had been a slave-owner before the Civil War, was unsparing in his criticism of the Court's acceptance of state segregation legislation. Although these laws were "cunningly devised to defeat legitimate results of the war, under the pretence of recognizing equality of rights," he predicted that "the thin disguise of 'equal' accommodations . . . will not mislead anyone, nor atone for the wrong this day done." Although the white race considers itself superior, he declared, "in view of the Constitution, in the eye of the law, there is in this country no superior, dominant, ruling class of citizens. There is no caste here. Our Constitution is color-blind, and neither knows nor tolerates classes among citizens. In respect of civil rights, all citizens are equal before the law." [67]

The Court had thus ended the crucial years of indecision on the Negro question. In 1899, it plugged the last remaining loophole by which the Fourteenth Amendment could impede the southern whites. It refused to require a southern school board to furnish equal educational facilities for Negroes and whites but rather allowed it to use its discretion in allocating funds.[68] It thus maintained the standard of "separate but equal," but removed any judicial yardstick for measuring equality. There was, unfortunately, no contemporary George Orwell to savor the irony of an opinion which stated, in effect, that although the accommodations for both races had to be equal, some could be more equal than others. The only man on the Court who might have been expected to expose the logical weakness of the majority's view

[66] *Plessy* v. *Ferguson, op. cit.*, 543, 544, 551, and 552.
[67] *Ibid.*, dissenting opinion, 560–561, 562, and 559.
[68] *Cumming* v. *County Board of Education*, 175 U.S. 528 (1899).

was the doughty Justice Harlan, who was not available for his accustomed role of dissenter because he himself had written the Court's opinion.

At this time, the Court acknowledged the political supremacy of the southern whites even more overtly by its interpretation of the Fifteenth Amendment. In the 1890's and in the first decade of the twentieth century, this hegemony was legitimized through a number of new state consitutions and laws, whose common purpose was to keep the Negro from even a shred of political power by effectively preventing his voting. When the charge of discrimination, for example, was leveled in the discussions at the Virginia constitutional convention, Carter Glass shot back: "Discrimination! Why that is precisely what we propose; that exactly is what the convention was elected for." [69] Among the most prominent of these discriminatory devices for limiting the franchise were the reading and comprehension tests the Court accepted as constitutional in 1898. It reasoned that they could not be considered violations of the Fifteenth Amendment since they did not specifically mention race or color.[70]

The rationalizations of these important decisions, particularly the seminal one of *Plessy* v. *Ferguson,* are significant not for their dialectical subtlety, but for their reflection of the racial attitudes of the American people. Alan F. Westin wrote that the Plessy decision was "an accurate reading of both local and national majority feeling in 1896, when the North had become bored with 'Negro strife,' the romantic antebellum South was enjoying a literary vogue, Southern political power had been restored in Washington and the national eye was turned toward imperial adventures following which brown and black peoples would be ruled as inferior wards of the white man." [71] Moreover, Frank has pointed out that if the Court had refused to recognize this

[69] Quoted in C. Vann Woodward, *Origins of the New South, 1877–1913* (Baton Rouge: Louisiana State University Press, 1951), p. 333.

[70] *Williams* v. *Mississippi,* 170 U.S. 213 (1898); see also *Giles* v. *Harris,* 189 U.S. 475 (1903).

[71] Alan F. Westin, "The Supreme Court and Group Conflict: Thoughts on Seeing Burke Put through the Mill," *American Political Science Review,* LII, 3 (September, 1958), 674. For the northern attitude towards the situation of the southern Negro in the 1890's, see C. Vann Woodward, *The Strange Career of Jim Crow* (New York: Oxford University Press, 1955), pp. 52–56.

shift of feeling and had continued to accept the Fourteenth Amendment at face value, its practical effect would have been highly doubtful: "National sentiment had abandoned the Negro population, and even if the powers of Congress had been upheld, they would not have been exercised or enforced; and if segregation had been declared illegal, the ruling would surely have been ignored." [72]

Since the Court's function is to adjust the words of the Constitution to the needs and opinions of each generation, it received the thankless responsibility of rationalizing the discrepancy between reality on the one hand, and the literal meaning and essential spirit of our constitutional heritage from the Civil War on the other. Thus in describing its role, C. Vann Woodward has written:

> When such a lag develops between popular convictions and constitutional commitments, and when that lapse cannot be conveniently rationalized by statutory or amendatory procedures, it becomes the embarrassing task of the Supreme Court of the United States to square ideals with practice, to effect a rationalization. The justices in this instance examined the words of the Fourteenth Amendment and, by what Justice John M. Harlan in a famous dissenting opinion called "subtle and ingenious verbal criticism," discovered that they did not at all mean what they seemed to mean, nor what their authors thought they meant. By a series of opinions beginning in 1873 the Court constricted the Fourteenth Amendment by a narrow interpretation which proclaimed that privileges and immunities we call civil rights were not placed under federal protection at all. In effect, they found that the commitment to equality had never really been made.[73]

The Court's reflection of national sentiment in the field of race relations continued into the twentieth century, when it generally supported the conservative political system with certain progressive interludes. Thus, challenges to southern white supremacy did receive some judicial recognition, but never enough to undermine its hold. On the question of "separate but equal," the Court in its most progressive phase of this era, 1908–1917, did indicate that such facilities would actually have to be equal. In 1927, however,

[72] Frank, *op. cit.*, p. 207.
[73] C. Vann Woodward, *The Burden of Southern History* (Baton Rouge: Louisiana State University Press, 1960), p. 84.

it did not pursue this line of development further, but instead returned to the 1899 rule that the facilities did not have to be identically equal.[74]

On the subject of franchise requirements, the Court's record was similarly not of one piece, although here it was consistently much less tolerant of restrictive southern practices than in the segregation cases. In 1915, a moderately liberal Court eliminated from state constitutions the "grandfather clauses" which were subterfuges to keep the Negro from the polls. In this instance, the Court refused to credit the contention that only a specific reference to race or color could render a state law or constitutional provision invalid. Even when the Court reverted to its more characteristic conservatism in the 1920's and 1930's, it still kept a sharp eye open for similar devices. In 1927 and 1932, it declared "white primary" laws unconstitutional because they violated the "equal protection of the laws" clause either directly or indirectly. The early New Deal Court, however, in the case of *Grovey* v. *Townsend*, did accept the white primary as constitutional in 1935 on the grounds that it was not an example of public discrimination by the state but rather discrimination by a private organization, the political party. Since no statute was involved, there could by definition be no violation of the equal protection of the laws.[75]

Despite elements of liberalism, white supremacy was still basically accepted by the Court in this period. Only in the late 1930's would it begin the process of constitutional reinterpretation that would fundamentally undermine the prevailing pattern of race relations in the South—and, in some measure, in the rest of the country as well.

The Court-packing Controversy

In the early twentieth century, as mentioned previously, the Supreme Court's function of balancing change and permanence

[74] *McCabe* v. *Atchison, Topeka & Santa Fe Railroad Co.*, 235 U.S. 151 (1914); *Gong Lum* v. *Rice*, 275 U.S. 78 (1927).

[75] *Guinn* v. *United States*, 238 U.S. 347 (1915), *Nixon* v. *Herndon*, 273 U.S. 536 (1927); *Nixon* v. *Condon*, 286 U.S. 73 (1932); *Grovey* v. *Townsend*, 295 U.S. 45 (1935).

was strained because it was committed to the support of a political system whose primary aim was to maintain the status quo by ignoring the forces of change. Thus, the Court's neglect of the traditional rules of judicial adaptation to change left it unable to adjust to drastic social transformation, especially such as that brought on by the Great Depression.

The traumatic economic experience of financial crisis, unemployment, and hunger forced a popular recognition of the nature of a modern economy and encouraged a changed conception of the relationship of government to society. The central figure in American life, the businessman, lost his footing by the failure of his ideology and the crumbling of his economy. His protective political system fell as a new majority, more egalitarian and less sympathetic to big business, was rising to dominate the politics of the next generation. The New Deal reflected the diverse demands of its various segments as well as the common urgent note of immediate economic amelioration. Despite wide national approval and enthusiasm, the New Deal found one stumbling block to its effective application, "the nine old men" of the Supreme Court.

In the first months of the recovery program, with the economic system still reverberating from its upheaval, the Court seemed willing to adjust to the new economic tides and to recognize the new dimensions of governmental activity.[76] This proved to be, however, only a short breathing spell for the New Deal, and by 1934, its main provisions, particularly the N.I.R.A. (National Industrial Recovery Act), faced a hostile judicial majority. For two memorable years, the Court followed a rigidly narrow interpretation of national powers and declared unconstitutional the major parts of a recovery program, a product of the needs of a great majority of the population as reflected by the demands of a determined administration and the hearty approval of Congress. Its victims were the Railway Retirement Act, the N.I.R.A., the first Agricultural Adjustment Act, and the Guffey Coal Act.[77]

[76] It accepted a number of controversial state and national emergency measures as constitutional such as a moratorium on mortgage foreclosures (*Home Building & Loan Association* v. *Blaisdell*, 290 U.S. 398 [1934]) and state regulation of minimum prices (*Nebbia* v. *New York*, 291 U.S. 502 [1934]).

[77] *Railroad Retirement Board* v. *Alton R. R. Co.*, 295 U.S. 330 (1935);

This remarkable display of judicial energy has been termed by one legal scholar as "the greatest degree of control over legislative policy that judges had ever claimed in the United States."[78] Never had the Court so openly challenged the political arms of government; never had it moved so contrary to the evident facts of national life.

Despite the fact that the Court's peculiar position in the preceding decades set the stage for such an impasse, the Court's exceptional behavior was not predetermined. Even the change of one of its members might have allowed it to reflect the country's political shift without crisis or conflict. Thus, the whole remarkable record of the early New Deal Court and the resultant "Court-packing" plan might have been averted if Wilson had appointed a Wilsonian liberal to the bench rather than his irascible, conservative attorney-general, James C. McReynolds; if one of Wilson's liberal appointees had not resigned to work for international peace, thereby allowing Harding the gratuitous opportunity to appoint a conservative—in addition to the three other Court appointments that he made in his one incompleted term; if the Senate liberals had not successfully forced the rejection of a nominee because of some scattered conservative blemishes on his otherwise liberal record; and finally, if Franklin Roosevelt—whose fortune in this respect was quite unlike Harding's—had had the opportunity to make one single appointment, let alone the presidential average of two, in his first term of office.

The four most conservative members of the Court, the hard core to which the waverers, Roberts and Hughes, usually attached themselves, were clearly products of a far different cultural and economic milieu than the America of the mid-1930's and they applied to the problems of a complex modern industrial society the economic preconceptions of rugged individualism gleaned from their frontier youth. Curtis has perceptively pointed out that while the liberal and the swing justices made their mark in the eastern urban centers of Boston, Philadelphia, and New

---

Schechter Poultry Corporation v. *United States*, 295 U.S. 495 (1935); *United States* v. *Butler, op. cit.; Carter* v. *Carter Coal Co.*, 298 U.S. 238 (1936).

[78] James Willard Hurst, *The Growth of American Law: The Law-makers* (Boston: Little, Brown, 1950), p. 28. See also McCloskey, *The American Supreme Court*, p. 165.

York, the background of their more conservative colleagues was fundamentally different.[79]

Even though the Court disagreed with both the administration and Congress, it still could have avoided a direct clash with them by utilizing some degree of prudence and evasion. Instead, it rushed into a direct conflict, thereby endangering its operation to a degree unmatched since the days of the Dred Scott decision. This was the period when Justice Stone, one of the minority of liberal justices—although Stone considered himself a conservative rather than a liberal because he believed that his dissenting position was more truly conserving of traditional values and institutions that the obdurate reactionary rigidity of his nominally "conservative" colleagues—warned his colleagues in a dissent that they should be more prudent since "the only check" upon the Court was its "own sense of self-restraint." [80]

The majority, however, shrugged its shoulders and, protesting its powerlessness in the face of constitutional injunctions, outdid all previous courts in its zeal for declaring legislation unconstitutional. Roosevelt, angered by its insouciant attitude and confident of his political strength after his overwhelming victory in the 1936 presidential election, was provoked into an overt attack upon the Court with the presentation of his plan to appoint a new member for every judge over seventy who did not retire.

Even though Roosevelt's Court-packing plan was defeated, he achieved his basic objective of a Supreme Court that would adjust to change and would not be a barrier to the expression of the popular will by the executive and legislative branches of government. While the plan was under consideration, the Court wisely began to shift its attitude toward New Deal legislation, and by upholding as constitutional such measures as the National Labor Relations Act and the Social Security Act, it eliminated the grounds for the president's complaints against it.[81] Then when one of the conservative justices, Van Devanter, announced his future retirement, it appeared to many that all need of the plan had ended.

[79] Curtis, *op. cit.*, p. 98.

[80] For Stone's dissent, see above, footnotes 3 and 4.

[81] *National Labor Relations Board* v. *Jones & Laughlin Steel Corporation*, 301 U.S. 1 (1937); *Steward Machine Co.* v. *Davis*, 301 U.S. 548 (1937); *Helvering* v. *Davis*, 301 U.S. 619 (1937).

The Implications of the New Court

The immediate result of the Court's change of heart was the validation of state and national legislation which previously had generally fallen foul of the Court's interpretation of the "due process" clause of the Fourteenth Amendment or of the commerce clause. No longer was the Court wedded to laissez-faire economics.

Even more significant than the substance of the Court's change, however, were its underlying implications. In acquiescing to the recognition of a fundamentally new economy, it was reasserting John Marshall's principle that a changing society need not be shackled in meeting its problems by a rigid interpretation of the Constitution. The Court was thus passing judgment not just upon the economic status quo but rather upon the whole political system of which it was an integral part. Because of the interrelationship of the various conservative interests within the system, the defeat of one would inevitably have an impact upon the others. We have already noted the Court's emphasis upon consistency in order to preserve the concept of a stable system of law. Thus, a Court which would no longer defend businessmen from the currents of change would not protect the southern whites and the farmers, because a constitution no longer being read as a charter of economic privilege would hardly be considered a defender of racial or geographical privilege. The sanctity of constitutional authority had been removed from what had been, in effect, a hierarchical system.

These implications were to a great extent obscured from contemporary observers because they concentrated their attention upon the techniques of judicial operation rather than its underlying significance. Thus, there were many who believed that the true importance of the Court's switch was the cessation of any judicial control over the legislature, the commitment that the judges would not, except under extraordinary circumstances, interfere with the work of the people's representatives. This was an important insight—but only a partial picture.

To appreciate the significance of the new Court that emerged from the Court-packing controversy, we should bear in mind the matrix of conflicting pressures of stability and change within which the Court operates as it attempts their resolution. Thus, the most meaningful classifications of the Supreme Courts of different periods or of their members at any one time is based on the tendency to move toward either one pole or the other.

There are, however, other useful standards with which to measure the judiciary, the most prevalent being the dichotomy between the judicial activists and the judicial self-restrainers. The activists maintain that by the nature of judicial review, the Court must reflect its values and philosophy. They are, furthermore, usually strongly committed to a particular scale of values. The activists, therefore, openly read their philosophy into the Constitution, and if this should differ from the opinions of legislative majorities, so much the worse for them.

The judicial self-restrainers, on the other hand, feel that judicial review can—and must—be exercised in a neutral fashion. They, thus, sublimate their own political values and philosophy to their judicial function by giving the benefit of the constitutional doubt to the legislative majorities except in the case of the most flagrant and obvious violations of the Constitution.

Each of these schools of thought is partially correct in its emphasis on one aspect of judicial review. The activists are justified in refusing to acknowledge that the most significant and contentious constitutional provisions have an objective, neutral meaning. This does not mean, however, that the justices are thus given an open license to become free-wheeling, independent super-legislators, able to read their views into the Constitution at will. The self-restrainers, on their part, are correct in recognizing the inhibitions on the Court's power, but miss much of the dynamism of the operation of judicial review by their strict adherence to its traditional myth. They are, thus, right in giving the legislatures their due, but wrong in refusing to recognize that all branches of government are actively involved in the process of adjustment to change.

The classification between judicial activists and self-restrainers is of limited use in securing a coherent historical pattern of judicial activity. The later New Deal Court, by acquiescing to the legislatures on economic matters, could be considered as exhibiting self-restraint in sharp contrast to the aggressive activism of the earlier conservative Court. Yet at the very time that it was "retreating" before the legislatures in the economic sphere, it initiated, in the face of determined congressional lethargy, a consistent process of questioning and striking down state segregation laws and practices. Moreover, it has more recently, by its decisions on apportionment, implicitly engaged in open conflict with the legislatures by branding their composition as illegitimate.

If, however, we return to the basic judicial division on adjustment to change, the Court's actions become more coherent. The later New Deal Court was unquestionably different from its predecessor, but its main point of distinction lay in adjusting to change—not in acquiescing to the legislatures. The Court "retreated" not because a legislature had legislated, but rather because it had adjusted to change. True to this commitment, the modern Court is still adjusting to change—but by means of an activist role because the legislatures, by the nature of their composition and power structure, have not acted themselves. If we concentrate upon the basic function of the Court, therefore, rather than upon the secondary methods by which that function is accomplished, we can discern this consistency of objective.

The Court's commitment to change, therefore, was the basic result of the 1937 crisis rather than the issue of judicial-legislative relation which, although of unquestioned importance, was nevertheless secondary in the long run. The Court hewed to a generally consistent path in this period whatever the predisposition of the legislative branches: whether Congress was in accordance with change as in the case of business regulation, whether Congress did not move at all but the state legislatures had acted against change as in the case of racial segregation, whether change was blocked by the inaction of both Congress and the state legislatures as in the case of reapportionment.

Civil Rights after the New Deal

In no field did the judicial commitment made in the New Deal period stand out as dramatically as in that of civil rights, and possibly no decisions in the Court's history were capable of changing the everyday life of more people than those which snuffed out legal segregation in the United States. Although the Court's role has been an unusually prominent one in influencing public and private behavior, it has been reflecting public opinion just as it did a half century earlier when it legitimized segregation. Dahl thus notes the paradox that "the Supreme Court seems not to have been opposed to a law-making majority either when it took the rights of Negroes away or when it gave them back." [82] The milieu in which the justices lived was deeply affected by the changed position of the American Negro after the turn of the century and, even more, by the changed reaction of the white population. Although racial prejudices still existed, a remarkable shift had occurred under the influence of the liberal atmosphere generated by the New Deal and the ideological character of World War II. An authority on international law has stated:

When the Supreme Court of the United States, in 1954, after a series of preparatory judgments, upset the interpretation of the 14th Amendment on the equality of races, given nearly half a century earlier, it partly responded to, and partly led, public opinion. It certainly could not have made the attempt—how successfully, is still an open question—unless the intervening period had brought a great change in the economic and educational status of the American Negro, and a corresponding evolution in the attitude of responsible individuals and important social groups, such as the armed forces, churches, universities, and at least part of organised labour.[83]

At the popular level, the manifestations of change in the 1950's were readily apparent. Where formerly it had been an accepted fact of life that Negroes were barred from professional baseball, this was the period when they could at last play our national sport. Even our concept of what was humorous had changed. "Amos n' Andy" was a highly popular Negro situation comedy in the 1930's even though it was not heard in parts of the South because it allegedly portrayed the Negro as too urbanized and sophisticated. In the 1940's, however, the show lost its former popularity because racial caricature was no longer considered a laughing matter. The core of the plot of the most popular musical comedy of the late 1940's, *South Pacific*, was the tested "boy meets girl, boy loses girl, boy gets girl." There was, however, a

[82] Dahl, *A Preface to Democratic Theory*, p. 121.
[83] W. [Wolfgang] Friedmann, *Law in a Changing Society* (Berkeley and Los Angeles: University of California Press, 1959), p. 12.

significant difference since the hero lost the heroine because of her shock at learning that he had married outside his race and that his children were the products of this miscegenation. He eventually got the girl back when she overcame her Little Rock prejudices and returned to him and his children.

The older sociological and anthropological theories that had emphasized the fundamental nature of racial distinctions were challenged and replaced by new currents of thought that accented cultural diffusion and development. With the weakening of this theoretical basis of discrimination came the inevitable concern as to the future of race relations in a country committed to an ideology of democracy and equality. Gunnar Myrdal, a Swedish economist, predicted in 1944 in his *An American Dilemma,* whose impact went beyond the community of sociologists or persons concerned with race relations, that the Negro would achieve full civil rights because he had the Constitution, the Declaration of Independence, and, indeed, our country's fundamental principles and ideals in his favor.[84]

The Court, thus, operated in accordance with its traditional role as it reflected the prevailing sentiment in the country. In addition, its manner of executing this judicial shift on segregation was also consistent with its typical pattern of constitutional interpretation. A similar gradual, step-by-step approach was used as in the years from the Slaughterhouse Cases to *Plessy* v. *Ferguson*— with, of course, a completely opposite conclusion.

On the question of Negro suffrage, in 1935 in *Grovey* v. *Townsend* the new Court accepted the white primary. In 1941, however, it declared, in a case having nothing whatever to do with Negro voting, that a primary could be considered an election within the meaning of federal law and the Constitution. Congress could thus regulate the primary because it was an "integral part" of the election process and, in fact, its most de-

[84] One of the leading figures responsible for the transition in anthropological thought was Franz Boas of Columbia University. See his article "Race" in the *Encyclopedia of the Social Sciences* (New York: Macmillan, 1934) vol. 13, pp. 25–36, and his *Race and Democratic Society* (New York: J. J. Augustin (1945). See also Ruth Benedict, *Race, Science and Politics* (New York: Modern Age Books, 1940) and Otto Klineberg, *Characteristics of the American Negro* (New York: Harper, 1944).

cisive stage.[85] This ruling obviously undermined the basis of the Grovey decision, which had held that a political party was only a private organization and consequently under no legal regulation as to the choice of its membership. In 1944, therefore, the Court specifically overruled its earlier decision and stated that a primary, when conducted under state authority, could not bar Negroes from participation because such a restriction would violate the Fifteenth Amendment.[86] Although the Court's shift in this instance was a more gradual one than in the field of economic regulation, it provoked Justice Roberts' disapproval of the break with precedent of nine years earlier.

On the interpretation of the "equal protection of the laws" clause, the judicial process of change was slower and more gradual. Nevertheless, the Court's 1954 decision in *Brown* v. *Board of Education* came under the similar attack of upsetting the principle of *stare decisis* since it overruled the "separate but equal" standard established in 1896. This charge, however, was correct only in a formal sense. Although "separate but equal" did not fall until the Brown case, its supporting ground had been steadily eroded since 1938 by a series of decisions.

In 1938, it declared that a segregated state was not fulfilling its obligation under the "equal protection of the laws" clause by offering to pay a Negro student for his professional school education outside the state. Ten years later in 1948, the Court underlined the significance of this decision by stating in a similar case that if a state denied its Negro students entrance to its law school, it would actually have to provide equal facilities for them.[87]

By 1950, however, when such a law school for the state of Texas did come under judicial scrutiny, the Court declared, in the case of *Sweatt* v. *Painter,* that it did not meet the constitutional standard of equality because its facilities were not truly equal to those of the regular white law school. In speaking for the Court, Chief Justice Vinson first pointed out that the Negro law school did not match the white one in terms of measurable physical and

[85] *United States* v. *Classic,* 313 U.S. 299 (1941).

[86] *Smith* v. *Allwright,* 321 U.S. 649 (1944).

[87] *Missouri ex rel. Gaines* v. *Canada,* 305 U.S. 337 (1938); *Sipuel* v. *University of Oklahoma,* 322 U.S. 631 (1948).

human resources, such as number of students, faculty members, library books, and buildings.[88] If Vinson had terminated his argument at that point, its impact for the future would have been of limited significance. It was, after all, in the realm of possibility that Texas could in time have secured enough students, teachers, books, and buildings for the Negro school to allow it to achieve parity with its white counterpart. Vinson went much further and, in effect, cut the ground from beneath the concept of "separate but equal" without, however, acknowledging the operation:

What is more important, the University of Texas Law School possesses to a far greater degree those qualities which are incapable of objective measurement but which make for greatness in a law school. Such qualities, to name but a few, include reputation of the faculty, experience of the administration, position and influence of the alumni, standing in the community, traditions and prestige.[89]

If the Court's point were too subtle to be recognized, Vinson also added that the Negro law student would be further handicapped because his lack of contact with a white student body would cut him off from "85% of the population of the State," which would "include most of the lawyers, witnesses, jurors, judges and other officials" with whom he would be dealing when a practicing lawyer.[90] The Supreme Court in 1950, therefore, while still refusing to reexamine the concept of "separate but equal," clearly turned against it because the most significant criteria by which the Negro school was inferior to the white one were obviously derived from its segregated character.

In a similar vein, the Court on that same day also held that the "equal protection of the laws" was not secured in the case of *McLaurin* v. *Oklahoma State Regents*.[91] Here, a Negro student was actually admitted to the white graduate school, but had at all times to sit segregated from the other students. Again speaking for the Court, Vinson believed that McLaurin was denied equality because he was deprived of a significant element in the educational process by not being able to come in contact with his fellow students. Thus, the Court once more held that it was the

---

[88] *Sweatt* v. *Painter*, 339 U.S. 629, 632–634 (1950).
[89] *Ibid.*, 634.   [90] *Ibid.*
[91] *McLaurin* v. *Oklahoma State Regents*, 339 U.S. 637 (1950).

quality of separation that prevented the attainment of a meaning-ful equality. Victor Rosenblum, in discussing similar decisions in the field of interstate commerce, wrote:

Consequently, while the Court spoke only of enforcing equality, the effect was to outlaw segregation. Facilities could not be both separate and equal at the same time. Expansion of the concept of equality had made coexistence of the two terms impossible in practice.[92]

In keeping with the conservatism of its judicial temperament, however, the Court still refused to invalidate the principle of "separate but equal."

In 1954, in the case of *Brown* v. *Board of Education,* the Supreme Court finally drew the consequences from the line of its previous decisions and overruled the principle of *Plessy* v. *Ferguson* by declaring that "in the field of public education the doctrine of 'separate but equal' has no place." Moreover, Chief Justice Warren, in this opinion of a unanimous court, explicitly stated what had been unmistakably implied before: "Separate educational facilities are inherently unequal." [93] After noting the emphasis upon intangible factors in the interpretation of "equality" in the 1950 cases, he added:

Such considerations apply with added force to children in grade and high schools. To separate them from others of similar age and qualifications solely because of their race generates a feeling of inferiority as to their status in the community that may affect their hearts and minds in a way unlikely ever to be undone.[94]

Thus, the Court not only overruled the Plessy opinion, but reversed as well its basic line of reasoning that segregated facilities did not entail legal discrimination, and that such invidious qualities were not found in the law itself but rather in the minds of the Negroes. The Warren Court maintained, on the other hand, that the psychological effect of these laws upon the Negroes reinforced their discriminatory character and shattered any pretense to equality.[95]

[92] Victor G. Rosenblum, *Law as a Political Instrument* (Garden City, N.Y: Doubleday, 1955), p. 57.
[93] *Brown* v. *Board of Education of Topeka,* 347 U.S. 483 (1954).
[94] *Ibid.,* 494.   [95] *Ibid.,* 494–495.

Warren initiated a wave of controversy when, in a footnote on this point, he cited works of sociological and psychological authorities, including Myrdal.[96] The opponents of the decision leaped upon these references as tangible proof for their view that the Court had been deflected from a truly judicial and impartial interpretation of the Constitution by the latest trends in sociology and psychology. Thus, they believed it to be a "sociological" rather than a judicial decision. "If the eternal verities as revealed through the writings of Gunnar Myrdal," wrote one critic in the *American Bar Association Journal,* "are to outweigh the words written in the constitution, the concept of the constitution as a solemn and binding contract is destroyed." [97]

In addition, the footnote upset persons who approved of the decision and thought that it distracted attention from the opinion's sound constitutional argument and gave an unnecessarily irritating scholarly flourish to the recognition of the most obvious aspects of reality. Charles Black, Jr., questioned how, even without the emphasis on sociological evidence, a court could ignore "a plain fact about the society of the United States—the fact that the social meaning of segregation is the putting of the Negro in a position of walled-off inferiority—or the other equally plain fact that such treatment is hurtful to human beings." [98] An even sharper critic of the Court's use of these sociological references was Edmond Cahn, who similarly emphasized the evident purpose of segregation throughout world history and the obvious effects upon those discriminated against. In addition, he believed that because of the changing nature of the principles of sociology and psychology, the reference to such evidence weakened rather than buttressed a guarantee of basic individual rights that deserved a more solid support in a democratic society.[99]

[96] *Ibid.,* n. 11.

[97] Ralph T. Catteral, "Judicial Self-restraint: The Obligation of the Judiciary," *American Bar Association Journal,* XXXX II, 9 (September, 1956), 832.

[98] Black, *op. cit.,* 427.

[99] See Edmond Cahn, "A Dangerous Myth in the School Segregation Cases," *1954 Annual Survey of American Law, New York Law Review,* XXX (1955), 150–169; and "The Lawyer, the Social Psychologist, and the Truth," *1955 Annual Survey of American Law, New York Law Review,* XXXI (1956), 182–194.

The wisdom of Warren's tactics is certainly open to question. They can easily be considered a blunder because they added an unnecessary element of controversy to a decision which would have been heavily controversial under any circumstances since it appeared to be breaking with precedent and overruling more than a half-century of decisions. The Court would undeniably have been more prudent if it had hewed to the judicial "straight and narrow."

In the broader perspective of the judicial process, however, Warren's approach was a breath of fresh air in removing some of the mysticism surrounding the Court's function. Although Albert Blaustein and Clarence Ferguson, Jr., admitted that including the findings of the social scientists was not necessary for the decision, they believed nevertheless that "where current economic or psychological thoughts influence judicial decisions, as they must, such influence should be exposed and identified." [100] By explicitly recognizing one of the factors in the world in which the Court and the country lived, Warren was only pointing out the obvious.

The decision was a truly sociological one not because it contained some specific scholarly references, but rather because it is impossible to interpret the word *equal* in the Fourteenth Amendment in regard to racial segregation without in some way referring to sociology. As we have seen, the Court's 1896 opinion in *Plessy* v. *Ferguson* was just as sociological—and psychological —as that in the Brown case. A particularly strong note of sociological valuation is also found in Justice McReynolds' dissent when the Court, in 1938, ordered Missouri to admit a Negro to a law school within the state. He predicted that, as one of the possible results, the state might "break down the settled practice concerning separate schools and thereby, as indicated by experience, damnify both races." [101]

The deeper insight into the nature of the judicial process comes with the realization that words like *liberty* and *equality* cannot be considered self-evident in their meaning but are rather

[100] Albert Blaustein and Clarence Ferguson, Jr., *Desegregation and the Law: The Meaning and Effect of the School Segregation Cases*, 2d ed. (New York: Vintage Books, 1962), pp. 135–136, 137.

[101] *Missouri ex rel. Gaines* v. *Canada, op. cit.*, 353, dissenting opinion.

open vessels in which are poured the experience and philosophy of an age. As Curtis has written:

We object to the Justices importing into the Constitution their own philosophy. It is not theirs only. It is ours. Some of us may object to the kind of philosophy it was, but that is a matter of dispute. We have cause to complain only when it is an obsolete philosophy, one that we have outgrown before the Justices have.[102]

The Aftermath of the Brown Decision

The Brown decision marked a milestone in the Court's history by its invalidation of the concept of "separate but equal." Although the Court was careful to limit its revocation of Plessy to the subject at issue in the case, public school education, the principle was soon applied to other fields such as recreation and transportation.[103] Despite this apparent reversal of precedent, it moved within a continuing trend of judicial interpretation. This character of gradualism and continuity was emphasized by the fact that the decision was not to be carried out immediately, but only after a year's delay to allow state legal officers opportunity to ponder how this drastic change of social relations could be effected as smoothly and peacefully as possible.[104] In reality, however, the year seemed to have been spent in many states in a regrouping of reactionary and racist forces to block the ruling altogether.

The effect of the Brown decision is incalculable, especially its impact upon the Negro population. If any one date is to be recognized as the beginning of the Negro Revolution, it should be May 17, 1954, because from that day forward the American Negro realized that the full attainment of his civil rights was within his reach. One can well understand why a Negro mechanic, when polled by a reporter in 1958 on his preferences in a congressional election, answered: "You really would like to know

[102] Curtis, op. cit., pp. 331–332.

[103] In recreation, Muir v. Louisville Park Theatrical Association, 347 U.S. 971 (1954); in transportation, Mayor and City Council of Baltimore City v. Dawson, 350 U.S. 877 (1955), Holmes v. Atlanta, 350 U.S. 879 (1955), Gayle v. Browder, 352 U.S. 903, 950 (1956), Owen v. Browder, 352 U.S. 903, 955 (1956).

[104] Brown v. Board of Education of Topeka, 349 U.S. 294 (1955).

how I'd like to vote? I'd like to vote for the whole United States Supreme Court, that's how I'd like to vote." [105]

The decision, however, did not guarantee that the quest for full equality would be a simple matter. On the contrary, one of its immediate effects was to heighten racial tension. Roy Wilkins, the executive secretary of the National Association for the Advancement of Colored People, would date the beginning of the Negro Revolution not from the Brown decision, but rather from the time that it was not followed by the responsible authorities in the southern states.[106] Even this interpretation, however, recognizes the Court's action as a watershed clearly dividing present Negro expectations from those in the past.

Within the governmental system, the Court's decision strongly affected the other branches by crystallizing the new national consensus on race. Within little more than a decade after the Brown decision, Congress produced the first significant civil rights legislation since the Reconstruction period. It was a felicitous turn of history when the Supreme Court, by its interpretation of the Fourteenth Amendment, led the way for Congress in this field. It was, after all, the Court which had, in the late nineteenth century, gravely weakened the amendment as a protection of Negro rights, the overriding purpose of its congressional advocates. In both instances, however, the Court was more attuned to public opinion than was Congress. Woodward has skillfully shown the irony of this historical paradox:

Once again there was a lag between popular conviction and constitutional interpretation. Only this time the trend ran the opposite way, and it was the Constitution that dawdled behind conviction. Again it proved unfeasible to close the gap by statutory or amendatory procedures, and again it became the embarrassing task of the Supreme Court to effect an accommodation, a rationalization. Once more the justices scrutinized the words of the Fourteenth Amendment, and this time they discovered that those words really meant what they said, and presumably had all along. The old debt that the Court had once declared invalid they now pronounced valid.[107]

[105] Quoted by Mario Einaudi in *The Roosevelt Revolution* (New York: Harcourt, Brace and World, 1959), p. 267.

[106] In a speech delivered at the American Political Science convention on September 10, 1964. Others would date the Negro Revolution from the Montgomery bus strike in December, 1955.

[107] Woodward, *The Burden of Southern History*, p. 85.

Legislative Apportionment

The courts played an even more prominent role in breaking the third and last bond of the old political order, that of rural domination of the legislatures. By necessity, this change was almost entirely carried out through the judicial process. The members of the state legislatures could not be expected to change the system by which they themselves were chosen, nor would they be likely to change the lines of congressional districts that they had originally drawn. Thus, the complaint that the rural areas were overrepresented fell upon the deaf ears of the legislative majority that represented the rural minority. Congress, in its turn, could not be expected to direct a more equitable form of representation because its own members had been elected under the prevailing system. Moreover, the nature of this problem gave little opportunity for the urban-oriented executive branch to exert pressure in favor of the cities. The conservative rural elements in control of the national and state legislatures were, therefore, in an almost impregnable position, open to attack from only one quarter, the judiciary.

This trap in which the cities found themselves was delineated sharply, if unintentionally, by Justice Frankfurter in 1946 in *Colegrove* v. *Green*. This case was pressed by urban voters in Illinois who claimed that the legislature had been so laggard in adjusting congressional apportionment to population changes that one district had as much as nine times the population of another. Frankfurter stated for the Court—technically a majority was secured for his disposition of the case rather than for his opinion—that congressional apportionment was a political issue rather than a judicial one and hence could be handled only by the political arms of government, particularly the legislature. "It is hostile to a democratic system," he averred, "to involve the judiciary in the politics of the people," by which he meant "party contests and party interest." In justifying the Court's action, he seemed to be warning future courts against involvement in anything touching upon representation because this "would cut very deep into the very being of Congress. Courts ought not to enter this political thicket." [108] Since relief could not be secured from

[108] *Colegrove* v. *Green*, 328 U.S. 549, 553–554, 556 (1946).

the courts, Frankfurter suggested that "the remedy for unfairness in districting is to secure State legislatures that will apportion properly, or to invoke the ample powers of Congress." As we have seen, however, there was little likelihood that these legislative bodies would take any such action.

Finally, in the early 1960's, the Court turned away from this policy and, rejecting his warning, entered the "political thicket." In a series of ringing decisions, it came down very heavily in support of the urban majority by affirming that the basic principle of legislative representation at both the state and national levels should be "one man, one vote."

Why did the Court execute this sudden shift, one of the most important in its history? It must have realized that, in acting as the leading precipitant of political change for the second time in a decade, it was imperiling its own position. It was undoubtedly aware of the fact that it would be attacked by conservative forces, traditional defenders of the judicial process. This provocation was additionally untimely since the number of the Court's enemies had appreciably increased because of its decisions on the side of the individual in civil liberty cases and because of its ruling against the use of prayers in the public schools.

The Court acted partly because of the interlocking nature of the various elements within the political system's hierarchical structure. As we have seen, the breaking of one bond meant the loosening of the others; thus, the elimination of racial inequality cut the ground from under rural political control.

The civil rights issue may have influenced the Court in still another way to act decisively since the judiciary had already witnessed the harmful effects of postponement in regard to the race problem. The obstruction in the legislative process which had prevented the pressures for change from being reflected into law intensified a bitterness that eventually broke society's law and order. Although the problems of the cities' population and the nature of urban discontent did not lend themselves directly and immediately to such outbreaks of violence, their effects upon all aspects of life within the shadow of the cities meant that their potential destructive capacity was great enough to shatter the country's basic social harmony. As in the case of civil rights, a postponement of urban problems in the name of law could undermine the very foundation of the law. Thus, the Court's observation of the dire consequences of postponing the recognition of one form of social change probably induced it to move in the field of apportionment even while the Negro Revolution was still the main topic of domestic concern.

This judicial process was hastened by the Court's decision in *Gomillion* v. *Lightfoot,* a case whose character pinpointed the basic similarity between Negro and urban discrimination.[109] It concerned the constitutionality of the Alabama legislature's redrawing the boundary lines of Tuskegee in such a way that neighboring localities secured portions of the city's former area. The sections removed contained practically the whole of its Negro population, which constituted a majority of the city's inhabitants. This remarkable act was a gerrymander designed to prevent the Negro numerical majority from becoming an electoral majority in full political control.

The whites felt pushed to this extremity not only by the number of Negroes, but also by their particular character. Many of the Negroes in Tuskegee and its county, Macon, were associated with Tuskegee Institute, founded by Booker T. Washington, and their continued exclusion from voting on the alleged grounds of illiteracy might have been difficult to sustain. A reporter prodded the chairman of the Board of Registrars of Macon County about its rejection from voting registration of some Negroes with Ph.D. degrees, and the account of the official's answer is a minor classic in irony:

"Well, they missed some part of the questionnaire. If a fella makes a mistake on his questionnaire, I'm not gonna discriminate in his favor just because he's got a Ph.D." He spoke righteously, a man who had found a cause: no discrimination in favor of Ph.D.'s. "We treat everybody alike, white or black," he went on. "Nobody can say we're not treatin' everybody exactly equal." [110]

The Court ruled in this case that an apportionment scheme with such an obviously discriminatory purpose was a violation of the "equal protection of the laws" clause of the Fourteenth Amendment. Justice Frankfurter, in his majority opinion, went to

[109] *Gomillion* v. *Lightfoot,* 364 U.S. 339 (1960).
[110] Bernard Taper, "A Reporter at Large: Gomillion versus Lightfoot," *The New Yorker,* XXXVII, 17 (June 10, 1961), 90.

great lengths to show that the Court could act upon this legislative districting proposal only because the discrimination involved was racial.[111] Despite the subtle distinction between the two types of inequality, the Court, in the Gomillion case, was moving counter to the Colegrove precedent of judicial inactivity on apportionment.

The actual break with Colegrove occurred in 1962 when the Court decided in the case of *Baker* v. *Carr* that the apportionment of state legislatures could legitimately come under judicial scrutiny.[112] The decision was of major importance because by opening the question of the basis of representation to public examination, it gave an implicit promise of eventual change. The significance of the case, therefore, did not lie in what was actually decided, since the Court merely stated that it would examine such questions and gave no guidelines as to what it would consider fair and unfair representation under the "equal protection of the laws" clause of the Fourteenth Amendment. The nature of the decision in this respect was similar to that of the Great Reform Bill of 1832, which initiated the process by which Great Britain developed into a democracy with full suffrage. In both historic instances the greatness lay not in the specifics, but in the promise for the future. The Court, therefore, was continuing the process begun in the late 1930's of facilitating political adaptation to social change. Thomas Emerson wrote that the "decision in *Baker* v. *Carr* is wholly in line with the direction that the Supreme Court must take and, with some lapses to be sure, has been taking for the past quarter of a century. In the impetus given this crucial development lies the real significance of the decision." [113]

The Court's decisive choice was not a unanimous one and Justice Frankfurter was predictably one of the two dissenters. Although his argument was similar to that in the Colegrove decision, his words, however, had a sharper edge since his colleagues were no longer heeding his counsel. Once more he warned against the judiciary's involvement in political matters,

---

[111] *Gomillion* v. *Lightfoot, op. cit.*, 346–347.

[112] *Baker* v. *Carr*, 369 U.S. 186 (1962).

[113] Thomas Emerson, "Malapportionment and Judicial Power," in "A Symposium on *Baker* v. *Carr*," *Yale Law Journal*, CXXII, 1 (November, 1962), p. 80.

and he reiterated his contention that the people could receive their salvation not through judicial remedy but "through an aroused popular conscience that sears the conscience of the people's representatives." [114] Thus, Frankfurter again failed to recognize that the people's representatives could hardly have their consciences seared because they were so well insulated from the temperature of popular feeling by the system of representation that was the very point at issue. Indeed, the prime criticism of the existing system was that "the people's representatives" did not really represent the people. Louis H. Pollak, in criticizing Frankfurter's view, said:

But the very heart of the problem is that the incumbent elective officials who have the power to make or block remedial laws are themselves not "the people's representatives." They are the faithful servants of muscular minorities whose continued control over state—and (though to a lesser extent) national—policy depends upon and will insure eternal vigilance against encircling majorities and eternal frustration of their attempted reforms. If the Court in *Baker* v. *Carr* had affirmed dismissal of the complaint, the Court would in effect have declared that the only power to arrest the pervasive systemic disorder of malapportionment lay in the hands of those who thrive on the malady. And this would have been an ominous declaration, for the malady is a grave one, a sclerosis which clogs the law-making heart of the American body politic. [115]

It required but a short time for the implications of the Baker decision to be developed by the Court. In the very next year, 1963, in *Gray* v. *Sanders*, it declared the notorious Georgia county unit system unconstitutional in statewide primaries because its discriminatory weighting of the vote against inhabitants of the cities violated the Fourteenth Amendment. [116] The Court thus revealed the egalitarian principles it would follow in considering the question of legislative apportionment itself.

The only element of surprise came in how quickly and how unreservedly the Court applied the rule of "one man, one vote."

[114] *Baker* v. *Carr, op. cit.,* dissenting opinion, 266, especially 267, 270, and 324, with the quotation from 270.

[115] Louis Pollak, "Judicial Power and the Politics of the People," in "A Symposium on *Baker* v. *Carr," op. cit.,* p. 88.

[116] *Gray* v. *Sanders,* 372 U.S. 368 (1963).

The next year, 1964, it declared in *Wesberry* v. *Sanders* that congressional districts would have to be virtually equal in population to insure proper representation. While analysts and politicians were pondering the significance and effects of this decision, the Court the same year held in *Reynolds* v. *Sims* that both houses of the state legislatures must have representation based upon the same equality.[117]

The Court, by these decisions, was attempting much more than checking the conservatism of the legislatures; it was actually trying to extract from them the very characteristics which had made them conservative strongholds. The consequences of this line of opinion could transform the nature of our legislatures, and, thus, guarantee the first foundation of a new political system. The daring of such a radical change left both critics and friends of the Court gasping in surprise. The modern Court, however, reflecting the character of its generation, was striking at the root inequality of the old system, just as earlier courts had upheld it.

Justice Black, speaking for the majority in *Wesberry* v. *Sanders*, obviously was reading into the Constitution much more than did former conservative colleagues when he referred to "our Constitution's plain objective of making equal representation for equal numbers of people the fundamental goal for the House of Representatives." Scholars might easily question the soundness of his historical analysis of the constitutional provision that members of the House of Representatives shall "be elected by the People of the several States." Few, however, would deny that he was reflecting the values of modern democratic American society in his view that it "means that as nearly as is practicable one man's vote in a congressional election is to be worth as much as another's." [118]

The Court's commitment to full equality of the vote was expressed in even more unequivocal language when Chief Justice Warren in *Reynolds* v. *Sims* declared any type of malapportionment of the state legislatures to be an unconstitutional violation of the Fourteenth Amendment's "equal protection of the laws" clause:

[117] *Wesberry* v. *Sanders*, 376 U.S. 1 (1964); *Reynolds* v. *Sims*, 377 U.S. 533 (1964).

[118] *Wesberry* v. *Sanders*, *op. cit.*, 18. 17–18, 7–8, respectively.

Legislators represent people, not trees or acres. Legislators are elected by voters, not farms or cities or economic interests. As long as ours is a representative form of government, and our legislatures are those instruments of government elected directly by and directly representative of the people, the right to elect legislators in a free and unimpaired fashion is a bedrock of our political system.[119]

In his opinion, Warren pointed out in simple language that the practical result of malapportionment was similar to allowing one group of a state's citizens more votes than another. He was unsympathetic, as we have seen in our chapter on legislatures and representation, to any special treatment accorded the inhabitants of any area: "A citizen, a qualified voter, is no more nor no less so because he lives in the city or on the farm." Similarly, he argued that the aggregate effect of such unfairness in the legislature would mean minority control and, thus, a limitation of majority rights. "Logically," he wrote, "in a society ostensibly grounded on representative government, it would seem reasonable that a majority of the people of a State could elect a majority of that State's legislators." [120] Thus, logic and reasonableness induced the Warren Court to interpret the Fourteenth Amendment's *equal* to mean mathematical equality in the voting booth just as logic and reasonableness induced earlier Courts, reflecting other values and other realities, to hold the opposite.

The Conservative Counterattack

Throughout the late 1950's the Supreme Court was a persistent target of a counterattack by conservative forces. Each time the Warren Court became involved in controversy—after the Brown decision in 1954 and after its 1957 decisions, particularly those pertaining to state antisubversive activities—laws and amendments were introduced in Congress to restrict the power of the Court. Although each wave was unsuccessful, each new one was more powerful than the last because of the cumulative increase in the Court's opponents.[121] Thus when the Court, in the reapportionment decisions, implicitly challenged the legislatures, it incurred an even stronger opposition with deep reserves of political power and acumen.

[119] *Reynolds* v. *Sims, op. cit.,* 562.   [120] *Ibid.,* 568, 565.
[121] Pritchett, *op. cit.,* esp. pp. 25–40.

In 1962, when the Court's decision in *Baker* v. *Carr* cast a threatening shadow over the state legislatures, they felt impelled to act. With great celerity, the Council of State Governments, a coordinating body of state officials and legislators, initiated a series of proposed constitutional amendments whose combined purpose was to check the power of the Court, expand the role of the state legislatures in the amending process, and protect the existing system of representation.[122] The state legislatures moved resolutely and quickly and the proposed amendments received the support of a number of them. They possibly moved, however, a little too quickly for their own good because they approved these broad and drastic changes in the Constitution with very little in the way of a national debate. Consequently, when the public became aware of the proposed changes, the effort appeared to be that of a small minority acting in a secretive, conspiratorial manner to keep itself in power at the expense of the majority. Under the light of such publicity, the campaign stalled.

The Court came under renewed attack, however, when it followed through with the implications of *Baker* v. *Carr* in its subsequent reapportionment decisions. Even some persons sympathetic to its basic predisposition watched with decreasing enthusiasm its steady movement toward committing the whole American representational structure, except for the constitutionally protected U.S. Senate, to the stark principle of virtually absolute equality. These critics would have felt more comfortable if the Court, upon approaching a subject of such overriding importance, had moved with its customary moderation and caution and had expressed itself in language less absolute and more amenable to flexible interpretation.

As we have seen, the Supreme Court has been no stranger to controversy and has met its share of opponents throughout its history. What is remarkable in this present phase, however, is the nature of the opposition. The Court has become the object of

[122] The first proposed amendment permitted two-thirds of the state legislatures to initiate an amendment directly; the second withdrew jurisdiction of state legislative apportionment cases from the federal courts; and the third established a "Court of the Union" composed of the chief judges from each state to review Supreme Court decisions affecting state powers. *Amending the United States Constitution to Strengthen the States in the Federal System* (Chicago: The Council of State Government, 1963).

attack even by state justices and by the American Bar Association—although the latter did partially retract. The bar has nearly always been in the forefront of the Court's clientele, a "constituency" formed, as McCloskey has noted, by those who approve of a particular series of decisions and by those who respect the Court as a symbol of the law and constitutional continuity. Thus lawyers and other judges have usually fulfilled both of these criteria of membership among the Court's supporters. The present bar and state judiciary, however, irritated by the liberal decisions, have deserted the Court despite its symbolism of law and constitutional continuity.[123] In this change of heart, they are reflecting conservative opinion and are duplicating the hostile action of conservative forces.

Some might think it unexceptional that a liberal Court should provoke a conservative opposition since many conservative ones have faced liberal attack. One's attitude toward judicial review, it is claimed, primarily depends upon whose ox is gored. Such it is, and such it will always be—and attempts of scholars to impose patterns of consistency will serve no other purpose than to show their separation from the practical world.

Despite the plausibility of this attitude, however, American conservatives do have a stake in the Supreme Court that transcends the content of a particular line of decisions, just as much as British Conservatives have in the House of Lords despite their opinion of its actions or of one of its eccentric members. The Court has been one of the main conservative institutions in our public life, and the stability of our political structure owes no small debt to it. Even though it adjusts to change in performing its function, its reference to tradition and precedence reflects conservative values. As C. Herman Pritchett has stated:

To speak of a conservative attack on the courts sounds like a contradiction in terms. Anyone who thinks of his political or philosophical position as conservative must of necessity find himself in a most anomalous situation when assaulting the judicial institution. For a true conservative should recognize an independent judiciary as one of the most effective and precious conservative forces in our culture. It is an interesting commentary on American conservative thought that some

[123] McCloskey, *The American Supreme Court*, pp. 71–72.

of its principal apostles had no difficulty in supporting and rationalizing the anti-Court campaign.[124]

Although the Court has made enemies and lost friends by its approach, it may have balanced this loss of so great a portion of its traditional constituency by tapping no less a reservoir of potential support than the majority of the country's population living in the metropolitan areas. Thus, the Warren Court may have gained by the fact that its majority opinions on segregation and apportionment have been phrased with a pointed directness and lack of subtlety. Such draftsmanship has evident disadvantages and has been criticized by legislators and scholars, but it does convey a clearer meaning to laymen than they can usually discern from the strange language of lawyers and the even stranger dialectics of judges.

The effectiveness of the Court's "educational" efforts may be gauged by the successive failures in 1964, 1965, and 1966 of conservative campaigns, led by the indefatigable Senator Everett Dirksen of Illinois, to secure laws that would prevent the courts from carrying out the directives of the Supreme Court or amendments that would protect at least one house of a state legislature from judicial scrutiny. Each defeat was, of course, a more significant event than the preceding one because with each year the yeast of reapportionment leavens the conservatism of our legislatures and renders increasingly unlikely an adverse judgment by them on this process of change.

The Court Today

The Court has become involved in controversy at a time when in the sharp light of legal realism it is bereft of much of its former supporting mythology and semireligious aura, which was lost during and after the Court-packing controversy. It is, therefore, an intriguing question as to whether the Court will be able to maintain its prestige and authority in the face of our more sophisticated recognition of its actual operation.

We noted earlier the disillusionment of some in discovering that the Court is not reading an absolute document, a secular

[124] Pritchett, *op. cit.*, pp. 123–124.

form of Holy Writ. They suspiciously consider that its attempt to balance stability and change is a somewhat shady form of legalistic juggling. This may, indeed, be the cause underlying the dissatisfaction of so many conservatives with the modern judiciary. They are no longer loyal to the Supreme Court today because it is not the unique institution they once respected and, in fact, revered. It is rather seen as a political instrument among other political instruments—and a liberal one at that. Yet these critics have mistaken the myth of the Court's operation for the reality and have lost sight of the fact that the Court, by constantly infusing the philosophy and values of each new generation into the words of the Constitution, is performing a task of fundamental importance in the preservation of our culture. They should bear in mind the wise words of James Willard Hurst: "Change is one of the few things men can be certain of. Any institution whose job is to deal directly, in as rational a way as possible, with this ceaseless flux, is to be counted one of the truly basic instruments of civilized living." [125]

The more realistic, therefore, our grasp of the Court's actual role, the greater—and certainly the healthier—will be our regard for it. We must realize that the Court cannot be considered a paternal guardian always vigilant to lead us aright whenever we err. Our true salvation lies not in the past, not in the Constitution, not in the Supreme Court, but in ourselves. Despite the prominence of the Court's activities, its apportionment and civil rights decisions and their aftermath have shown the wisdom of Loren Beth's view: "Perhaps we no longer expect judicial review to save us, but only to help us save ourselves." [126]

[125] Hurst, *op. cit.*, p. 19.

[126] Loren P. Beth, "The Supreme Court and the Future of Judicial Review," *Political Science Quarterly*, LXXVI, 1 (March, 1961), 23.

Chapter VII

The Demands of the Future

This description and analysis of twentieth-century American politics has emphasized the manner and the degree to which our political institutions have adjusted to wide-sweeping social, economic, and intellectual change, indeed to the transformation of our society. This fundamental political shift has occurred through a continuing clash between those who desired to maintain the status quo and those committed to its change. The modern conflict began about the turn of the century when the future outlines of an industrial urban America were already clearly evident. The conservative forces at that time set the stage for the struggle by establishing a rigid political system as a protective device to contain change and to inhibit its political effects. Tension was thus inevitable as, with each succeeding decade, the forces restricted by the system and identified with the wave of change were pressing with increased intensity for political expression against the apparent implacability of the institutional structure. In essence, as we have seen, the drama of these years was that of a society attempting to bring its politics in line with its changing character, a people striving to secure the satisfaction of its needs from a political system expressly designed for the interests and values of a previous century, a nation trying to break through its own preconceptions and rationalizations in order to perceive the real world.

We have followed this drama through its various phases, from the beginning when there seemed little hope of significant change until today when such evidence is unmistakable. After briefly noting the heightening of tension in the Wilson era and in the 1920's, we paid particular attention to the New Deal period when the political system began to capitulate to change and the under-lying hierarchical structure of the nation became undermined. The conflict in the succeeding years had the formerly conserva-tive forces on the defensive in the face of a liberal tide which consciously attempted to secure a program of social and eco-nomic reform, and rather unconsciously tried to construct a new political system that would be more attuned to reality than its discredited and fragmented predecessor. We have carried this historical account until the present, when attempts to reverse the tide, such as the Goldwater movement and the campaign to check the Supreme Court, have proven unsuccessful. At the same time, by 1967, the Johnson administration had achieved a remarkable record, comparable in this century only to that of Wilson's and Franklin Roosevelt's first terms, in securing the passage of liberal legislation which had been pending for years. Each measure was a reflection of the political adjustment to the modern character of the country; each was a coffin nail in the former political agree-ment of the old elites; and each was a response to a particular element in the present dominant liberal Democratic coalition: a Medicare bill for the aged, the establishment of a cabinet depart-ment for urban affairs, a broad voting rights bill for the southern Negroes, and an immigration bill that eliminated the quota sys-tem which had for more than forty years set an invidious distinc-tion of admission against immigrants from southern and eastern Europe. Thus, the last gasp of the old conservatism and the ful-fillment of the implications of the New Deal can be considered the inception of a new political system.

This transition from one system to another has been obscured by the comparatively slight change in the political structure itself and by the solidity of its institutions. The impact of outside pressures was felt at all levels of the structure and was reflected in the tension between its institutions. In the resultant process of adjustment, the institutions have changed in nature and function even though they have remained stable.

We have noted that the localism and conservatism of Con-gress expanded the powers of the president and aided in his de-velopment as the chief instrument and symbol of urban industrial America. Similarly, within the framework of the existing federal system, the reluctance of the states to adjust to the modern world increased the power and authority of the national government. This nationalizing trend, although more gradual, was also evident in our political parties. The courts, as well, recognized the character of modern society in their interpretation of the Constitution, particularly in the major fields of economic regulation, race relations, and legislative reapportionment. Indeed, by this flexible interpretation they were reproducing at their own level the whole historical process by which stable institutions and values adjusted to the needs of each generation. At the last stage of the development of our political institutions we saw that the liberal role of the executive and the judiciary exerted an effect upon even the composition and operation of Congress and the state legislatures.,

A phenomenon similar to this flexibility of our permanent institutions is recognized by O. Kahn-Freund in his introduction to Karl Renner's *The Institutions of Private Law and Their Social Functions*. In explaining Renner's conception of the stability of the institutions of private law as they performed different functions in different periods, Kahn-Freund writes that Renner thought of these institutions as similar to the building blocks used by a child. With these blocks, he erects a different set of constructions. Since the number of blocks is limited, he must each time tear down the old to begin the new. The constructions, therefore, are new; but the blocks, of course, always remain the same.[1] This process is a subtler one in actual operation than this analogy indicates, since the changes are more gradual than can be assumed from such phrases as "tear down the old" and "begin the new." The changes are rather accomplished block by block. Thus, we are often not aware of the most significant transformations as they are taking place.

The flexibility of these institutions and the shift of the political system have preserved our fundamental political structure and values. It is difficult to overestimate this contribution. To the philosopher Alfred North Whitehead, the necessity of adjustment to change was nothing less than the basic predicament of civilization itself: "Those societies which cannot combine reverence to their symbols with freedom of revision, must ultimately decay

[1] Kahn-Freund, introduction to his edition of Karl Renner, *The Institutions of Private Law and Their Social Functions*, trans. Agnes Schwarzschild (London: Routledge & Kegan Paul, 1949), p. 6.

either from anarchy or from the slow atrophy of a life stifled by useless shadows." [2]

Since this problem of adjustment is a general one, other countries have faced challenges similar to our own. The political systems of France in the Third and Fourth Republics, especially in the long-lived Third (1870–1940), were excellent examples of the failure to adjust to significant social and economic change. Although the old France of the peasantry and the small-town tradesmen was being shunted aside by the forces of industrialism, there was little recognition of this in the political arena. The locus of political power, particularly in the omnipotent national legislature, remained frozen in the rural villages and small towns despite the increase in wealth and population in the more dynamic areas of the country. With each succeeding year, the disparity between "political" France and the "real" France became greater. Correspondingly greater, as well, was the gap between what was achieved politically and what the country actually needed to meet the problems of a modern society. The result was that the political system became alienated from an increasingly cynical people and was unable to withstand the pressure of military defeat in the Third Republic and colonial revolt in the Fourth.

On the other hand, in Great Britain the opposite has generally been true. Although British history has unquestionably been marked by strains and conflicts, what strikes the observer is that in the long run the eventual accommodation has been made. As a result, her political institutions, which developed from the twelfth century, if not earlier, and which were instruments of royal and noble rule, have survived because they have accepted and absorbed new social and economic developments rather than resisting and battling them.

By bearing in mind the example of these two countries, almost polar extremes on this fundamental issue, we are aided in placing our own experience in perspective. As in the case of France, the political power of the rural areas and small towns has been noted throughout this work in contrast to their declining economic and demographic importance. Similarly, this disproportion has pre-

---

[2] Alfred North Whitehead, *Symbolism: Its Meaning and Effect* (New York: Macmillan, 1927), p. 88.

sented an unreal world in the legislature and has handicapped the country in the solution of its problems. But the basic trend of our political development has been toward the ready institutional adjustment of British practice.

During the decades while the political structure has adjusted to the urban and industrial character of twentieth-century America, even greater technological, social, and economic changes have been occurring. The technological revolution, in itself, has been termed "a transformation that is, in all likelihood, bigger, deeper, and more important than the industrial revolution." [3] The cumulative effect of such changes has put renewed pressure upon the political apparatus. Thus, after securing the passage of significant social welfare legislation, which should have been passed decades ago, we are now confronted with the newer problem of automation, which does not directly lend itself to legislative remedy. After the southern Negro has at long last a real opportunity to secure his civil rights, the effects of years of bitterness and frustration have made his full integration into society more difficult and, in some instances, less appealing. Moreover, our justifiable concentration upon the flagrant and open legal segregation of the Negro in the South caused us to overlook the subtler and insidious problems of prejudice he faced in the large northern city. Now that the metropolitan areas are on the threshold of a greater degree of governmental recognition and legislative representation, their problems of health, transportation, water, welfare, crime, and pollution of air and water have assumed such proportions that they demand an extraordinary use of imagination and resources as well as a more flexible organization of the governmental structure if a civilized life is to be maintained within their limits—and the limits themselves are expanding at an uncontrollable pace. History is a remorseless creditor and one borrows time only at compound interest.

We are thus in no position for complacency, because despite the degree to which our political institutions have adjusted to change, there are still greater hurdles for them to overcome. Thus, in evaluating our record in this century, the difference between the optimist and the pessimist is largely between the one

[3] Alvin Toffler, "The Future as a Way of Life," *Horizon*, VII, 3 (Summer, 1965), 110.

who accents what we have already accomplished and the one who emphasizes what yet has to be done, between the one who sees the glass half full and the one who sees it half empty. Those optimists, however, who advise halting instead of advancing in order to consolidate and digest our unprecedented gains misjudge the treadmill of historical change. We can well repeat what the Red Queen said to Alice: "In our country you have to run as fast as you can to stay where you are; if you want to get anywhere you have to run twice as fast."

Thus, to meet the needs of modern society in succeeding years we must recognize clearly its nature. Our civilization is an urban one and our main concentration must be upon the problems of the city because there is no possibility of evading them in a rural past or in a stratospheric future. As Morton and Lucia White wrote: "The wilderness, the isolated farm, the plantation, the self-contained New England town, the detached neighborhood are things of the American past. All the world's a city now and there is no escaping urbanization, not even in outer space." [4]

The necessity of consciously keying our political system to this reality does not render us passive slaves to history. On the contrary, the ones who are truly slaves to historical change are those who refuse to recognize it and are, therefore, pushed and pummeled by its forces with little conscious control or direction. Thus we must be wary of rationalizations that deflect us from acting in accordance with the recognition of our environment. "We cannot unfreeze our politics," wrote James MacGregor Burns, "until we unfreeze our minds." [5]

We have already seen how persistently persuasive have been such concepts as the freedom of the states from national control, protection for the minority against the rule of the majority, and legislative representation for each locality. The antimajoritarian strain in American political thought and practice unquestionably still possesses a strong appeal. A sophisticated version of the anti-majoritarian theory can be discerned in the view that the genius of our politics lies in balance, in the maintenance of an equilib-

[4] Morton and Lucia White, *The Intellectual versus the City* (Cambridge: Harvard University Press and M.I.T. Press, 1962), p. 239.

[5] James MacGregor Burns, *Deadlock of Democracy: Four-Party Politics in America* (Englewood Cliffs, N.J.: Prentice-Hall, 1963), p. 7.

rium between its principal institutions and forces, between the cities and the rural areas, between the states and the nation, between the executive and the legislature. Such a principle, however, gives a misleading comfort in neat, mathematically balanced solutions. The equilibrium of our politics has undoubtedly been of major importance—but not for the sake of balance itself. It has been significant in recent American political history because it has checked the more backward and provincial characteristics of our politics and mitigated their influence. The balance of power can, however, easily swing in the other direction and end its progressive tendency.

An example of this attempt to secure a balanced political system is the use of the federal formula for state legislative representation, a "half a loaf" compromise in which, as in the national Congress, one house based upon population can be a check upon the other based upon area. This solution assumes that the representation of separate and sovereign states is similar to the representation of counties and towns in the legislature of a state to which they are legally subordinate. Aside from this constitutional restraint, such an approach violates the basic principle of a politics primarily designed to reflect reality. If a small minority does not deserve a majority of representatives in both houses of the state legislature, is practicality—to say nothing of justice— served by giving it a majority in one? We would once more be immersed in the sticky question examined earlier, "Why this minority and not that?" The achievement of a state of adequacy by splitting the difference between success and failure is no recipe for political wisdom. Just as in a former national crisis, the country could not survive "half slave and half free," we must now realize that there are times when a clear understanding of fundamental principles overrides the political inclination toward compromise.

Such clarity of thought does not, however, guarantee success. By a clear apprehension, without illusion, of our society and our politics, we will secure only the *means* to operate as efficiently as we are able. A utopia will not be created overnight; our legislatures will not suddenly be packed by Aristotles and Websters; the decisions of an increasingly powerful presidency will not always be the wisest; and, most important, the massive weight of our problems will not dissolve. If the advocates of legislative reapportionment and a strengthened presidency entertain such hopes, they will surely be as disappointed as were the most enthusiastic advocates of woman suffrage and the direct primary.

Despite this modest appraisal of what can be achieved, the survival of our society is dependent upon our continuing quest for a more rational politics. Our failures in this respect have been difficult for us to appreciate because our nation has always prided itself upon its practicality, and its spur to greatness lay in this direction rather than in theory. The first American was rightfully Benjamin Franklin, memorably described as "a man . . . less concerned with the golden pavements of the City of God than that the cobblestones on Chestnut Street in Philadelphia should be well and evenly laid. . . ." [6] Will not future historians be amazed at the remarkable dichotomy between the brilliance of our technical achievements and the relative poverty of our political and social arrangements? They will certainly ponder long over the question of how a culture could master the complex problem of reaching the moon, yet not manage a satisfactory solution to the simple problems of life on earth, such as a fair distribution of wealth, the maintenance of good health and educational standards, and the checking of crime.

Our fate is in our ability to order our lives as rationally as possible in a world marked by huge and precipitous changes. The future of American principles and institutions that began their development in a fundamentally different period lies ultimately in their adjustability to these changes. This challenge, which underlies all others, is a great one befitting a great people, and derives from change, the essence of life itself.

[6] Vernon Louis Parrington, *Main Currents in American Thought: An Interpretation of American Literature from the Beginning to 1920* (New York: Harcourt, Brace, 1927), I, 178.

Bibliography

In addition to the books and articles directly pertinent to this work—including some items not listed in the footnotes—this bibliography attempts to include further readings on the main topics covered for those whose interest has been whetted. The list is, of course, far from comprehensive or exhaustive, and the author is the first to realize how arbitrary his standards of inclusion and exclusion might appear. Usually, the editions cited are those most easily available to students.

General History

AGAR, HERBERT, *The Price of Union.* Boston: Houghton Mifflin, 1950.

BROGAN, DENIS, *Politics in America.* Garden City, N.Y.: Anchor Books, 1960.

CHAMBERS, WILLIAM NISBET, *Political Parties in a New Nation: The American Experience, 1776–1809.* New York: Oxford University Press, 1963.

FAULKNER, HAROLD U., *Politics, Reform and Expansion, 1890–1900.* New York: Harper and Row, 1959.

FORCEY, CHARLES, *The Crossroads of Liberalism.* New York: Oxford University Press, 1961.

GOLDMAN, ERIC F., *Rendezvous with Destiny: A History of Modern American Reform,* rev. and abr. ed. New York: Vintage Books, 1956.

HANDLIN, OSCAR, *Al Smith and His America.* Boston: Little, Brown, 1958.

———, *The Uprooted: The Epic Story of the Great Migrations That Made the American People.* New York: Grosset and Dunlap, 1951.

HAYS, SAMUEL P., *The Response to Industrialism, 1885–1914.* Chicago: University of Chicago Press, 1957.

HICKS, JOHN D., *The Populist Revolt.* Minneapolis: University of Minnesota Press, 1931.

———, *Republican Ascendancy, 1921–1933.* New York: Harper and Row, 1960.

HIGHAM, JOHN, *Strangers in the Land: Patterns of American Nativism, 1860–1925*. New Brunswick, N.J.: Rutgers University Press, 1955.

HOFSTADTER, RICHARD, *The American Political Tradition and the Men Who Made It*. New York: Vintage Books, 1956.

————, *The Age of Reform from Bryan to F.D.R.* New York: Knopf, 1956.

LATHAM, EARL, ed., *The Philosophy and Policies of Woodrow Wilson*. Chicago: University of Chicago Press, 1958.

LINK, ARTHUR S., "The South and the New Freedom: An Interpretation," *The American Scholar*, XX, 3 (Summer, 1951), 314–324.

————, *Woodrow Wilson and the Progressive Era, 1910–1917*. New York: Harper and Row, 1954.

NUGENT, WALTER T. K., *The Tolerant Populists: Kansas Populism and Nativism*. Chicago: University of Chicago Press, 1963.

PARKES, HENRY BAMFORD, *The American Experience: An Interpretation of the History and Civilization of the American People*. New York: Vintage Books, 1959.

PARRINGTON, VERNON L., *Main Currents in American Thought: An Interpretation of American Literature from the Beginning to 1920*. New York: Harcourt, Brace, 1927.

POLLACK, NORMAN, *The Populist Response to Industrial America: Midwestern Political Thought*. Cambridge: Harvard University Press, 1962.

SMITH, HENRY NASH, *Virgin Land: The American West as Symbol and Myth*. Cambridge: Harvard University Press, 1950.

WOODWARD, C. VANN, *Origins of the New South, 1877–1913*. Baton Rouge: Louisiana State University Press, 1951. Volume IX of the series, Wendell Holmes Stephenson and E. Merton Coulter, eds. *A History of the South*.

————, *Reunion and Reaction: The Compromise of 1877 and the End of Reconstruction*, 2d ed. Garden City, N.Y.: Anchor Books, 1956.

American Political Theory

ADAMS, JOHN, *The Political Writings of John Adams: Representative Selections*, ed. George Peek, Jr. New York: Liberal Arts Press, 1954.

BOORSTIN, DANIEL J., *The Genius of American Politics*. Chicago: University of Chicago Press, 1953.

BURNS, JAMES MACGREGOR, *The Deadlock of Democracy: Four-party Politics in America*. Englewood Cliffs, N.J.: Prentice-Hall, 1963.

CALHOUN, JOHN, *A Disquisition on Government and Selections from the Discourse,* ed. C. Gordon Post. New York: Liberal Arts Press, 1953.

COMMAGER, HENRY STEELE, *Majority Rule and Minority Rights.* New York: Peter Smith, 1950.

DAHL, ROBERT, *A Preface to Democratic Theory.* Chicago: University of Chicago Press, 1956.

The Federalist, available in many editions, but see especially the one edited by Edward Mead Earle (New York: Modern Library, 1937).

FISCHER, JOHN. "Unwritten Rules of American Politics," *Harper's,* CXCVII (November, 1948), 27–36.

HARTZ, LOUIS, *The Liberal Tradition in America: An Interpretation of American Political Thought since the Revolution.* New York: Harcourt, Brace and World, 1955.

LIPPMANN, WALTER, *Essays in the Public Philosophy.* Boston: Little, Brown, 1955.

MORGENTHAU, HANS, *The Purpose of American Politics.* New York: Knopf, 1960.

NIEBUHR, REINHOLD, *The Irony of American History.* New York: Scribner's, 1952.

ROSSITER, CLINTON, and JAMES LARE, eds., *The Essential Lippmann: A Political Philosophy for Liberal Democracy.* New York: Random House, 1963.

Roosevelt and the New Deal

BURNS, JAMES MACGREGOR, *Roosevelt: The Lion and the Fox.* New York: Harcourt, Brace and World, 1956.

EINAUDI, MARIO, *The Roosevelt Revolution.* New York: Harcourt, Brace and World, 1959.

FARLEY, JAMES A., *Jim Farley's Story: The Roosevelt Years.* New York: McGraw-Hill, 1948.

FLYNN, EDWARD J., *You're the Boss: The Practice of American Politics.* New York: Viking, 1947.

FREIDEL, FRANK, *Franklin D. Roosevelt* (Boston: Little, Brown). Vol. III: *The Triumph* (1956).

ICKES, HAROLD L., *The Secret Diary of Harold L. Ickes.* New York: Simon and Schuster. Vol. I: *The First Thousand Days, 1933–1936* (1953). Vol. II: *The Inside Struggle, 1936–1939* (1954). Vol. III: *The Lowering Clouds, 1939–1941* (1954).

PERKINS, FRANCES, *The Roosevelt I Knew.* New York: Viking, 1946.

ROSENMAN, SAMUEL I., *Working with Roosevelt*. London: Rupert Hart-Davis, 1952.

SCHLESINGER, ARTHUR M., JR., *The Age of Roosevelt*. Boston: Houghton Mifflin. Vol. I: *The Crisis of the Old Order, 1919–1933*, (1957). Vol. II: *The Coming of the New Deal*, (1959). Vol. III: *The Politics of Upheaval* (1960).

TUGWELL, REXFORD GUY, *The Democratic Roosevelt: A Biography of Franklin D. Roosevelt*. Garden City, N.Y.: Doubleday, 1957.

The Shift in American Politics

BELL, DANIEL, ed., *The Radical Right*. Garden City, N.Y.: Doubleday, 1963.

BURNHAM, WALTER DEAN, "The Changing Shape of the American Political Universe," *American Political Science Review*, LIX, 1, (March, 1965), 7–28.

CORNWELL, ELMER, JR., "Bosses, Machines, and Ethnic Groups," *Annals of the American Academy of Political and Social Science*, 353 (May, 1964), 27–39.

EISENHOWER, DWIGHT D., *The White House Years*. Garden City, N.Y.: Doubleday. Vol. I: *Mandate for Change, 1953–1956* (1963). Vol. II: *Waging Peace, 1956–1961* (1965).

ELDERSVELD, SAMUEL J., "The Influence of Metropolitan Party Pluralities in Presidential Elections since 1920," *American Political Science Review*, XLIII, 6 (December, 1949), 1189–1206.

FENTON, JOHN H., "Liberal-Conservative Divisions by Sections of the United States," *Annals of the American Academy of Political and Social Science*, 344 (November, 1962), 122–127.

FUCHS, L. H., *The Political Behavior of American Jews*. Glencoe, Ill.: Free Press, 1956.

GLAZER, NATHAN, and MOYNIHAN, DANIEL PATRICK, *Beyond the Melting Pot: The Negroes, Puerto Ricans, Jews, Italians, and Irish of New York City*. Cambridge: M.I.T. Press and Harvard University Press, 1963.

GREENSTEIN, FRED, "The Changing Pattern of Urban Party Politics," *Annals of the American Academy of Political and Social Science*, 353 (May, 1964), 1–13.

GRIMES, ALAN P., *Equality in America: Religion, Race and the Urban Majority*. New York: Oxford University Press, 1964.

HAVARD, WILLIAM C. "From Bossism to Cosmopolitanism: Changes in the Relationship of Urban Leadership to State Politics," *Annals of the American Academy of Political and Social Science*, 353 (May, 1964), 84–94.

HEILBRONER, ROBERT, "Carmine De Sapio: The Smile on the Face of the Tiger," *Harper's*, CCIX (July, 1954), 23–33.

HUGHES, EMMET JOHN, *The Ordeal of Power: A Political Memoir of the Eisenhower Years*. New York: Atheneum, 1963.

JOHNSON, DONALD BRUCE, *The Republican Party and Wendell Willkie*. Urbana: University of Illinois Press, 1960.

LUBELL, SAMUEL, *The Future of American Politics*, 2d ed. Garden City, N.Y.: Anchor Books, 1956.

MOON, HENRY LEE, *Balance of Power: The Negro Vote*. Garden City, N.Y.: Doubleday, 1948.

MOSCOW, WARREN, *Politics in the Empire State*. New York: Knopf, 1948.

SCHLESINGER, ARTHUR M., JR., *A Thousand Days: John F. Kennedy in the White House*. Boston: Houghton Mifflin, 1965.

SILVERMAN, CORINNE, "The Little Rock Story," *Case Studies in American Government*, "Inter-University Case Program," ed. Edwin A. Bock, and Alan K. Campbell. Englewood Cliffs, N.J.: Prentice-Hall, 1964.

SORENSEN, THEODORE C., *Kennedy*. New York: Harper and Row, 1965.

TRUMAN, HARRY S., *Memoirs by Harry S. Truman*. Garden City, N.Y.: Doubleday. Vol. I: *Year of Decisions* (1955). Vol. II: *Years of Trial and Hope* (1956).

WHITE, THEODORE H., *The Making of the President, 1960*. New York: Atheneum, 1961.

———, *The Making of the President, 1964*. New York: Atheneum, 1965.

WHITE, WILLIAM S., *The Taft Story*. New York: Harper and Row, 1954.

WILSON, JAMES Q., *The Amateur Democrat*. Chicago: University of Chicago Press, 1962.

Representation and Apportionment

"A Symposium on *Baker* v. *Carr*," *Yale Law Journal*, LXXII (November, 1962). See particularly E. E. Schattschneider, "Urbanization and Reapportionment," pp. 7–12, and Allan P. Sindler, "*Baker* v. *Carr*: How to 'Sear the Conscience' of Legislators," pp. 23–38.

ADVISORY COMMISSION ON INTERGOVERNMENTAL RELATIONS, *Apportionment of State Legislatures*, Washington, D.C., December, 1962.

BIBLIOGRAPHY

BAKER, GORDON E., *Rural versus Urban Political Power: The Nature and Consequences of Unbalanced Representation.* Garden City, N.Y.: Doubleday, 1955.

———, *The Reapportionment Revolution: Representation, Political Power, and the Supreme Court.* New York: Random House, 1966.

BICKEL, ALEXANDER M., "Reapportionment & Liberal Myths," *Commentary*, XXXV, 6 (June, 1963), 483–491.

DERGE, DAVID, "Metropolitan and Outstate Alignments in Illinois and Missouri Legislative Delegations," *American Political Science Review*, LII, 4 (December, 1958), 1051–1965. See comments on Derge's article by Richard T. Frost, *American Political Science Review*, LIII, 3 (September, 1959), 792–795.

DOUGLAS, SENATOR PAUL H. Speech in the Senate, March 26, 1956, *Congressional Record*, vol. 102, pt. 4 (Washington: Government Printing Office, 1956), pp. 5535–5574.

FRIEDMAN, ROBERT S. "The Urban-Rural Conflict Revisited," *The Western Political Quarterly*, XIV (June, 1961), 481–495.

HACKER, ANDREW, *Congressional Districting: The Issue of Equal Representation*, rev. ed., Washington: The Brookings Institution, 1964.

HAMILTON, HOWARD D., ed., *Legislative Apportionment: Key to Power.* New York: Harper and Row, 1964.

HANSON, ROYCE, *The Political Thicket: Reapportionment and Constitutional Democracy.* Englewood Cliffs, N.J.: Prentice-Hall, 1966.

JEWELL, MALCOLM E., ed., *The Politics of Reapportionment.* New York: Atherton Press, Prentice-Hall, 1962.

MCCLOSKEY, ROBERT G. "Foreword: The Reapportionment Case," *Harvard Law Review*, LXXVI (November, 1962), 54–74.

"On State Legislature Malapportionment: Rural Overrepresentation Acute in State Legislatures," *Congressional Quarterly*, XX, 5 (February 2, 1962), 170–178.

"On Urban-Rural Representation: Suburban Areas Most Underrepresented in House," *Congressional Quarterly*, XX, 5 (February 2, 1962), 153–169.

PERRIN, NOEL, "In Defense of Country Votes," *Yale Review*, LII, 1 (Autumn, 1962), 16–24.

PRITCHETT, C. HERMAN, "Equal Protection and the Urban Majority," *American Political Science Review*, LVIII, 4 (December, 1964), 869–875.

SCHUBERT, GLENDON, *Reapportionment*, New York: Scribner, 1965.

SILVA, RUTH C., "Apportionment of the New York State Legislature," *American Political Science Review*, LV, 4 (December, 1961), 870–881.

[254]

WELLS, DAVID, *Legislative Representation in New York State.* New York: International Ladies Garment Workers' Union, 1963.

Congress

BAILEY, STEPHEN K., *Congress Makes a Law: The Story Behind the Employment Act of 1946,* New York: Columbia University Press, 1950.

BERMAN, DANIEL M., *A Bill Becomes a Law: Congress Enacts Civil Rights Legislation,* 2d ed., New York: Macmillan, 1966.

————, *In Congress Assembled: The Legislative Process in the National Government,* New York: Macmillan, 1964.

BURNS, JAMES MACGREGOR, *Congress on Trial: The Legislative Process and the Administrative State.* New York: Harper and Row, 1949.

CLARK, JOSEPH S., ed., *Congressional Reform: Problems and Prospects,* New York: Thomas Y. Crowell, 1965.

———— (and other senators), *The Senate Establishment.* New York: Hill and Wang, 1963.

FENNO, RICHARD E., JR., "The House Appropriations Committee as a Political System: The Problem of Integration," *American Political Science Review,* LVI, 2 (June, 1962), 310–324.

FROMAN, LEWIS, JR., *Congressmen and Their Constituencies.* Chicago: Rand McNally, 1963.

GALLOWAY, GEORGE B., *History of the House of Representatives.* New York: Thomas Y. Crowell, 1962.

————, *The Legislative Process in Congress.* New York: Thomas Y. Crowell, 1953.

GOODWIN, GEORGE, JR., "The Seniority System in Congress," *American Political Science Review,* LIII, 2 (June, 1959), 412–436.

GROSS, BERTRAM M., *The Legislative Struggle: A Study in Social Combat.* New York: McGraw-Hill, 1953.

JONES, CHARLES O., "Representation in Congress: The Case of the House Agriculture Committee," *American Political Science Review,* LV, 2 (June, 1961), 345–357.

KEEFE, WILLIAM J., and MORRIS S. OGUL, *The American Legislative Process: Congress and the States.* Englewood Cliffs, N.J.: Prentice-Hall, 1964.

LOWI, THEODORE J., *Legislative Politics U.S.A.,* 2d ed. Boston: Little, Brown, 1965.

MASTERS, NICHOLAS A., "Committee Assignments in the House of Representatives," *American Political Science Review,* LV, 2 (June, 1961), 345–357.

MATTHEWS, DONALD R., *U.S. Senators and Their World*. New York: Vintage Books, 1960.

PEABODY, ROBERT L., and NELSON W. POLSBY, eds., *New Perspectives on the House of Representatives*. Chicago: Rand McNally, 1963.

ROBINSON, JAMES A., *The House Rules Committee*. Indianapolis: Bobbs-Merrill, 1963.

ROGERS, LINDSAY, *The American Senate*. New York: Knopf, 1926.

————, "Barrier Against Steamrollers," *The Reporter*, XX (January 8, 1959), 21–23.

SHILS, EDWARD A., "Congressional Investigations: The Legislator and His Environment," *University of Chicago Law Review*, XVIII (Spring, 1951), 571–584.

SHUMAN, HOWARD E., "Senate Rules and the Civil Rights Bill: A Case Study," *American Political Science Review*, LI, 4 (December, 1957), 955–975.

TRUMAN, DAVID, *The Governmental Process: Political Interests and Public Opinion*. New York: Knopf, 1964.

WHITE, WILLIAM S., *Citadel: The Story of the U.S. Senate*. New York: Harper and Row, 1956, 1957.

WILSON, WOODROW, *Congressional Government: A Study in American Politics*. New York: Meridian Books, 1956.

WOLFINGER, RAYMOND E., and JOAN HEIFETZ, "Safe Seats, Seniority, and Power in Congress," *American Political Science Review*, LIX, 2 (June, 1965), 337–349.

Federalism

The Commission on Intergovernmental Relations, *A Report to the President for Transmittal to the Congress* (June, 1955).

ELAZAR, DANIEL J., *American Federalism: A View from the States*. New York: Thomas Y. Crowell, 1966.

————, *The American Partnership: Intergovernmental Co-operation in the Nineteenth-Century United States*. Chicago: University of Chicago Press, 1962.

GOLDWIN, ROBERT A., ed., *A Nation of States: Essays on the American Federal System*. Chicago: Rand McNally, 1964.

MACMAHON, ARTHUR W., ed., *Federalism: Mature and Emergent*. Garden City, N.Y.: Doubleday, 1955.

RIKER, WILLIAM H., *Federalism: Origin, Operation, Significance*. Boston: Little, Brown, 1964.

Political Parties

BINKLEY, WILFRED E., *American Political Parties.* New York: Knopf, 1949.

CAMPBELL, ANGUS, *et al., The American Vote* (New York: Wiley, 1960).

———, and H. C. COOPER, *Group Differences in Attitudes and Votes.* Ann Arbor, Mich.: Survey Research Center, 1956.

Committee on Political Parties of the American Political Science Association (E. E. Schattschneider, chairman). *Towards a More Responsible Two-party System,* issued as a supplement to *American Political Science Review,* XLIV, 3 (September, 1950).

DAVID, PAUL T., "The Changing Political Parties," in Marian D. Irish, ed., *Continuing Crisis in American Politics,* pp. 47–66. Englewood Cliffs, N.J.: Prentice-Hall, 1963.

HEARD, ALEXANDER, *A Two-party South?* Chapel Hill: University of North Carolina Press, 1952.

HERRING, PENDLETON, *The Politics of Democracy: American Parties in Action.* New York: Rinehart, 1940.

HINDERAKER, IVAN, *Party Politics.* New York: Holt, Rinehart and Winston, 1956.

KEY, V. O., JR., *American State Politics: An Introduction.* New York: Knopf, 1956.

———, *Politics, Parties, and Pressure Groups,* 5th ed., New York: Thomas Y. Crowell, 1964.

———, *Southern Politics in State and Nation.* New York: Knopf, 1950.

PENNOCK, J. ROLAND, "Responsiveness, Responsibility, and Majority Rule," *American Political Science Review,* XLVI, 3 (September, 1952), 790–807.

RANNEY, AUSTIN, "Towards a More Responsible Two-Party System: A Commentary," *American Political Science Review,* XLV, 2 (June, 1951), 488–499.

———, and WILLMORE KENDALL, *Democracy and the American Party System.* New York: Harcourt, Brace and World, 1956.

ROSSITER, CLINTON, *Parties and Politics in America.* Ithaca, N.Y.: Cornell University Press, 1960.

SCHATTSCHNEIDER, E. E., *Party Government.* New York: Rinehart, 1942.

———, *The Semisovereign People: A Realist's View of Democracy in America.* New York: Holt, Rinehart and Winston, 1960.

STEDMAN, MURRAY S., and HERBERT SONTHOFF, "Party Responsibility —A Critical Inquiry," *Western Political Quarterly,* IV (September, 1951), 454–468.

The Presidency

BURNS, JAMES MACGREGOR, *Presidential Government: The Crucible of Leadership.* Boston: Houghton Mifflin, 1966.

CORWIN, EDWARD S., *The President.* New York: New York University Press, 1957.

FINER, HERMAN, *The Presidency: Crisis and Regeneration: An Essay in Possibilities.* Chicago: University of Chicago Press, 1960.

KOENIG, LOUIS W., *The Chief Executive.* New York: Harcourt, Brace and World, 1964.

LONGAKER, RICHARD P., *The Presidency and Individual Liberties.* Ithaca, N.Y.: Cornell University Press, 1961.

NEUSTADT, RICHARD E., *Presidential Power.* New York: Wiley, 1960.

ROCHE, JOHN P., and LEONARD W. LEVY, eds., *The Presidency.* New York: Harcourt, Brace and World, 1964.

ROSSITER, CLINTON, "President and Congress in the 1960's," in Marian D. Irish, ed., *Continuing Crisis in American Politics,* pp. 86–108. Englewood Cliffs, N.J.: Prentice-Hall, 1963.

———, *The American Presidency.* 2d. ed. New York: New American Library, 1960.

TUGWELL, REXFORD GUY, *The Enlargement of the Presidency.* Garden City, N.Y.: Doubleday, 1960.

The Supreme Court and Judicial Review

ABRAHAM, HENRY J., *The Judicial Process: An Introductory Analysis of the Courts of the United States, England, and France.* New York: Oxford University Press, 1962.

BETH, LOREN P. "The Supreme Court and the Future of Judicial Review," *Political Science Quarterly,* LXXVI, 1 (March, 1961), 11–23.

BICKEL, ALEXANDER M., *The Least Dangerous Branch: The Supreme Court at the Bar of Politics.* Indianapolis: Bobbs-Merrill, 1962.

CARDOZO, BENJAMIN N., *The Nature of the Judicial Process.* New Haven: Yale University Press, 1921.

CLAYTON, JAMES E., *The Making of Justice: The Supreme Court in Action.* New York: Dutton, 1964.

The Constitution of the United States of America: Analysis and Interpretation (Annotations of Cases Decided by the Supreme Court of the United States to June 30, 1952), ed. Edward S. Corwin, Prepared by the Legislative Reference Service, Library of Congress, 82d Cong., 2d sess., S. Doc. No. 170. Washington: Government Printing Office, 1953.

CORWIN, EDWARD S., *Court Over Constitution: A Study of Judicial Review as an Instrument of Popular Government.* Princeton: Princeton University Press, 1938.

CURTIS, CHARLES P., JR., *Lions Under the Throne.* Boston: Houghton Mifflin, 1947.

DAHL, ROBERT A., "Decision-Making in a Democracy: The Role of the Supreme Court as a National Policy-Maker," *Journal of Public Law*, VI (1957), 279–295.

FRANK, JOHN P., *Marble Palace: The Supreme Court in American Life.* New York: Knopf, 1958.

FREUND, PAUL A., *The Supreme Court of the United States: Its Business, Purposes, and Performance.* Cleveland: World; Meridian Books, 1961.

FRIEDMANN, WOLFGANG, *Law in a Changing Society.* Berkeley and Los Angeles: University of California Press, 1959.

HAMILTON, WALTON, "The Path of Due Process of Law," in Conyers Read, *The Constitution Reconsidered*, pp. 167–190. New York: Columbia University Press, 1938.

HAND, LEARNED, *The Bill of Rights.* Cambridge: Harvard University Press, 1958.

HURST, JAMES WILLARD, *The Growth of American Law: The Law Makers.* Boston: Little, Brown, 1950.

KURLAND, PHILIP B., "Foreword: Equal in Origin and Equal in Title to the Legislative and Executive Branches of the Government," *Harvard Law Review*, LXXVIII, 1 (November, 1964), 143–176.

LERNER, MAX, *The Mind and Faith of Justice Holmes: His Speeches, Essays, Letters and Judicial Opinions.* Garden City, N.Y.: Halcyon House, 1943, 1948.

———, "The Supreme Court and American Capitalism," *Yale Law Journal*, XLII (1933), 668–701.

MCCLOSKEY, ROBERT G., *The American Supreme Court, 1789–1960.* Chicago: University of Chicago Press, 1960.

———, ed., *Essays in Constitutional Law.* New York: Vintage Books, 1957.

MASON, ALPHEUS, *Harlan Fiske Stone: Pillar of the Law.* New York: Viking, 1956.

[259]

———, *The Supreme Court: Palladium of Freedom*. Ann Arbor: University of Michigan Press, 1962.

———, and William M. Beaney. *American Constitutional Law: Introductory Essays and Selected Cases*. Englewood Cliffs, N.J.: Prentice-Hall, 1954.

MENDELSON, WALLACE, *Justices Black and Frankfurter: Conflict in the Court*. Chicago: University of Chicago Press, 1961.

———, "Justices Black and Frankfurter: Supreme Court Majority and Minority Trends," *Journal of Politics*, XII (February, 1950), 66–92.

PELTASON, JACK W., *Federal Courts in the Political Process*. New York: Random House, 1955.

PRITCHETT, C. HERMAN, *Civil Liberties and the Vinson Court*. Chicago: University of Chicago Press, 1954.

———, *Congress Versus the Supreme Court: 1957–1960*. Minneapolis: University of Minnesota Press, 1961.

ROCHE, JOHN P., "Judicial Self-restraint," *American Political Science Review*, XLIX (September, 1955), 762–772.

RODELL, FRED, *Nine Men: A Political History of the Supreme Court from 1790 to 1955*. New York: Random House, 1955.

SCHMIDHAUSER, J. R., *The Supreme Court: Its Politics, Personalities, and Procedures*. New York: Holt, Rinehart and Winston, 1960.

SCHUBERT, GLENDON A., *Constitutional Politics: The Political Behavior of Supreme Court Justices and the Constitutional Policies That They Make*. New York: Holt, Rinehart, and Winston, 1960.

———, *Judicial Policy-Making: The Political Role of the Courts*. Chicago: Scott, Foresman, 1965.

SWISHER, CARL B., *American Constitutional Development*, 2d ed. Boston: Houghton Mifflin, 1954.

WECHSLER, HERBERT, *Principles, Politics, and Fundamental Law: Selected Essays*. Cambridge: Harvard University Press, 1961.

Civil Rights

BLACK, CHARLES, JR., "The Lawfulness of the Segregation Decisions," *The Yale Law Journal*, LXIX, 3 (January, 1960), 421–430.

BLAUSTEIN, ALBERT, and CLARENCE FERGUSON, JR., *Desegregation and the Law: The Meaning and Effect of the School Segregation Cases*, 2d ed. New York: Vintage Books, 1962.

CAHN, EDMOND, "A Dangerous Myth in the School Segregation Cases," *1954 Annual Survey of American Law, New York Law Review*, XXX (1955), 150–169.

————, "The Lawyer, the Social Psychologist, and the Truth," *1955 Annual Survey of American Law, New York Law Review*, XXXI (1956), 182–194.

CATTERAL, RALPH T., "Judicial Self-Restraint: The Obligation of the Judiciary," *American Bar Association Journal*, XLII, 9 (September, 1956), 829–833.

COOK, EUGENE, and WILLIAM I. POTTER, "The School Segregation Cases: Opposing the Opinion of the Supreme Court," *American Bar Association Journal*, XLII, 4 (April, 1956), 313–317, 391.

HUMPHREY, HUBERT H., ed., *School Desegregation: Documents and Commentaries*. New York: Thomas Y. Crowell, 1964.

IRION, H. GIFFORD, "The Constitutional Clock: A Horological Inquiry," *Georgetown Law Journal*, XLVI (Spring, 1958), 443–458.

LEWIS, ANTHONY, and *The New York Times, Portrait of a Decade: The Second American Revolution*. New York: Random House, 1964.

MYRDAL, GUNNAR (with the assistance of RICHARD STERNER and ARNOLD ROSE), *An American Dilemma: The Negro Problem and Modern Democracy*. New York: Harper and Row, 1944.

ROSENBLUM, VICTOR G., *Law as a Political Instrument*. Garden City, N.Y.: Doubleday, 1955.

To Secure These Rights: The Report of the President's Committee on Civil Rights. Washington: Government Printing Office, 1947.

TAPER, BERNARD, *Gomillion versus Lightfoot: The Tuskegee Gerrymander Case*. New York: McGraw-Hill, 1962.

WOODWARD, C. VANN, *The Burden of Southern History*. Baton Rouge: Louisiana State University Press, 1960.

————, *The Strange Career of Jim Crow*. New York: Oxford University Press, 1955.

ZIEGLER, BENJAMIN MUNN, ed., *Desegregation and the Supreme Court*. Boston: D. C. Heath, 1958.

Index

Adams, John, 24
Adkins v. *Children's Hospital,* 206n
Africa, 74
Agricultural Adjustment Act, 214
agriculture:
    early political dominance of, 4,
        5, 10, 11, 41, 42
    in interrelated economy, 197
    and the New Deal, 41
    and party politics, 64, 76, 159
    political decline of, 33, 92
    and slavery, 11
    and urban growth, 16
    and Wilsonian liberalism, 29
Alabama, 117, 231
Alaska, 107
Alsop, Joseph, 75
Alsop, Stewart, 75
American Bar Association, 237
American Bar Association Journal,
    225
Anglo-Saxonism, 4, 17, 19, 28, 47,
    60, 82, 83
    see also ethnic minorities
anti-Catholicism, 15, 38
anti-Communism, 47
antimajoritarianism, 21–25, 88, 94,
    97–98, 245
anti-Semitism, 38
antitrust, 26, 30, 203
antiunionism, 75

antiurbanism: *see* ruralism
apportionment: *see* representation,
    apportionment of
Arizona, 117
Arkansas, 79, 117
armed services, desegregation of, 79
Articles of Confederation, 174
Asia, 74
Attlee, Clement Richard, 68
authoritarianism, 56

"backlash vote," 86
Bacon, Francis, 190
Bailey v. *Drexel Furniture Com-*
    pany, 205n
Baker, Gordon, quoted, 105
Baker v. *Carr,* 78, 151n, 232–233,
    236
Barden, Graham, 120
Barton, Bruce, 71
Beaney, William, 202
Bell, Daniel, quoted, 32
Benson, George C. S., 145
Beth, Loren P., 239
Bickel, Alexander M., quoted, 99,
    108–109
Bill of Rights, 141
Black, Charles, Jr., 209, 225, 234
Black, Hugo, 234
Blaustein, Albert, quoted, 226
Boorstin, Daniel, quoted, 2

bossism, 28–29, 45
Brandeis, Louis D., 205
Bricker, John W., 67, 74, 173–174
Bricker amendment, 74, 173–174
Brogan, Denis W., *Politics in America*, 33
Brown, Henry, 209
Brown v. *Board of Education of Topeka*, 77–78, 222, 224, 227
Bryan, William Jennings, 14, 25, 36, 37, 41, 42
Buchanan, James, 179
Bunting v. *Oregon*, 205n
Burns, James MacGregor, quoted, 21–22; 114, 245
business:
    big, 10, 17, 18, 29, 73, 76–77, 146, 200–206
    Eisenhower and, 73
    government regulation of, 12, 13, 63, 65–66, 144, 200–206
    and the New Deal, 41, 65–66, 214, 217
    and political conservatism, 17, 18, 76–77
    small, 41, 65
    and Supreme Court, 77, 200–206
    and Wilsonian liberalism, 29
Butler, Paul, 154
Byrnes, James F., 156

Cahn, Edmond, 225
Calhoun, John C., 21, 88, 94;
    theory of concurrent majority, 24
California, 37, 41, 69, 82, 97, 176
Calvinism, 30
Cannon, Clarence, 131
Cardozo, Benjamin N., 193
Carter v. *Carter Coal Co.*, 198n
Cater, Douglass, quoted, 118
census:
    1790–1960, compared, 3; 1860, 3; 1890, 2, 34; 1910, 1920, 34
Chiang Kai-shek, 75

Chicago, 41, 176
Chicago, Milwaukee and St. Paul R.R. v. *Minnesota*, 202n
child labor laws, 193, 205, 207
China, 111
civil rights:
    and federal balance, 79, 139, 140, 141
    and the judiciary, 56, 74, 77–79, 82, 141, 206–213, 219–228
    and the legislature, 7, 120–126, 228
    and the New Deal, 48–51
    and party cleavage, 156–161
    post-Civil War, 168, 206–213
    post-New Deal, 76–81, 219–227
    and state compliance, 79
Civil Rights Act of 1957, 78
Civil Rights Act of 1960, 78
Civil Rights Act of 1964, 78, 80, 158, 228
Civil Rights Act of 1965, 228
civil rights bills:
    1956, 121; 1957, 79, 121, 122; 1960, 79; 1964, 140
Civil Rights Cases, of 1883, 208
Civil War, the, 10–14, 24, 81, 159, 200
Clark, Joseph, *The Senate Establishment*, 119, 129–130
Clayton Antitrust Act, 30
cloture rule, 122–126 *passim*, 130
Colegrove v. *Green*, 191n, 229, 232
Commission on Organization of the Executive Branch of the Government: *see* Hoover Commission
communications, frontier, 92
communications industries, 33, 146
Communism, 75
concurrent majority, theory of, 24
confederation, 137
Congress:
    attack on Supreme Court by, 235–238

Congress (*cont.*)
    committee system, 60, 113–119, 127–128
    conservative domination of, 50, 57, 59–62, 72–87 *passim*, 241
    environmental distortions of, 126–234 *passim*
    "operating rule" of, 115
    parochialism of, 113
    and party organization, 153
    and presidential power, 58, 165, 172–173, 175
    representational inequities in, 105–112, 135–136
    and rules of procedure, 120–122, 130
    and seniority system, 114–119
congressional elections:
    1918, 169; 1934, 54; 1938, 59–62
Connecticut, 97
consensus, group, versus abstract majority, 21
conservatism:
    and antimajoritarianism, 124
    attack on judiciary, 235–238
    checked by Supreme Court, 234
    Congress as last stronghold of, 81, 57–59, 71–87
    contextual meanings of, 52–54
    dependence on malapportionment, 88
    as dominant twentieth-century theme, 76
    and federal balance, 140, 143–145
    legislative, and changing concept of federalism, 136
    and local autonomies, 18
    and New Deal, 40–44, 54–55, 59–62
    political ascendancy of, 13–20
    and post-New Deal, 71–87
    as product of federalism, 148–149
    Progressive, 26–29

conservatism (*cont.*)
    and Republican party, 63–64
    self-defeating character of, 166–167
    southern strains of, 15, 86
    Supreme Court's reflection of, 203–206
Constitution, the, structure of, and judiciary function, 22–23, 55–56, 137–138, 182–186, 195–198, 217
Constitutional Convention, 146, 197
constitution(s), state:
    and apportionment, 17
    and executive power, 161
Coolidge, Calvin, 73, 74
"cooperative federalism," 148
Corwin, Edward S., quoted, 192
Council of State Governments, 236
"Court-packing" bill, 55–56, 60, 213–216, 238
"cross of gold, the," 14
Cummings v. *County Board of Education*, 210*n*
Curtis, Charles, Jr., 190
Cushman, Robert, 195

Dahl, Robert, quoted, 112, 192, 220; 188, 189
Darrow, Clarence, 36
Darwinism, 25, 35–36
Daughters of the American Revolution, 43
Davis, John William, 37
Delaware, 117
Democratic Advisory Council, 154
Democratic party:
    and agrarian alliance, 13
    convention, 1896, 14; 1924, 37–38; 1948, 156–157
    ideological cleavage in, 156–160
    as instrument of New Deal, 40–41, 47
    in Jacksonian period, 11
    and nationalization of policy, 154–155

Democratic party (*cont.*)
    post-World War I split, 36–38
    pre-New Deal prejudices of, 43
    Roosevelt's "purge," 57–60, 153
    Senate domination, 117, 119
    southern bloc, 50–51, 156–157
    and two-thirds rule, 51
    and urban vote, 38, 40–48, 50–51, 156–160
    and Wilsonian liberalism, 29–31, 152, 171
Democratic Steering Committee, 119
Depression, Great, the, 15, 40, 49, 77, 142, 143, 171, 214
Dewey, Thomas E., 61, 66–67, 69, 71–72
Dicey, A. V., 149, 198
Dirksen, Everett, 80, 238
Disraeli, Benjamin, 68, 71
Dixon-Yates controversy, 75
Douglas, Paul, 105, 108, 123
Dred Scott case, 216
"due process," 217
Dunne, Finley Peter, 189, 190

Eastland, James O., 120–121
economy:
    and Civil War, 10–14, 200
    class clashes within, 22
    government involvement in, 6, 11, 12, 137–139, 142, 148, 150, 203, 205
    interrelatedness of, 4, 5–7, 205
    and New Deal, 41–44
    and technological revolution, 1, 2, 5, 244
education, and civil rights, 222–224
Eisenhower, Dwight D.:
    and business, 73
    and civil rights, 78, 79
    and conservative reaction, 74–76, 144–145
    and power of the presidency, 174–175
elections: *see* presidential elections; congressional elections
Electoral College, 39, 175–178

electoral reform, 177–178
electoral vote, 50–51
Emerson, Thomas, 232
Employment Act of 1946, 75
"equal protection of the laws," 12, 202, 207, 213, 222, 223, 232, 234
equality:
    abstract, 24
    political distortion of, 19
ethnic minorities:
    and conservative bias, 27, 82
    and Democratic party, 36–39
    Negro prejudice among, 86
    and New Deal, 43–46
    and new federal balance, 144
    political emergence of, 10, 11, 25, 32, 36–39
    politically victimized, 18, 19, 27–29, 76–77
    second, third generation, 47
Europe:
    migration from, 4
    post-World War II, 74–75
executive reorganization bill, 57, 60

"faction," 21
Fair Deal, the, 73, 118
Falkland, Viscount Lucius Cary, 66
Faulkner, Harold, 5
Federal Bureau of Investigation, 142
Federal Reserve System, 29
Federal Trade Commission, 29
federalism:
    built-in conservatism of, 148–151
    changed concept of, 136
    and conformist pressures, 146–147
    conservative defense of, 146, 150
    defined by balance of forces, 79, 136–137
    flexibility of, 137
    inadequacies of, 148–149
    liberal criticism of, 150

federalism (*cont.*)
    and nationalizing process, 136–
      138, 145–147
    problem-solving within context
      of, 147–148
    and separation of powers, 88,
      137–139
    states' role in context of, 136
    utilitarian purpose of, 145–146
    viability of, 145, 148
Federalist party, 10
Fenno, Richard, Jr., 128
Fenton, John H., 65
Ferguson, Clarence, Jr., 226
Fifteenth Amendment, 208, 211–212,
    222
filibuster, 80, 111, 122–126
Finer, Herman, quoted, 178
Fish, Hamilton, 71
Florida, 97, 117
foreign policy:
    post-World War II, 74–75
    and presidental power, 74, 173–
      174
Fourteenth Amendment:
    and apportionment, 232–233
    and free enterprise, 194–197,
      200–206
    and Negro civil rights, 12, 13,
      207–213, 220, 226
    passage of, 141
France, Third, Fourth Republics of,
    132, 243
Frank, John P., quoted, 204; 203,
    207, 211–212
Frankfurter, Felix, 141*n*, 188, 191,
    193, 229–230, 231–233
Franklin, Benjamin, 247
freedom:
    individual, as limitation of ac-
      tion by state, 22
    meaning of, 7
    and political power, 23
Froman, Lewis, Jr., 115
frontier, official ending of, 2
fundamentalism, religious, 25, 33–
    36

Gaitskell, Hugh, 70–71
Garner, John Nance, 41
Gayle v. *Browder*, 227*n*
"general welfare," 138
George, Walter, 121
Georgia, 37, 117
Georgia Railroad . . . v. Smith,
    202*n*
Germany, proportional representa-
    tion in, 90
gerrymandering, 93–94, 129, 231
Gibbons v. *Ogden*, 197
Giles v. *Harris*, 211*n*
Glass, Carter, 211
Glazer, Nathan, 35
gold reserves, 111
Goldman, Eric, quoted, 43–44
Goldwater, Barry, 64, 67, 85–86,
    158, 241
Gomillion v. *Lightfoot*, 231–232
Gong Lum v. *Rice*, 213*n*
"Grand Old Party," 6
"grandfather clauses," 213
Granger laws, 204
grant-in-aid programs, 137–139, 148,
    150
Gray v. *Sanders*, 233
Great Britain:
    cabinet system of, 165–166,
      178, 180
    Conservative party of, 67–70,
      237
    example of, 23, 243
    House of Commons of, 23,
      165
    Labour party of, 68–71
    plural vote system, 102
    prime minister, 166, 179
    representational system of, 90,
      91, 95–96
"Great Commoner," the, 36
Great Reform Bill of 1832, 20, 95–
    96, 232
Gremillion, Jack P. F., 140
Grovey v. *Townsend*, 213 and *n*,
    221–222
Guffey Coal Act, 215

Guinn v. *United States,* 213n
Gunther, John, quoted, 110

Hacker, Louis, 4
Hall v. *De Cuir,* 208n
Hamilton, Alexander, 11, 197
Hammer v. *Dagenhart,* 193, 205n
Harding, Warren G., 73, 74, 215
Harlan, John M., 210, 211, 212
Hartz, Louis, *The Liberal Tradition in America,* 22–23
Hayden, Carl, 131
Helvering v. *Davis,* 216n
Hirabayashi v. *United States,* 191n
Hirschfield, Robert, quoted, 135–136; 151
Hofstadter, Richard, 12; quoted, 27
Holmes, Oliver Wendell, Jr., 183, 185, 207
Hoke v. *United States,* 207
Home Building & Loan Association v. *Blaisdell,* 214
Homestead Act, 12
Hoover Commission (Commission on Organization of Executive Branch of the Government), 57
Hoover, Herbert, 38, 48, 57
House of Representatives:
    Agricultural Committee, 113
    Appropriations Committee, 128, 131
    Democratic Committee on Committees, 118
    majority floor leader, 118
    reapportionment of, 177
    representational function of, 107
    Rules Committee, 58, 118, 120
    rural overrepresentation in, 105
    suburban underrepresentation in, 106–107
    Speaker, 26, 118
    Ways and Means Committee, 118, 128–129
Hughes, Charles E., 215
Hugo, Victor, 80
Humphrey, Hubert, 157, 158
Hungary, 75

Hurst, James Willard, quoted, 1; 92, 239

Illinois, 176, 229
immigrants: *see* ethnic minorities
immigration:
    and Anglo-American tradition, 83
    and industrial capitalism, 12
    restriction of, 27–28, 34–35, 73, 241
    southern, eastern European, 4, 16, 34–35, 83
    and urban growth, 3, 4
Indonesia, 137
industrialization:
    beginnings, 4–6, 10
    and Civil War, 10–14, 200
    government regulation of, 64–66
    and immigration, 12
    malapportionment encouraged by, 17, 92, 109–111
    and New Deal, 42
    and progressive middle class, 26
    and rural-conservative leadership, 17
    and Wilsonian liberalism, 29
interstate commerce, 137, 197, 203, 205, 207–208, 224
interventionism, 63
Iowa, 117
Irish, the, and machine control, 37, 46, 48, 82
isolationism, 36, 63, 170
Italians, the, and machine control, 46, 48

Jackson, Andrew, 41
Jackson, Robert, 186
Jacksonian era, 11, 163, 164, 166
Jacksonian ideal, 29
Japanese Americans, and World War II, 62
Jefferson, Thomas, 11, 13, 41, 162, 164

Jeffersonian ideal, 29
Jews, the, and machine control, 46, 48
Johnson, Edwin C., 131
Johnson, Lyndon B.:
  accomplishments, 241
  civil rights, 78, 80–81, 139
  as Senate Majority Leader, 78, 80, 114n, 130
  symbolism of, 84, 158
  as vice president, 80
judiciary, the:
  and change in concept of justice, 141
  executive support of, 79
  and federal courts, 141
  and transformation of power structure, 82
  see also Supreme Court

Kahn-Freund, O., 242
Kaltenborn, H. V., 146–147
Keefe, William J., 120
Kendrick, Benjamin, 4
Kennedy, John F.:
  and civil rights, 78, 79, 80
  style, 84
  symbolism, 81–83
Kestnbaum, Meyer, 144–145
Kestnbaum Report, 144n, 145
Key, V. O., Jr., 149
Keynes, John Maynard, *General Theory of Employment, Interest, and Money*, 194; quoted, 192; 52–53, 194
Keynesian economics, and democratic world, 53
Koenig, Louis, 167
Krock, Arthur, 125–126
Ku Klux Klan, 25, 37–38

labor:
  and immigration, 16, 34–35
  and industrialization, 12
  and New Deal, 41, 73
labor leaders, 41

labor unions, 73
laissez-faire, 6, 8, 30, 77, 194, 202–203, 217
land grants, 12
Landau, Martin, quoted, 147; 151n
Landon, Alfred M., 55
law enforcement:
  federal, and civil rights, 79
  local distortions of, 140, 142
League of Nations, 169
legislative apportionment: see representation, apportionment of
legislator, the:
  insulated environment of, 126–131
  perceptual distortions of, 131–134
legislature(s), state:
  antimajoritarianism, 92–93, 135–136
  and civil rights, 77
  decline of, 161–166
  and reapportionment controversy, 236–239
  rural-urban disparities in, 95–100, 103–104
  see also representation, apportionment of
Lehman, Herbert H., 61, 131
Leites, Nathan, 132
Lerner, Max, 201
liberalism:
  as compromise, 52
  compensating action of forces of, 135–136
  of New Deal, 45–46
  party representation of, 57–59
  Populist limits of, 36
  post–New Deal, 72–87 *passim*
  and Republican party, 63–64
  and Supreme Court, 205–206
  Wilsonian, 29–31
liberum veto, 22
Lincoln, Abraham, 12, 49, 80, 167, 179, 180
Lippmann, Walter, quoted, 5, 6n, 42, 104, 123
literacy, and progressive reform, 27

Little Rock (Ark.), 79
localism:
    congressional, 92, 94, 113, 241
    diminution of, 136
    and New Deal, 57–58
    replaced by nationalism, 147
    see also ruralism
Lochner v. New York, 203
Loewenstern, Karl, 145
Los Angeles, 176
Louisiana, 117, 140
Louisville, New Orleans, and Texas
    Railway v. Mississippi, 208n
Lubell, Samuel, 38, 156
Lucas v. Colorado, 99

McAdoo, William Gibbs, 37
McCabe v. Atchison, Topeka, and
    Santa Fe R.R. Co., 213n
McCarran-Walter Act, 73
McCarthy era, 47
McCloskey, Robert G., quoted,
    192n, 199, 206; 237
McCooey, John, 45
McCulloch v. Maryland, 196–197
McLaurin v. Oklahoma State Re-
    gents, 223
McReynolds, James C., 215, 226
Madison, James, 21–24, 88, 94, 162n,
    179
Madisonian philosophy, the, 21–25,
    97, 122
Magnuson, Warren, 124n
Maine, 54
majority:
    abstract, versus group consen-
        sus, 21
    permanent, 19
    rule, and minority rights, 98,
        102–104
    theory of concurrent, 24
    unpropertied, 22
    see also antimajoritarianism;
        minority
malapportionment: see representa-
    tion, apportionment of
Malaysia, 137

Mali Federation, 137
Manion, Clarence, 144–145
Manion-Kestnbaum Report contro-
    versy, 76, 144–145
Marshall, John, 137, 196, 197, 217
Marshall Plan, 74
"Martin, Barton, and Fish," 71
Martin, Joseph, 71
Mason, Alpheus Thomas, 192, 202–
    203
Mason-Dixon Line, 81
Massachusetts, 117
Masters, Nicholas, 128
Matsu, 75
Matthews, D. R., U. S. Senators and
    Their World, 127
Mayor . . . of Baltimore City v.
    Dawson, 227n
Medicare, 241
Melnik, Constantin, 132
mercantilism, 11
Mexico, 111
Michigan, 117
Middle Atlantic states, 10
Midwest, the:
    conservative, liberal identifica-
        tion of, 64
    decline of Populism in, 15, 16
    Democratic party resurgence
        in, 160
    isolationism, 31, 36, 63–64
    and malapportionment, 17
    Progressive movement in, 26,
        63
minimum wage laws, 184, 206
Minnesota, 202
minority:
    aggregates, 98
    antimajoritarian, 24
    economic interests, 109–112
    elitist rule of, 98–103
    permanent, 19
    privileged, 22, 149
    "protection," 122–126
    and vestigial majority, 100,
        103–106
    see also ethnic minorities; ma-
        jority; antimajoritarianism

Mississippi:
  segregation, 208
  and Senate seniority, 117
  voting rights, 139–140
Missouri, 78, 118, 226
Missouri ex rel. Gaines v. *Canada*, 222
"Mr. Republican," 72
"monkey trial," 35–36
Montesquieu, Baron de la Brède et de, 23
Moon, Henry Lee, 49
morality, legislation of, 26–28, 32–33
Morgenthau, Henry, Jr., 111
Moynihan, Daniel Patrick, 35
Mugler v. *Kansas*, 202
Muir v. *Louisville Park Theatrical Association*, 227n
Muller v. *Oregon*, 205n
Mundt-Coudert proposal, 177–178
municipal reform, 26
Munn v. *Illinois*, 202n
Myrdal, Gunnar, *An American Dilemma*, 221, 225

National Association for the Advancement of Colored People (NAACP), 49, 228
national character, turning point of, 5
National Industrial Recovery Act (N.I.R.A.), 214
National Labor Relations Act, 216
National Labor Relations Board v. *Jones & Laughlin Steel Corp.*, 216n
nationalization, 15, 164, 136–138, 145–147
nativism, 34, 37, 38
naturalization, literacy qualifications for, 27
Nebbia v. *New York*, 214n
Negro, the:
  and civil rights legislation, 50, 77–81, 84
  and Democratic party, 159–160

Negro, the (*cont.*)
  and Ku Klux Klan, 37–38
  and machine politics, 27–28
  and New Deal, 48–49
  and new federal balance, 144
  political emergence of, 39, 160
  and school integration, 210, 222–224, 227–228
  and Senate "minority" protection, 110
  and southern judiciary, 140
  and urban migration, 34–35
  and voting rights, 18, 139, 207, 211–212, 222, 231
  and Wilsonian liberalism, 30
  and World War II, 63
Negro Revolution, the, 227–228, 231
Neumann, Franz, 149
Nevada, 96, 107
New Deal, the:
  and civil rights, 216–227 *passim*
  and congressional opposition, 57–59, 72–87 *passim*
  and conservatism, 40–44, 59–62, 72
  and Court-packing controversy, 55–56, 187, 194, 213–219
  decade preceding, 32–39
  and Democratic party, 41, 57–58, 153
  durability of, 74–76
  and the executive, 164
  and federal balance, 142–144, 171–174
  and industry, 65–66
  philosophical ambiguities of, 51–53
  and Republican party, 54–55, 57–59, 63–72
  silver policy of, 111
  spirit of, and World War II, 62–63
  Truman's extension of, 72–73
  and urban population, 42–43, 47–48
New England:
  early urbanism of, 10

New England (*cont.*)
ethnic minorities in, 46
Democratic party resurgence in, 160
New Jersey, 46, 148
New York:
machine politics, 27, 37, 46
rural-urban disparities, 147–148, 176
Senate representation of, 107
New York City:
electoral power of, 176
state representation of, 95, 147–148
Nigeria, 137
Nixon, Richard M., 82, 180
Nixon v. *Condon*, 213n
Nixon v. *Herndon*, 213n
"noble experiment, the," 34
Norris, George, 53
North Atlantic Treaty, 75
North Dakota, 117
Northeast, the:
malapportionment in, 17
Negro migration to, 35
political impotence of Negro in, 18
Notre Dame Law School, 144
nuclear armaments race, 74–75
Nyasaland, 137

obiter dicta, 198
O'Connor, John, 58, 118
Ogul, Morris S., 120
Ohio, 61
"one man, one vote," 230, 233
one-partyism, 116–117, 160, 177
Oregon, 117
Orwell, George, 210
Owen v. *Browder*, 227

pacificism, 3
"parliamentary democracy," 165
parliamentary systems, 23
patronage, federal, and the New Deal, 44

Patterson, Joe T., 139
Payne, Frederick, 131
Pennsylvania, 119, 176
Pennsylvania Dutch, the, 17
Perrin, Noel, quoted, 94–95
Peters v. *Hobby*, 191n
Philadelphia, 148
Philadelphia Convention, 22
Plato, 36, 101, 133–134
Plessy v. *Ferguson*, 208–210, 211, 221, 224, 226
plural vote system, 102
Point Four Aid Program, 75
Poland, 22
political campaigns, sub rosa issues of, 25
political dualism, 26–29
political institutions, effective, 1, 8, 9
political machines:
basic conservatism of, 46
and ethnic minorities, 28
and New Deal, 44–45, 47–48
and patronage, 44
and Roosevelt nomination, 41
and rural conservatism, 18
and Stevenson nomination, 47
and Truman nomination, 78
and urban Democratic party, 13, 36–39, 41, 47, 153
and urban reform, 26–27
political parties:
campaign contributions, 153
and historical process, 152
and ideological consistency, 154–155
leadership, 154
national, state power structure, 58–59
nationalization of, 151–161
and party discipline, 155–158
prototype of successful, 11
and segregation, 222
see also specific parties
political philosophers, American, 24
political tradition, permanent, transitory, 8, 9
Pollak, Louis H., 233

Pollock v. *Farmer's Loan and Trust Co.*, 203n
population:
    ethnic structure of, 17, 27–28
    mobility, and state, national loyalty, 138–139
    patterns, and political outlook, 1–9
    representation, 96–97
Populist movement, 14–16, 25–26, 36–37
Pound, Roscoe, quoted, 182
presidency, the:
    antithird term tradition, 61, 74
    candidates for, 179–180
    continuum of power growth in office of, 167–172, 174–178
    future of, 178–181
    limitations imposed on, 164, 172–174
    power of, 50, 57, 72–84 *passim*, 161–167, 170, 241
presidential elections:
    1860, 1896, 87; 1928, 38, 42, 48; 1932, 54, 87, 42; 1936, 42, 54, 59; 1952, 47, 73; 1956, 47; 1960, 82; 1964, 86–87
President's Committee on Civil Rights, 79
Pritchett, C. Herman, 237
Progressive movement; Progressivism, 26–31, 34, 64, 207
prohibition, 15, 26–27, 32–34, 37
proportional representation system (political), 89–93
    see also representation, apportionment of
Protestantism, 32–33, 47, 83
Prussia, 102
psychology, 224–226
Puerto Ricans, and the New Deal, 48
Puritanism, 17, 26, 207

Quemoy, 75
quota system, 73, 241

racism, 15, 34, 158, 221

railroads:
    fixing of rates of, 202, 204
    segregation of, 208
Railway Retirement Act, 214
Railroad Retirement Board v. *Alton R.R. Co.*, 214
Rayburn, Sam, 129
reapportionment: *see* representation, apportionment of
recession, of 1937, 1938, 57
Reconstruction, 37, 78, 208
reform movement, early twentieth-century pattern of failure, 31
religion: *see* fundamentalism; Protestantism; Roman Catholicism; Jews, the
Renner, Karl, *The Institutions of Private Law and Their Social Functions*, 242
representation, apportionment of:
    elitist concepts, 100–102
    and federal balance, 143
    and Fourteenth Amendment, 243
    function and purpose, 88–89
    geographical versus political systems of, 89–92, 95–96, 139, 230
    and minority groups, 76–77, 98, 231
    and New Deal, 56–57
    problem of diversity, 92–93, 95, 97, 100, 110, 129
    rural-urban disparities in, 17, 18, 92–104, 105–107
    and strengthened executive, 85, 163
    and Supreme Court, 150, 177, 191, 219, 229–235
    and vestigial majorities, 100, 103–104, 105
Republican party:
    business orientation of, 206
    candidates characterized, 42
    compared to British Conservative party, 67–70; Labour party, 69–71

Republican party (*cont.*)
  congressional record of, 54, 59–
    62, 71–72
  conventions, 1944, 1948, 67;
    1952, 64, 66; 1964, 67
  formation of, 11, 12
  hegemony, 63–65, 76–77
  liberal, conservative wings, 64–
    67
  and Negro vote, 48–49
  and New Deal, 45, 48–49, 54–
    55, 75–76, 172
  and new federal balance, 143–
    145
  1912 split, 29
  1928 victory, 38
  1960 election, 82
  1964 election, 85
  and party loyalty, 155–156
  post-Civil War, 13, 15–20
  post-Reconstruction, 208
  and power of presidency, 18,
    174–175
  Senate control by, 117
  and the South, 78, 86, 158–160
Revolutionary War, 92
Reynolds v. *Sims,* 234–235
Rhodesia, 137
Ribnik v. *McBride,* 206
Richards, Allan, quoted, 161
Riker, William H., 147, 149
Roberts, Owen J., 183–185, 189,
  215, 222
Roche, John P., quoted, 83
Rockefeller, Nelson, 69
Rogers, Lindsay, quoted, 108
Roman Catholicism, 37, 82
Roosevelt, Eleanor, 49
Roosevelt, Franklin D.:
  death of, 47, 72, 76
  eclecticism, 53
  enmities, 43–44, 61
  humanity, 43
  and the machines, 44–47
  nomination, 41
  and party reform, 57–59, 118,
    153, 156

Roosevelt, Franklin D. (*cont.*)
  patronage, 44
  and presidential power, 164,
    170–174, 241
  and the South, 50–51
  successors, 72–84
  symbolism of, 49
  underestimation of, 42
  see also New Deal, the
Roosevelt, Theodore, 26, 167–169
Rosenblum, Victor, 224
Rossiter, Clinton, 164, 169, 173
ruralism:
  and apportionment, 17–20, 229–
    230
  contemporary irrelevance of,
    245
  and Democratic party, 36–39
  as early political determinant,
    1–10 *passim*
  and New Deal, 64–65, 81
  and 1924 Democratic conven-
    tion, 38
  1938 congressional resurgence,
    60–62
  and post-World War I reaction,
    32–39
  and Supreme Court, 207

Santa Clara County v. *Southern Pacific Railroad Co.,* 202n
Schattschneider, E. E., quoted, 40–
  41
Schlesinger, Arthur M., Jr., 52, 53,
  111, 186
school prayers, 187, 230
Scopes case, 35–36
Secretary of State, 64
Senate:
  Appropriations Committee, 119,
    131
  defenders of, 108–109
  establishment, 119, 129, 130
  filibuster, 109, 122–126, 130
  Foreign Relations Committee,
    119

Senate (*cont.*)
 inequities of equal membership, 107–108, 112
 Judiciary Committee, 121, 122
 seniority system, 114n, 117, 119
Senate Establishment, The, 119
seniority system, 57–58, 60, 114–120
"separate but equal," 208–210, 212, 222–224
separation of powers, 88, 137, 165, 175
Sherman Antitrust Act, 203
Shuman, Howard E., 121
silver-mining industry, 109–111
Silver Purchase Act, the, 111
single-member constituency system (geographical), 89–93, 95–97, 230
Slaughter, Roger, 118
Slaughterhouse Cases, 201–202, 207, 208, 221
slavery, political, economic effect of, 11, 12
Smith, Alfred E., 37–38, 41, 82
Smith, Howard W., 120
Smith v. *Allwright,* 187, 222
social security, 65, 75–76
Social Security Act, 216
social workers, 41
Socialism, 69
sociology, 224–226
South, the:
 and civil rights, 80–81, 156–157, 206–213
 and conservatism, 76
 Democratic monopoly in, 15, 50–51, 156–157
 and government aid, 7
 and John F. Kennedy, 78
 and the judiciary, 140
 local law enforcement in, 140
 and the Negro, 18, 35, 79
 and the New Deal, 50–51, 55
 and Populist movement, 15
 and Republican party, 38, 48–49, 86, 158–160

South, the (*cont.*)
 romanticizing of, 211
 self-defeatism of, 140
 white supremacy, 30
South Carolina, 117, 157
South Pacific, 220
Southwest, federal aid to, 50
Spanish-American War, 15
Spencer, Herbert, 194
Spingarn, Joel E., 49
"spirit of the laws, the," 23
Stafford v. *Wallace,* 205n
stare decisis, 199, 222
state government:
 business regulation, 200–206
 executive strength in, 161–163
 police powers, 202
 segregation laws, 208
 see also legislature(s), state
Staten Island, 94
states' rights:
 and civil rights legislation, 139–140
 and federal balance, 142–145, 164
 and grants-in-aid, 137–139
States' Rights party, 157
status quo, 17–20, 31–33, 36, 54, 214
Stevenson, Adlai E., 47, 83, 180
Steward Machine Co. v. *Davis,* 216n
Stewart, Potter, 99
Stone, Harlan Fiske, 184, 216
sugar industry, 109–110, 203
Supreme Court:
 adaptation to change, 142–143
 appointment of justices, 188–189
 and apportionment, 99, 101, 150, 177, 191, 219, 229–235
 attempted restrictions on, 184–185, 213–216, 236, 238–239
 and business regulation, 77, 200–206
 and civil rights, 12, 13, 77–82,

Supreme Court (*cont.*)
134, 195, 202, 206–213, 219–227
division of opinion of, 186
function of, 135–136, 182–195, 198–200, 212
judicial activism, 218–219
judicial avoidance of issue, judgement, 190–192
judicial reversal, 186–187, 193, 194–195
judicial self-restraint, 184, 190, 218–219
majoritarian position of, 188–190, 192, 220
and New Deal, 55–57, 74, 187, 194, 197, 213–219
and policy making, 183–187
and separation of powers, 137
tenure, 189–190
and writ of certiorari, 190 and *n*
Sutherland, George, 184, 185
Sweatt v. *Painter*, 222–223
Swift v. *United States,* 205*n*

Taft, Robert A., 61–62, 64, 66–67, 72
Taft-Hartley Act, 73
Taft, William H., 167*n*, 168, 188
Tammany Hall, 27, 37
tariff, 29, 41
tax, federal income, 203
"taxation without representation," 92
Tennessee, 35–36
Tennessee Valley Authority, 50, 53, 75
territorial expansion, 2, 11
Texas, 41, 222, 223
third parties, 14, 19
three-part franchise system, 102
Thurmond, Strom, 157
To Secure These Rights (report), 79
totalitarianism, 23, 56, 57, 90, 146, 166
trade unions, 34, 65
Treaty of Versailles, 169
Trevelyan, George M., 20, 21*n*

Trevor-Roper, H. R., quoted, 129
Truman, Harry S.:
and civil rights, 78, 79
and conservative revival, 72–74
domestic policies, 75–76
Fair Deal, 73, 118
foreign policy, 74–75
and power of the presidency, 174–175
and states' rights South, 156, 157
Truman Doctrine, the, 74
Tugwell, Rexford G., quoted, 171, 173
Tuskegee Institute, 231
Twenty-second Amendment, 74, 172–174

Union of Soviet Socialist Republics, 74
United States v. *Butler,* 183–184, 198*n*
United States v. *Classic,* 222
United States v. *Cruikshank,* 208
United States v. *Darby,* 193
United States v. *Reese,* 208
University of Texas Law School, 223
urban-industrial community:
beginnings and effects, 1–9, 16, 17
and apportionment, 106–107, 229–230
diversity of, 94–99
electoral power of, 92–93, 110, 113, 175–178
and government expenditures, 105
irrelevance of geography, 139
and middle class progressives, 26
and New Deal, 41–42, 64–65
and political power structure, 17–20, 81–84
ruralist attack on, 32–39
and Democratic party, 36–37
and state loyalties, 147–148
and Wilsonian liberalism, 29–31

Vandenberg, Arthur, 131
Van Devanter, Willis, 216
Vann, Robert, 49
Vermont, 54, 95, 97, 117
Vinson, Fred M., 222, 223
Virginia, 117, 211
vote, the:
    elitist systems, 102
    equality of, and diverse minority, 99–101
    Negro, 35, 207–208, 211–212
    qualifications for, 27, 139, 211
    registration and, 79, 139, 231
    white primary, 213, 221, 222
Voting Rights Act of 1965, 78, 139
voting rights bill, 80, 241

Wages and Hours Act of 1938, 57
Wagner, Robert F., 94
Wallace, Henry, 78, 156
Warren, Earl, 69, 101, 187, 224–226, 234–235, 238
Washington, 117
Washington, Booker T., 168, 231
Washington, D.C., 30
"wasps," 60
Wechsler, Herbert, 105, 148
Wesberry v. *Sanders*, 177, 234
West, the:
    appeal of Republican party to, 10, 12
    and Democratic rural alliance, 30
    and 1960 election, 82

West Coast Hotel Co. v. *Parrish,* 185*n*
West Indian Federation, 137
West Virginia, 37
Westin, Alan F., 211
White, Lucia, 245
White, Morton, 245
white supremacy, 13, 15, 30, 37, 76, 77, 209, 210
White, Theodore, 83
White, William S., 127–128, 131
Whitehead, Alfred North, 242
Wickard v. *Filburn,* 198*n*
Wiker, Tom, 131
Wilkins, Roy, 228
Williams v. *Mississippi,* 211*n*
Willkie, Wendell, 59, 64, 71, 179
Wilson, Woodrow:
    beginning legislation, 29–30
    Democratic party gains, 36, 41, 240
    final phase of administration, 31–32, 37
    and party reform, 152–153
    and the power of the presidency, 164, 168–171
    and Supreme Court, 215
Wolf v. *Colorado,* 141
woman suffrage, 15, 26, 27
Woodward, C. Vann, *The Burden of Southern History,* 81; quoted, 212; 15
World War I, 31–39, 62, 90, 169
World War II, 62, 63, 68, 74, 137, 172, 220
writ of certiorari, 190 and *n*